YOUR ULTIMATE CONNECTION AWAITS

YOUR ULTIMATE CONNECTION AWAITS

Once you embrace the blueprint for romantic bliss!

Mark Worthington

First published 2026 by Mark Worthington.

www.mark-worthington.com

Cover design by Julia Kuris, Designerbility designerbility.com.au

Internal design by Zena Shapter, zenashapter.com

Diagrams and Pictures by Bill Shapter, posbycheckout.com

CONTENTS

BE TRUE TO YOU
Remember the True You and the Loving Power of Pain
Mark Worthington
WHERE YOUR HAPPINESS HIDES
Once you know, you'll never let it go!
Finding Unshakeable Happiness
FROM PAIN TO POSSIBILITY
Mark Worthington
Remember the Power of Love
Mark Worthington
THE TRUTH ABOUT LOVE
And the lost secrets of true love!
Understanding the Power of Love
Advanced Leadership
Mark Worthington
SHOW ME THE HARMONY
Discover the true superpower of new-age leaders!
Mark Worthington
YOUR ULTIMATE CONNECTION AWAITS
Once you embrace the blueprint for romantic bliss!
Mastering Romantic Relationships
... AND CREATE A LIFE YOU'LL REALLY LOVE!
Mark Worthington
Transformational Coaching & Consulting
Clarity. Alignment. Better Outcomes.
www.mark-worthington.com

I dedicate this book to a world that silently craves more harmony and balance between the masculine and feminine.

In a world where wars and other disasters seem to be never ending, we must strive for peace in our romantic relationships and homes.

Let's put down the swords and knock down the walls that keep us apart, and our families under siege.

The ultimate, creative power on this planet is love, and it's waiting to show us what is possible when we connect with ourselves, and with others, with purity and passion. And when we shine a light on the ignorant charade that we currently call our 'love lives'.

We owe it to ourselves to be consciously open to new and wonderful possibilities.

The cover of this book was intentionally displayed in the colour of violet. Violet is the highest frequency colour in the rainbow, and it has always been associated with the offering of true love to another. It is time for us to paint and light up the world of romantic relationships in a more violet way, as we choose to love more freely and without fear. There is much gold at the end of this rainbow for us all, should we choose to rediscover it.

Mark Worthington
Author

INTRODUCTION

The Missing Piece in the Relationship Puzzle

The Insanity of Humanity

We live in a world where human beings live so much in their minds that they have seemingly lost their minds. There are many examples of insane situations unfolding daily.

But there is no greater representation of this insanity, than our collective inability to create happiness within our so-called love lives, despite romantic love being one of our deepest human desires. Our lack of conscious awareness has become a crisis, and in many cases, it is proving to be highly detrimental to the relationships that define the quality of our lives.

The age-old power struggle between the sexes continues unabated, relegating love into the background as our egos compete to become complete; and we have become blind to this reality as we seek safety and success, over the passion and purity of love itself. We say that love is blind, but truly we are the blind ones.

A lover's role is not to compete with you or complete you, but to allow you to become more complete within yourself. And herein lies a core paradigm that we must now embrace.

As you read this book, I welcome you to consider the wisdom that I have learned through the pain of disconnection in relationships.

He or she who needs nothing gets everything!
Love is no-thing, and the person who has already connected to it within themselves does not need it from another.
And this is where true freedom begins to reshape our relationship with love, and those lovers with whom we were meant to journey.

What Ifs, Why Nots and Who Knows

What if all the trials and tribulations of our love lives so far could be transformed in the miraculous energy of love itself? And what if the doorway to a better place could be opened wide for all of us to walk through, by dropping the need to control love, and by placing our romantic futures in the hands of love's natural curiosity?

That is the point of this book.

I have written it to help lovers, and would-be lovers, imagine and prepare for a more positive future, rich in new possibilities. It does not seek to judge anyone for where they are, or what has come before now. Frankly, I would be a first-class hypocrite to do that, as my stories go on to explain. Instead, it seeks to put forward propositions and new paradigms of love in the energy of discernment, so we can make better choices in our romantic relationships going forward.

I'm not putting forward any new rules, just new possibilities.

In my book, *Where Your Happiness Hides*, I put forward the possibility of living in the energy of wonder, rather than worry. Now this is of course easier said than done, but it seems to me that our love lives could do with an infusion of wonder to make them more wonderful.

So, to set the scene for this book and to show you up front, where my words are designed to take you, consider these questions before you read on:

What Ifs?

What if you are exactly where you need to be, and all that came before now was meant to show you how you could take your love life to a whole new level?

What if you learned from the pain of the past, and allowed it to show you a brighter future in love?

What if your greatest experiences in love are yet to come with the kind of lover you always dreamt about?

What if this book has the answers, you have been waiting for all your life?

Why Nots?

Why not open your heart to love from a fresh place, armed with new perspectives, and protected by new levels of awareness about love?

Why not be grateful for all the joy that love has given you, and be compassionate to your past and present partners who, like me, did their best to find love with you?

Why not explore the wisdom on love that this book has to offer you?

Who Knows?

Who knows what adventures your heart has in store for you, if you choose to follow its purest desires, and surrender to its mysteries?

Who knows how good love can be with another if you trust more than ever, and live from a higher version of love?

Who knows how the words you are about to read could change your love life for the better?

When you finish this book, I hope you will be able to answer these questions and more. You might even say to yourself: who knew that my love life could be so wonderful, simply by opening my heart to live from the wonders of love itself!

The Bold and Italic Me

Where I use my own experiences in this book to assist my readers with examples that relate to my life, the words are shown in bold/italics, to distinguish them from my other views.

I am not a psychologist who has learned all the answers in a

well-known university course. I have been to the university of life, the one with lots of hard knocks and relationship disappointments that originally knocked me down, and forced me to go inward then outward, to discover the truths about love and relationships in our modern world. I have studied widely, observed intensely and turned my relationship pain and darkness into the wisdom in this book, for all to simply consider on their own journeys.

All I ask for is your curiosity to explore my views. I don't need you to believe me, just open yourself up to your own intuition on the important topics I ponder and present. The more we all remember the experience of love, the more wonderful the world of romance can become.

Your Sexual Persuasion is Irrelevant

This book is for the benefit of all, regardless of your sexual persuasion or the nature of your loving relationship. We are all a mix of masculine and feminine energies. Accordingly, the concepts in this book can be applied to all.

For simplicity, however, I will refer to men and women throughout my words, rather than constantly referring to the differing mixes of masculine and feminine energies that we all possess. When I refer to men, I am truly referring to people who identify predominantly with masculine energies, and when I refer to women, I am referring to those who identify as being mainly in feminine energies.

Masculine and feminine energies are defined more clearly later in this book. They may sound simple and obvious to understand, because most of us have bodies that identify us as being inherently male or female, but this is a misnomer.

Is it Time to Choose a Saner Way Forward?

As this book portrays, there is too much pain and mediocrity in many romantic relationships, which could be so much more fulfilling if we applied a higher dose of compassion and awareness. Many of the issues in the dating and relating world are hidden in plain view but contribute to a complex web of confusion.

For those readers who desire a more joyous path in love, this book provides the natural blueprints to making this possible, individually and collectively.

I believe it would be wise to now choose the path we really want, and end the suffering that we were taught to choose. Time, like love, is of the essence.

We can continue to do what we are doing now, and suffer into perpetuity, by just trying to fix relationship flare ups on a case-by-case basis, when they become serious enough to put individual relationships on 'life support'. And people can continue to go to see counsellors and psychologists when all hope seems lost, hide their pain from their family and friends behind a veil of secrecy, and then, most likely, contact their divorce lawyers, like I had to do, twice.

Then they can spend the next 10 years wondering 'what the hell' went wrong, and questioning whether they ever want to try to love again. But frankly, this paradigm is not working for many people, and although it has great intentions, the normal system of relationship repair will, in my view, only ever result in incremental change to a difficult situation, and not substantially change the landscape of love.

Alternatively, we can get our 'heads out of the sand', see this dilemma for the opportunity that it is, and embrace a new paradigm of relating and dating, which will transform our pain into new possibilities, and help our children avoid the 'junk' through which many of us have had to wade.

We can't add days to our lives, but we can add life to our days, when we allow love and peace be the foundations of our romantic interactions.

We live in a world in which change is said to be a constant. Like death and taxes, change is somewhat inevitable. But how well do we cope with it in our love lives, without carrying the pain of past experiences?

I contend that we need more than change in our romantic landscapes. We need transformation, which is change on steroids, to bring us the happiness that we so richly deserve. And rapid transformation can only come from higher intelligence, and our willingness to reframe our many pasts, from one of pain to one rich in learnings and wonder.

We tend to view our past relationships through the lens of being a victim or a martyr. This is the handy work of our insidious egos, which want to deflect us away from what is possible. I urge us all to evolve our love lives, by seeing them as an opportunity to become victors, not victims, in union with each other. Humanity has seen fit to reward those who have suffered for a cause for centuries and called them martyrs. But do we really want to love this way? True love does not tolerate suffering, for it knows that we can unite for the sake of love without the need to tear each other apart. We need to stop seeing the opposite sex as some kind of opponent and see them as our joint benefactors of our journeys into love. It's time we focussed on connections, not superficial interactions.

The non-clinical and commonly used definition of insanity is doing the same thing repeatedly and expecting a different outcome. Can you see how this definition may apply to our current love-lives? What we resist will persist, but not without great and unnecessary pain and suffering. So please read on, for your heart wants you to see the future of loving relationships on this planet.

Welcome aboard mighty hearts, for this journey into the unknown is for you, if you choose it.

Achievement Without Fulfilment, Creates Fragility

One of the key messages I want to convey to readers in this book is that, when we go after some concept of achievement in our relationships, without first knowing what fulfils us, and whilst acting from that perspective, we open ourselves up to fragility and disappointment, because our hearts and minds fall out of alignment. Current imbalances between us needing to find happiness within us, and expecting others to give it to us, is a core reason for our relationship problems.

To attain anything that we want in life, we can fake it, take it or make it. Isn't it time we learned to really make loving relationships a part of our lives, and stopped approaching them in a fake and needy way.

The dating and relating worlds are rife with people subconsciously trying to turn their love lives into successful 'projects' and basing their decisions on preconditioned beliefs about what they are worthy of, without having their hearts truly engaged in what takes place. Presence has been replaced by the need for presents, you might say.

And when their romantic experiences don't work out as they expected them to, their dented egos place them in the story as victims and refuse to let go of something that they could learn from and move past into big and better experiences. In the energy of love, we will never do this to ourselves. Egos create casualties, hearts create curious and confident creators.

Many people are subconsciously programmed to look externally for happiness, rather than internally. If we are in a relationship, we are prone to attribute our happiness to our partner, particularly in the early stages of a relationship, then blame them for our unhappiness as the relationship unfolds, rather than being aware of this unfair anomaly. Does this make sense if we have not consciously set the path forward with shared intent, and faced our issues together?

Do we ignore the reality that happiness must start within ourselves first? And that if our relationship is deteriorating it may be a good idea to work on our own sense of self, or with our partner on improving the situation that we have created together, rather than going outside of the relationship to start again with another person. Do we make our happiness the victim of our righteousness?

And are we addicted to the excitement of new relationships, but find longer term relationships become toxic, because they start to lack the initial bouts of excitement and the associated hormonal boosts, that we so badly need to feel happy? And do we create conflict instead of peace, because that reflects our inner states of disconnection from our own true selves.

I contend that we tend to focus on external measures of happiness that can never give us the joy that our hearts truly desire, and this creates the never-ending cycle of union, back to separation.

Can our partner's apparent success, or looks, even if they are positives, really fill the holes in our inner sense of self-worth and happiness? The answer is 'no', not in the long run. Yet this is how we behave, because we are subconsciously programmed to seek our happiness within the offerings of others. We then blame others, who we once claimed to love, when they fail to complete the 'project' that was essentially not theirs to own, and was impossible for them to complete. In short, our own happiness is hiding, where only we can feel it, and no one else can access it.

Life has a way of punishing decisions made for success, and not fulfilment, and romantic relationships entered to attain some form of recognition, or to win in some way, will inevitably feel hollow or superficial in the end. If we are in a relationship with someone primarily because of temporary things that they own – like their wealth, status, external looks, or reputations – we are, almost certainly, acting out of fear and attraction, and not love. This crazy imbalance is what we need to address to make our love lives more authentic and stable.

Fulfilling relationships take shape when both partners have high levels of self-esteem and self-love, and express these attributes with each other, with the primary intent of sharing love and passion together. In this place, the material and superficial obsessions of our fearful minds take a backseat and are dominated by love. Fear not, this kind of love awaits your attention, and commitment.

Of course, attraction matters, and success doesn't hurt. But when we try to succeed without the feeling of fulfilment being present first, we are on a slippery pathway to pain. It's all a matter of balance. Why not love who we are, then let this joy bring forth the relationships, which can simply add to this fulfillment?

If we continue to relate out of fear, we may as well just witness our relationships for what they are becoming, for some – transactional arrangements primarily based on value, and some kind of return on investment. In other words, they are just projections of need, and not pathways to sustainable joy.

Have We Failed in Love?

We have a confusing landscape on our hands when it comes to romantic relationships. But changing this is the opportunity of our lifetimes. Confusion always precedes clarity and herein lies the 'silver lining' in our relationship clouds. We will only 'fail' if we fail to learn from our current and past mistakes, and if we continue to repeat our ignorant and unsophisticated ways of loving ourselves, and each other. Isn't it time that we prepared to succeed in love, not keep searching for convenient reasons to give up, or entertain the blame game as victims and martyrs of our own ignorance?

The divine blueprint for a fulfilling love life lies in the pages before you. I urge you to prepare to love, and be loved, like you've never been loved before. Victory without competition is yours to enjoy.

Your heart already knows what you are about to read. And it wants to remind your mind of what is possible, when you remember how to love in a more natural, not normal, way.

We Tend to Love in Fear

A fundamental reason why our love lives, like other aspects of our lives, are not proving to be as successful or fulfilling as we want them to be stems from the relationship between love and fear. Essentially, we are trying to love in the energy of fear, and not in the pure energy of love itself. And this is no more than a learned behaviour, which we can change with a dose of commitment, humility and remembrance.

Love is ever-present in this world. It is all around us. But the big issue we face is that we are loving from preconditioned and fearful mindsets that keep us trapped in paradigms of what love is meant to look like.

Love is a feeling, not a thought, so when we determine in advance what it should look and even feel like, we do not let love create its own endless possibilities. Instead, we wrestle it to the ground, put it in a 'headlock' and subdue it in a cage of conditioning that we call normality.

The propensity to live from this place of fear then effects all parts of human life, not just our love lives. Collectively, we have been taught to play safe and live from a set of predetermined mindsets, but this is stopping our lives from being the adventure they are meant to be. Our homes, businesses, political systems and more, are steeped in fear, and this is leading us into pain, rather than what is truly possible.

We are leading our lives, but are we loving our lives?

For many people the answer is unfortunately 'no', and this is leading us into fragile relationships and experiences that are prone to suffer, and even fragment, under the stress of our many commitments.

I experienced this multiple times, and it hurt.

In this dark place, we are essentially approaching relationships in the energy of lack and a fear of failure, rather than from one of abundance and adventure, as we constantly compare our lives to those we see around us. So is it any wonder that we have ended up where we have. And this is why so many relationships unravel in despair, rather than unfold in happiness.

The reality is that we can probably all remember and recognise the feeling of love within us. For those who have children, can you remember the feeling you had when you held your newborn baby in your arms for the first time? And for those who are married, can you recall that deep feeling of love you may have had when you stared into the eyes of your beloved partner and said your wedding vows? Or can you remember being younger, and the love you felt when you experienced the joy of playing an exciting new game with your friends, and your heart burst forth with joy?

When life gets busy and intense, as modern life can so often get, we are prone to forget these beautiful moments, when we connected to the love in our hearts so fully. We all know love, and we sometimes just need a reminder that it is one of, if not, the most important and compelling components of our lives. We can learn in life from the many experiences we encounter, and many of them are giving us the opportunity to simply remember how wonderful we can feel when we allow love to flow through us and activate our sense of joy and spontaneity.

This book speaks of higher awareness and learning how to love again with force, but for most of us this is truly just a remembering process, and not an intellectual exam we need to pass. And it is so core to us that it can be like riding a bike again, for it is the essence of us. We just need to remember that when we love with our overflowing and unconstrained hearts, there is nothing more fulfilling in our lives, and this can put everything else we have been taught to pursue, or do, into a clearer context.

The question is, do you really want to live more from love, and reignite your heart in its full expression, such that this way of living becomes our default way of seeing ourselves and the world?

If so, read on and discover the adventure that relating from the natural forces of love, not the normal forces of fear, can bestow upon your lives. The balance between love and fear needs to be reimagined, in the knowing that love has the power to cast our fears aside when we trust it.

I want this book to bring new possibilities to our romantic relationships, and form the basis of a new oasis where our love for each other can thrive and be nourished all over again.

True love, and the bliss we all deserve, is within our grasp, when we know how to let it into our lives. It is waiting patiently for our attention.

The Loving Cure for Our Shared Crisis of Consciousness

Our evolutionary psychology is essentially a form of programming, which has led us to much fear, neediness and suffering in romantic relationships, and other walks of life.

We are all the product of human evolution that has led humanity away from its natural ways of existing. Our truth has been lost in the distorted ways we have been taught throughout the centuries to witness ourselves, and the world around us.

Evolution, whether it's through pleasure or pain, is the primary purpose of our lives. And as intelligent beings with the ability to connect to two different operating systems within us – one being of higher intelligence, and one being of a lesser capability, as this book goes on to explain – we have our evolutionary destinies in our own hands. We can continue as we have been doing and pay a hefty price for dysfunction in relationships, or we can evolve to new heights, and love the lives that we live. The choice is ours.

If you like, our natural programming has been 'scrubbed' or altered and replaced by conditioned programming that is limiting our possibilities as a race. This programming can, however, be reversed when we know how to do so.

There are two core levels to this conditioning, being collective and individual. We are all a product of the experiences we have in our own lives, but also the stories and paradigms we witness in the world around us. And we tend to be strongly conditioned by both these sets of mindsets.

Collective conditioning is generally passed down from generation to generation, although it does evolve over time. And this becomes embedded within us in different ways.

Individual conditioning is learned directly from our own personal experiences.

Both can change, although changing collective consciousness is something that is much harder to alter than individual mindsets and perceptions, because of its sheer scale.

This book points out some of the bigger picture, conditioned mindsets that are corrupting the way we interrelate romantically. And once you see them you won't be able to unsee them. But of course, on top of these paradigms, we all have our own limiting beliefs and attachment patterns that apply to our own love lives. It is a complex web of distortions, but it is a web we can escape from if we desire.

The source of this programming dates back for centuries, however there are some core human misconceptions that limit our ability to reverse them.

Firstly, we live in a world where we principally believe in what we can see and touch. Physical and mental concepts are the default position of most human minds. But we have lost sight of this reality: all is metaphysical before it is physical.

In other words, our adopted consciousness creates everything, including our own bodies and minds, and the world we inhabit over time. And our true centre of consciousness is not in our minds, but in our hearts, which we have complete access to, but which we have been largely taught to ignore. Intellect has replaced intuition as our principal way of perceiving our world, and our lives, for thousands of years. And this is a departure from the natural human blueprint by which we were intended to live and love. Our hearts are meant to choose our lives, and our minds are meant to be the orchestrators of our desires. But our hearts have become the silent, and often vanquished, partners.

So, if consciousness determines it all, then by definition it determines our biology, habits, thoughts and ways that we relate to each other. Make no mistake, our souls, or hearts, have the power to change everything if we connect to them and allow them to lead us to wiser choices. Everything is a thought before it manifests into reality. And behind every thought sits a set of beliefs.

I often hear scientists expressing the view that many of the ways that we behave and think are determined by instincts and biology, and I do not disagree with this. However, consciousness is the force that determines these factors, and other drivers of our lives, and we can alter our consciousness. But what if this consciousness has become 'corrupted' and depleted by limiting human belief structures?

Consider wild animals in a jungle. They are driven by instincts and evolution, but their pure consciousness, or nature, essentially drives every behaviour they exhibit and the bodies they inhabit. They do not go to school or watch documentaries that tell them how to be or what to think. They just are what they are, and nature itself is the pure source of the evolution to which they are subjected over time. And this makes them different to humans, who can choose the level of consciousness into which we tune ourselves.

When we stopped – thousands of years ago, on mass – to access our higher intelligence capabilities, we opened ourselves up to become the victims of limited understandings of what is possible. We don't see it this way collectively, because it takes higher levels of wisdom to see what we currently can't perceive about ourselves. And many of our common relationship problems stem from this limitation, meaning no one can truly be blamed for what is taking place. It just is and should not be judged, just reconsidered and upgraded.

You may ask how I know this. I have spent at least a decade studying higher consciousness, or love, and applying it to my own life. This book was written because of this research and years of practice, and because I want to give lovers and would-be lovers this opportunity to improve their love lives in the best ways possible. What matters isn't matter, but we have seemingly lost sight of this truth.

Readers can of course form their own views on the topic – and should not just trust my personal experiences and views – by referencing the key principles of quantum physics and the views put forward by experts such as Dr Bruce Lipton in his book *The Biology of Belief* (first published in 2005).

Put simply, Mr Lipton put forward evidence to confirm that our beliefs, and perceptions, ultimately create our cellular structures, or DNA, and determine our physical and mental realities on Earth. Personal and societal transformation, he concluded, is therefore dependent on the relationship between our minds, bodies and souls, with our beliefs being critical in all aspects of life.

In addition, when we experience issues in this world, and in our own lives, we tend to try to 'rethink' our way out of issues. The problem with this is that our level of consciousness determines our beliefs, and these beliefs determine our thoughts, and ultimately our actions. So, unless we change our inherent belief structures, the level of change in our lives is only ever likely to be incremental, and could in fact be adverse.

Asking our minds to alter what they have ignorantly and already accepted to be true is a dichotomy upon which we are falsely prone to rely. True transformation happens much faster, and more thoroughly, when it arises from higher levels of conscious awareness.

So, what does this all mean for the malaise of dating and relating issues that we struggle to overcome as a society? What it means is that there is a great opportunity for transformation to take place in a very positive way, if we want it to. But we must take the blinkers off and step away from the 'auto-pilot' approach through which we tend to relate. When we can look at what is going on from a higher perspective and see the patterns and habits to which we have become addicted – on an individual and collective level – then, and only then, can we make the positive steps forward that we need to make.

There are many learned people who assist others every day to deal with the pain and despair that our relationship paradigms are creating.

I salute these endeavours. But what we truly need to see is that we have the power to reverse this unfortunate dilemma, and step into a far more positive set of experiences, together.

Once we identify and dissolve the conditioned thinking that we currently impose upon love, we can set it free to transform our world, relationship by relationship. This will take time, but we must all start somewhere.

Balancing Within Duality and Polarity

The Earth is a place of opposites, and human beings are no different. Everything is physical and metaphysical, we can choose from our hearts or minds, we can love something or hate it, we can need something or want it. This list is endless. Our individual and shared destinies are dependent upon what we choose, as life's circumstances unfold.

We all have the power of free will. But are we choosing wisely?

Balance is critical to creating the harmony in life that we all want and need in order to be happy and feel fulfilled. Our romantic relationships lack harmony on a mass scale – ***as I so readily experienced too*** – because we lack balance within ourselves, individually and collectively. And this is a massive issue we need to finally face, because it is tearing us apart, separation by separation, tear by tear.

Every action has an equal and opposite reaction on Earth, and therefore we get what we put out into this remarkable 3D environment. This is its unique and grand design, in a universe of infinite possibilities.

So, let's be clear here…

If aspects of our lives, including our romantic relationships, are not fulfilling or happy, we are choosing that reality out of sheer ignorance. There is no place to hide from this truth, and we must take accountability for the realities that we have created, as foreign as this may feel.

This is not a soft and fluffy book about love and romance, like a Mills and Boon novel, with a predetermined ending that we all know is coming, and which will satisfy our long-held and delusional beliefs. What it offers a reader is a true and natural way to find the deep connections of love that we so readily say we want in life. And for those who really want it, it provides the blueprint to attain the highly prized version of love that we call true love.

Not everyone is likely to accept or choose the wisdom in this book, so that they can make the natural transition that is possible, back to the kind of love we are collectively capable of experiencing. Why? Because this is a choice that every reader will need to consciously make, with an open heart and a willing mind, by trusting in the natural solutions that you have probably never been shown before.

It will require courage, commitment, and a willingness to put down the swords of regret, and release the subconscious need to suffer that many of us have been taught to cling to and accept as permanent.

If you want the fantastic connection with a lover that you have always dreamt about, this book contains a natural pathway back to that possibility.

Our culture does not love the true feeling of love. It loves the idea of love. And these two options offer us very different propositions.

If you have made 'bad' decisions in past relationships, which have not worked out in the way you had hoped, there is a simple solution that we can all now take to remedy this reality. And that is: to make different decisions next time.

Let me show you how!

Our Past is Still Haunting Us

We have witnessed thousands of years of suppression of feminine energies on this planet at the hands of patriarchal societies and laws. And this imbalance has meant that key aspects of our lives – which have until recently been controlled by cisgender heterosexual men – have become battlegrounds for male and female egos alike. This is not the fault of any man or woman alive today, it is a by-product of an ignorant 'system' handed down from past generations. This includes politics, the worlds of business and finance, international geopolitical affairs, expectations of marriage and parenthood, human rights, and even fashion.

Since the dawn of time, the civilisations that have successfully harmonised the power of masculine and feminine energies, both within individuals and across the population, have been the ones that thrived. Most of these documented societies – like the Bugis Society in Sulawesi (Indonesia), the Mosuo of Southwest China, and the North American Indian system known as the Haudenosaunee – were what we refer to as ancient civilisations; and in those civilisations matriarchy was revered, not just patriarchy.

Men and women shared the important roles required to create a harmonious society, and the embodiment and nurturing of both male and female energies was actively encouraged, both on a macro and micro basis. Even the Ancient Egyptians had Pharaohs who were women, although modern day Egypt has a male-dominated culture, based on what I witnessed when I went there recently.

We think of ourselves as modern, but when it comes to societal pressures, let alone romantic relationships, we appear to be the ones in need of some wise evolution.

We have lived in a male-dominated world for centuries, with feminine energies and intelligences suppressed, to the detriment of many communities of people. Accordingly, our world has become overly competitive, money focussed, goal oriented, and uncaring as we collectively strive to prove that we are worthy of being loved, by deploying primarily masculine energies.

Big businesses are run with a primary focus on winning and getting rich, and we generally deprioritise the importance of human interactions and love in the various cultures that we create. Across our western societies, we fear the full expression of emotions, for many people, mainly men, have become divorced through habit from their feelings, and the expression of love in deep connections.

Essentially, for thousands of years, the balancing of sexual energies has been prevented by a world that trapped us all in different cages of conditioning. Men have been expected to meet the image of certain masculine archetypes, and women have been expected to be purely feminine, largely for the benefit of men and children. Make no mistake, men were in control of this world for centuries, and women were treated as second-class citizens for far too long.

But this old-fashioned way of thinking is now ceding to the advent of greater choice and self-determination for all, at least in many Western countries.

So that we can all get on the same page, I have defined in Chapter 5 what exactly constitutes the core masculine and feminine energies. Understanding these is important, because it will give you an insight into what has been damaging the harmony between human beings for thousands of years.

To be frank, we have created a world full of ego-centric relationships tuned to outdated masculine ways of thinking, which operate from fear and a core belief that winning and having power over others, makes us more valuable.

This way of life needs to shift, and under new modern forces that are now driving us towards greater equality, we are heading in a direction that can bring us more fulfilment in our lives, through more reciprocal relationships, once we master it. And master it we can, if we start with a dose of humility. But first we need to get there, and the pathway to what we seek is proving painful to traverse.

Our modern romantic relationships continue to suffer from our old habits. With egoic energies flowing through them, is it any wonder that love has ceded to concepts of value, and that superficial and materialistic priorities have become barriers to the sacred union that romance is supposed to engender and bring forth?

The feminine energies that men can develop have been deeply discouraged, by a world that expects them to always be strong and assertive but not overly focussed on being caring and compassionate.

And women are being given the long overdue opportunity to express both their masculine and feminine energies in a world, which is finally giving them the right to express their genius in all areas of life, including the business world, politics and government, rather than just forcing them to be nurturers and homemakers. This has allowed their feminine energies to be more infused into new walks of life, and this is having a positive impact on our world.

But with this rebalancing in progress, are we keeping up with it, and giving ourselves the best opportunity for harmonies between men and women to be more fully achieved? I think not. And yet this is a fertile place for new possibilities to arise.

Unchecked male energies have been responsible for so much damage and unhappiness in this world, with their obsession with doing, winning, making money, having power over others, and suppressing our natural abilities to feel and freely express emotion. The natural power of feminine intuition has been largely overwhelmed by this masculine prioritisation, effectively blocking our ability to flow in a loving and creative way as a world.

At its worst representation is the plethora of wars that mankind has endured, most of which have been initiated by the wounded egos of men, trying to create a legacy at the expense of peace. And these experiences have stained the souls of those who were forced to participate or even bear the brunt of post-war pains.

We have created wonderful cities and technologies, but we are yet to seemingly master, on a widespread basis, one of the core things we all crave – fulfilling romantic love.

My Offering of Love to Love

This book is my attempt to assist with what I witness to be centuries of imbalance and disharmony between masculine and feminine energies on this planet.

I witnessed it growing up, and my initial ignorance on the subject

has left me with many scars and bruises to bear, including two painful divorces. And I know that I am not alone on this pathway of pain. It's more like a crowded highway.

The ongoing tension between the sexes has seemingly reached new heights of disappointment and despair, despite our never-ending hope, as new modern forces collide with established ways of believing and behaving. The advent of social media has seemingly inflamed this tension, particularly amongst younger generations who access it more regularly. We owe it to ourselves, and to our children, to address this.

Greater awareness about what both sexes want, and need, is a powerful starting point, and would be far more constructive than the constant sharing of pain that currently appears on millions of devices across the world every day.

Many people profess that cisgender heterosexual men ('men') prioritise sex and intimacy in their romantic relationships, and that cisgender heterosexual women ('women') prioritise financial security in their romantic relationships, both preferring to select partners who can give them external sources of validation. This book investigates these propositions and reframes them with higher wisdom.

Although many unconscious people may relate this way and have contributed to these stereotypes, it's not the natural outcomes of love itself. Love does not create relationships like this. They are predominantly derived from normal conditioned ways of thinking, derived from ancestors who knew no better, and who related in a different world in which equality was not even remotely present between the sexes, and higher consciousness was a trait only available to prophets and monks.

I don't seek to judge, or take a side on these stereotypes, for they are just the outcomes of traditions and egoic patterns of human survival from which we continue to suffer. ***And to be frank, I embodied them all at one stage.***

We all want and deserve love. We are also all capable of unconditioned love, since we are all born from and are love itself. Our self-imposed limitations are not inevitable. So, with even just a little bit of higher intelligence, we can all take our love lives to a new level.

The famous author Shakespeare once wrote:

> "Love is not the words we say when everything feels bright.
> Love is the quiet decision to stay through every darker night.
> For passion burns like summer flame,
> And fades with passing weather,
> But hearts that learn the art of grace,
> Are the ones that last forever."

In other words, when we love with feeling, awareness and commitment to each other, anything is possible.

Women with the power of love in their hearts don't just chase men with financial success, they commit to a man they love and forge an enduring relationship with the love in their hearts, even if life gets tough.

Similarly, men who have dealt with their psychological woundings, value far more than sex and beauty in their partnerships with women, and seek to establish deep connections.

Highly self-aware people know how to love in a conscious way. They are self-centred, which means they operate from a place of healthy self-esteem, because they have embodied high doses of:

- Self-love
- Self-acceptance
- Self-forgiveness
- Self-awareness
- Self-respect
- Self-honour, and
- Self-trust

Lots of 'self's, as you can see. People who are closely connected in this way to their true selves can be more natural with their approaches to romantic relationships. And these many healthy energies of self that they embody, then allow them to bring forth healthy relationships that can thrive, not just struggle to survive.

What truly matters in romantic relationships is our connections with others, and this can vary by person. But the connection of love between two hearts is what we naturally desire to experience, not the many surrogates we may have deemed to represent this precious experience.

Integrating Known Truths About Love

My book *The Truth About Love* thoroughly explores the true metaphysical properties of love. Love is deployed by the universe through our hearts to further the purpose of our existence on this planet, which is: to evolve us all, individually and collectively, back to love in all that we are, and do.

This book seeks to practically apply the principles in *The Truth About Love,* specifically to the world of relationships. It is grounded in everything I have witnessed and learned from over the years, in the hope of helping lovers to enjoy their love lives more fully.

The sheer complexity of the topic being addressed in this book is immense, so I make no apology for giving the issues and solutions ample respect and consideration. It deserves a thorough examination, for there is too much at stake for us all.

It is my gift to a world that thinks it needs more love, when in fact it is truly already overflowing with it.

PROLOGUE

Paying for My Learnings in Love

I Did What I Was Taught to Do

Most of us start out in life determined to find the love of our lives, settle down, raise a beautiful family and live happily ever after. This is the paradigm we are all promised.

I was no different.

I grew up in Australia in the 1960s. Life was simpler in many ways, primarily because technology was more rudimentary; and from what I observed, so too were romantic relationships. They were controlled by strict societal norms and rules, and perhaps people were also more compliant back then, or were wearing masks to cover up their true experiences.

My parents were quite traditional in this, so I was taught from childhood – primarily by my mother – to follow the relationship paradigms of the time. I was encouraged to become the epitome of the 'perfect young man' in both relationships and life. I was taught the principles of chivalry. I was primed to be the knight in shining armour for a woman, who would be swept off her feet by my romantic gestures, strong values, and my commitment to security and success. I was taught to be caring and compassionate for my lover. But was I taught how love truly worked or felt? Definitely not.

Accordingly, I became determined to be the good provider, a nice caring man, a good father who was always committed to his career and family, for the benefit of all who relied upon him. And for the most part, this was what I became, buying into the expectations of my family and a relatively conservative society.

In return, I was taught that I would receive love from a beautiful and soft woman, who would have my children with a reciprocal desire to share my romantic dreams and grow old in my arms.

I applied great energy to what I was taught and who I was expected to be. But, alas, my relationship dreams were ultimately shattered through two divorces, and multiple relationship disappointments. Each of these outcomes were energetically, emotionally and financially expensive, particularly the two divorces. However, those who follow my work will know that I believe that one of the core reasons we are alive is to expand our consciousness levels.

I therefore consider the costs of my missteps to be payments for learning, and triggers to the expansion of my own self-awareness. So, I fully accept these outcomes, being reflections of my own limitations and learned behaviours at the time – in particular a lack of self-respect and self-honour, and the naïve, ignorant and unskilled nature of the relationship paradigms and stories we were all taught would serve us well. They did not!

I take full responsibility for my role in the demise of all my romantic relationships. After seeing through the mist of my own relationship misadventures and being transparent with my past, I choose love over continued suffering, and a new life, over old habits.

The contemporary dating and mating world is becoming increasingly complex to successfully navigate, with relationship stress and 'failure' seemingly getting worse. I particularly feel for today's young people, who seem very confused, and who must seemingly endure more broken family structures than any earlier generation, except maybe war-torn generations.

So, I have been compelled to write this book. After years of studying human belief structures, love and conscious awareness, I truly believe that a higher awareness and a commitment to higher levels of harmony and forgiveness can improve this situation. As a father of five young adults embarking on their own love lives, I want my research and new awareness levels to influence the lives of my children, and grandchildren.

Which is why, after much deep personal introspection to understand why both of my divorces happened, I am now passionate about helping others avoid the intense pain and losses that I endured.

Of course, I am obviously a man and have a limited perspective due to my predominantly masculine energies. But other perspectives are also included in this book, to ensure its content has balance. I have closely observed the conditioning and paradigms that women, and those with more feminine energies, have been exposed to, and have consulted with both; for I want this book to be a blueprint for greater relationship success for us all.

This book is designed to provide solutions for the sub-standard relationships that many of us are experiencing and enduring. It does not seek to judge anyone, because that kind of response is not helpful, *and I know all too well how unhelpful and soul-destroying that can be.*

The subliminal message in this book is one of recovery and rebirth. It outlines the opportunity that we all have to always draw a line in the sand and start again, with a dose of grit and compassion, in all that we do.

My life was punctuated by more than relationship disharmony. I also endured job losses, wealth meltdowns, and the pain of a significant muscle disease that lasted for over 40 years, or 15,000 days. But most of them were caused by romantic dysfunction, for it was my strongest source of validation, and where I felt like a failure most of all.

That's a lot of pain. While I was seen as successful by many, the true me felt deeply unfulfilled for many years. I just hid it well, as I became a victim in my own mind.

But eventually I found my way through it all and allowed it to be my inspiration to come back home to a greater sense of happiness than

I had ever known before. This has been an intense transformational journey, but there was no greater area of disappointment for me than my love life. I am proud of the fact that I never gave up, but instead, I totally owned my experiences and found a way to grow through them. You can too.

I hope that my down-payments and close encounters with pain have not been in vain. I have always dreamt of living in a more loving world, and I will not give up trying to make this a possibility for those who share my dream.

Let the dreams begin…

Part A

OUR DISTORTED RELATIONSHIP DYNAMICS

Chapter 1

Are We Choosing to Suffer, Together?

The Battlefields of Pain

The landscape of contemporary families and romantic encounters have both become battlefields, in which fear and need are dominant, and where love is the absent general that we rarely allow to call the shots. Our pre-conditioned version of love is dominated by silent humiliations and separations, rather than the transparent expressions of truth for the sake of wonderful union.

But is this what we really want?

Humans have a propensity to accept suffering in their lives, because we believe it is virtuous to do so, and collectively this seems to be the case in our romantic relationships. All is a choice, however, whether we believe that or not.

Loving and 'losing' can be very painful, and expensive, if it's not done with compassion and the best of intentions. We won't always get relationships right of course, because not all relationships are meant to be 'forever'. But if all we are trying to do is manipulate the so-called 'game of love' and its existing rules, without reconsidering if we really want to play this style of game, then we stand to lose much more than we could if we were more intelligent about the current dynamics.

The reality is that the more you see through the current situation, the more you start to crave a different 'game' – one that has less hidden rules and expectations.

Love is the patient and infinite master of romantic relationships, and until we master it, it will continue to deal with us as it sees fit, as my book *The Truth About Love* explains. Love witnesses our love lives in quiet observation, never judging what we do, but always leading us towards a lighter, brighter place.

Unfortunately, many people have lost trust in love, because they have witnessed such painfully conditional love in their lives, and so many relationships end up 'failing'.

On a planet where the natural passions between men and women can be so beautifully expressed through love making, and the sheer power of the unity of both sexes is so potent, that it can create new people, the potential for relationship balance and harmony – and balance and harmony on a societal level – has been desecrated by ignorance, and our inability to come together to solve this heart-breaking dilemma.

Only the fortunate few, skilled in the art of love, are currently thriving in this difficult situation, and I admire their ability to do so. Truly happy and lasting relationships are possible, but have become all too rare, as later chapters illustrate.

To coin a common phrase – which I heard from frustrated younger generations throughout my research – the contemporary dating world has become a sh#t show, which they are reluctantly choosing to abandon, in contravention of all their natural instincts to be in union. And this is so sad!

It's time we opened ourselves up to new possibilities, to bring real love to our 'love lives'. Equality is seemingly upon us, and it deserves to be unstoppable, as it is an essential part of unconditional love. So, isn't it time that we truly let it into our lives, and allow it to express itself through our romantic relationships?

There Has to Be a Better Way

Many relationships sadly end or break down without fulfilling our initial dreams and expectations. On the one hand, this can be for our own good, because relationships are meant to test and change us into the people we need, and deserve, to become. But on the other hand, the dating and relating world has become a test of our self-esteem, and in some cases has 'crushed our spirits'.

Many of us have struggled in romantic relationships, not because we didn't try hard, but because we were not taught how they can be successfully managed. This is not a surprise, because many of our 'teachers', or mentors, lacked the wisdom to guide us forward in an intelligent way.

Maintaining peace and passion for extended periods of time with another person is one of the greatest challenges we will face, yet it's a challenge we rarely acknowledge or explore because we are so drawn to the idea of being 'in love'. And I believe it is proving harder than it needs to be.

We are prone to live with enduring hope, driven by our primal desires for intimacy and our natural compulsion to love and be loved. However, when our dreams are dashed, and our relationships either end in separation or atrophy to a level of disinterest, there can be much confusion, humiliation, or shame – all of which harms our sense of self.

Many of us have not been taught how to deal with the pain that follows from relationship issues, for it can so-often send us the subliminal message that we are simply not enough, when nothing could be further from the truth. There is no need to feel this way, because it's a wonderful thing to grow and learn more about yourself, and as human beings we usually do that best through our mistakes. ***But this is easier said than done, as I discovered the hard way.***

The trouble is that relationships often end in the 'blame game', which can morph into shame for one or more of the partners. No human being deserves to feel humiliated or shamed by another, but then our own egos can often take us to this dark place.

We are collectively programmed to avoid failure. Not only because it doesn't feel nice, but because when we fail, we so often conclude that we have somehow become less lovable. And this can impair our personalities, making us less positive about our own lives, which can then have an impact on future relationships by introducing new fears into our repertoire of unwarranted emotions.

The many dating and relating worlds are not areas driven by high levels of skill. Our education systems rarely teach us how to navigate the twists and turns we will invariably face in romantic relationships, and we are often left to learn from what we witness growing up. Our unskilled relatives, and the world in which we inhabit, teach us largely through osmosis. As children, we cannot feasibly control or influence this process, even though what we witness is often not impressive or wise.

Of course, a fortunate few do have different experiences. Some may, however, just remain oblivious to the undetonated limiting beliefs that remain dormant within them and their partner, and may be more vulnerable to relationship disappointment than they truly know. But, either way, the key is to acknowledge and accept this lack of guidance, which many of us have encountered, and to seek to educate ourselves on the possibilities that await our attention.

Many relationships may feel like puzzles we simply cannot solve, despite our best endeavours and our deep desires. But the missing piece of the puzzle might be closer than you think!

The Missing Puzzle Piece

Love is everywhere and in everything, but to a large degree we have forgotten its infinite powers.

Most romantic relationships involve high levels of attraction. The world is full of attractive people, particularly given how many of us go out of our way to ensure that we present as well as possible to the opposite sex (or to the cohort of people we seek to impress).

Unfortunately, attraction is not love and never can be, and yet we have become unskilled as a race at telling attraction and love apart. And physical attraction is one of the first 'hooks' that so often brings us into connection with another person, because we are drawn to their appearance, or demeanour.

The greatest problem in this, is that love cannot be thought. It must be felt, and our ability to feel it is determined by the relevant part of ourselves from which we make choices.

When we operate primarily from our minds or egos, we get trapped within conditioned mindsets that can lead us away from love, and more fully into the energy of attraction, and our mind-based illusions, or mental 'checklists', of what love needs to look like, rather than feel like. This is a common attribute of modern life. Many people have largely lost the ability to get in contact with their feelings, and discern what those feelings are trying to tell them.

In this ever-demanding world where there is so much pressure on people both financially, administratively and emotionally, the opportunity to connect to the love in our hearts is a constant struggle. Feeling love is not easy in such a hectic world that validates people on what they do and have, rather than what and who they are, and this discourages us from connecting to, and understanding, our feelings.

All this means is that we are primarily slaves to the fickle components of success and attraction in relationships, and to feelings that we often don't understand. Some people may suppress their feelings, whilst others may be beholden to them. Either way they dismiss the opportunity to benefit from the wisdom that flows through their bodies. It is hard to see or acknowledge the more intelligent and enduring energy that emanates within us, known as love, when we do not fully honour our feelings.

This is where relationships unravel so easily, in the density and murkiness of human thought, not in the purity and passion of love.

I am reminded of the concept in the movie called *The Matrix* (Wachowski, 1999), in which love was so aptly depicted as an unpredictable and irrational glitch in the machine, which was built from logic to control humankind. Is it time we explored love more deeply, because it is more real than the logical but limited apparatus we try to use to describe and control it: our egoic minds?

Is This a Silent Apocalypse?

Many disasters have been recorded in the annals of history, and we of course empathise with those who have suffered through their participation in these events. The tangled mess of romantic relationships is every bit as tragic; yet it seems to go on, coldly sinking our self-worth with titanic proportions.

Just think for a moment about all the separations and divorces around you. Perhaps you have suffered in this as well? You probably know others who have. We have all seen nice, kind and generous people – who tried incredibly hard to love – seemingly struggle to have the relationships they deserved, despite their incredible commitment levels.

Why is this?

The pain and suffering experienced in relationships that 'fail' in this way, or which are mediocre at best, can often feel like an unspoken 'cancer' of human life.

Love is supposed to be blind, but have we become blind to it? So many hearts are broken or are on the verge of breaking. Yet how do we react to this unmitigated disaster, which destroys so many lives and is 'ponying' up to destroy more?

Some of us are living in fear that our relationship will be the next to fall, ignorant to the fact that those fears are the very things making it so probable.

We must first recognise the magnitude of this problem. Otherwise, as a society, we cannot take the steps we need to take to learn from our mistakes. If we bury our collective heads in the 'sand' and hope that it won't happen to us, nothing will change. More importantly, it won't set a good example for the next generation of lovers.

We constantly want more in our modern lives, but for some reason our obsession with more is rarely considered in the context of relationship balance and harmony. We want to own more, or be seen as more important, yet don't we seek to be more, or to love each other more. We blindly roll the dice every day, in every family, then wonder why we so often lose! Are we unknowingly gambling with our love lives?

Relationships are meant to challenge us to grow, but they are not meant to destroy our self-esteem. They are meant to make us wiser and wealthier in the things that really matter, which are not actually tangible matter. Unfortunately, our fragile egos often don't perceive it this way.

Instead, we need to let the pain of romantic relationships educate us, so we can emerge better and stronger than ever before. Being traumatised is not an excuse to stay stuck in the quicksand that just keeps trapping generation after generation in relationship pain. Not when this trauma can end in the wisdom of higher awareness and in defeating the conditioned beliefs that we all share, but to which we are often blind.

Let's approach this situation with wonder, not worry, about what is possible. Let's care more about the happiness of our family units than about impressing our neighbours, who are probably only pretending to be happy, and most likely, don't really care how happy you are anyway!

Love does not have to be blind to flourish. It can be intentional and guided by awareness and a dose of skill. For too many of us, hope alone is not working, and frankly on its own, never will.

Knowing You, Knowing Me

Self-awareness is collectively low among the general human population on this planet, although this too is shifting for those seeking to take responsibility for, and learn from, their own experiences.

A core issue is that few people really know their true selves to any great extent. They know of the personality they were taught to be, the body they have been born within, and the stories of their life thus far. But this is not their true self, which is capable of higher versions of love.

So, I ask you this: if a person does not know the truth of themselves to any significant extent, how can they possibly express their authenticity in a relationship with another person, and expect it to be a satisfying experience? And what is the possibility of true love being experienced, if both people in the relationship are not true to themselves?

Let's not sugar-coat this. The answer is that they simply can't. And herein lies a core issue that has been present for centuries, and which renders romantic relationships substantially fragile, often shattering them completely.

'No' is a complete sentence, and it's time we simply said a short and sharp 'no' to this ludicrous illusion we all buy into with ignorance.

Relationship experts can argue about how attraction can be understood or manipulated until they are 'blue in the face', but unless we realise that all we so-often do is mould and manipulate fake and unnatural identities to get our needs met, we will continue to experience a litany of failed relationships, and what we naïvely refer to as 'broken' hearts.

The truth is that hearts don't break, only our egos do. Our egoic minds are always the source of any romantic pain that we feel in our bodies. Our hearts are our eternal source of joy. Until we understand this, we will never move forward to create harmony between the masculine and feminine.

Ignorance is said to be bliss, but not when it comes to love!

Similarly, love is said to be blind, yet nothing sees clearer than pure love in its infinite wisdom.

When two people in a romantic relationship do not know themselves to any great extent, they will be at the whim of the many subconscious belief structures that reside within them. It is like playing Russian roulette with each other, with three bullets in the chambers, because at any moment their subconscious belief structures, which they are yet to understand, can be triggered and explode within their relationship.

Unless we grow from our painful pasts, we are also highly unlikely to create pain-free futures, for ourselves or our children. But if we listen to love, it can be both beautiful and brutal in the wisdom that it offers us. If we can understand the power of love and truth in relationships more fully, it can help us reframe 'setbacks' as 'steps forward', and ruthless outcomes as ruthless truths that we should not ignore.

Our love lives could collectively be described as a kind of jungle. At present this jungle is full of fear, but with new rules and a dose of reality, we can change this jungle into one that captivates our hearts. As espoused by the famous song from the stage play, *The Lion King*, 'Can You Feel The Love Tonight' by Elton John, the feeling of love is enough to make kings and vagabonds believe the very best.

Now isn't that the kind of jungle within which we all want to be set free?

Mirror, Mirror on the Wall

A key thing we need to understand when we think about romantic relationships, is that they are essentially universal 'experiments' designed to help us really know and experience the love that we already are at our core.

Relationships hold a magic mirror up to both parties in the relationship to help them see themselves more clearly. And I don't mean physically, I mean seeing the truths about their beliefs and insecurities. This is why our souls often match us with the 'right, wrong' person, to enhance the power of this self-awareness journey.

Loving relationships require a commitment to transparency and truth, not denial, and this is so often in short supply. Typically, we all have an attachment pattern that we apply when relating to the opposite sex, which typically remains hidden, particularly to ourselves, because we are often not wise enough to look for it, and refine it through knowing. It's safer not to, so we hide within the shadows of our own sense of righteousness and deflect our pain onto others.

How many people carry the stories within them of a destructive ex-partner, without being able to see that ultimately that story is about them, and what they have been prepared to accept, reflect or project.

One truth in life is that you always get back what you put out. Dishonour yourself, and others will be sure to dishonour you in turn. That's a given.

And to be frank, this was the greatest lesson I learned in my many years of romantic relationships, in a very painful way.

Relationships can so often either bring you higher self-esteem or harm your sense of self. Unfortunately, what we are seeing is too many people getting hurt in romantic relationships, because they are not approaching them in a conscious way, and are instead holding on to negative stories that limit their potential for happiness.

This is not their fault, because they are unknowingly playing out historic patterns that they witnessed, and which were programmed into them.

What we have seen, and been surrounded by for centuries, is countless relationships based on mutual incompleteness. And, to be frank, we are choosing this unhappy mindset.

Many people say that they want a partner to complete them. But there is great toxicity in this perspective, because the truth is that no one else can ever complete you. Only you can do this for yourself. So, if you hear this comment on a first date, my advice is to take a step back, before going forward.

Fortunately, both partners can complete themselves, and share this in harmony with another, if they set this intention and act upon it with authenticity.

The real power lies within us, not outside of us, when we empower ourselves to love, and become more aligned with our own truths.

Do We Really Understand Each Other?

In general, men and women are largely clueless about each other's psychologies, simply because we don't learn from each other. Both genders are constantly in tension with each other because of a lack of transparency, and because of conditioned mindsets that date back over millennia. But power plays and subtle control are inconsistent with the energy of love and are best avoided in relationships.

Our Egos are Dating, Mating and Relating

When we are not making our feelings of love a key component in our choice of romantic partners, but instead relying on our ideas of love, we are essentially outsourcing that choice to our egos.

Unfortunately, our egos are artificial representations of our true selves. They are individuated identities, that our experiences have taught us that we are, rather than the truth of our existence. We are spirits, or metaphysical fields of awareness, having a physical experience, and we are all connected through our hearts. Unfortunately, we have collectively forgotten this, and this is colouring the way we interact with each other, in a negative way.

In this world, we are embarking on a new era of AI. We fear the impacts of Artificial Intelligence, because it may disrupt our lives in some, if not many, ways. Yet we ignorantly hand our lives over to the more insidious version of AI that directly impacts every aspect of our interactions with this world: our own Artificial Identities, which live in our heads and think they know what we truly desire. They do not!

Would you trust an illusory being that has thoughts, generated from limiting and hidden beliefs, to create the more important aspects of your life; or would you prefer to give it to the intelligent centre of truth within you, which knows you and others better than your ego ever could?

Two artificial personalities thinking they can create true love together – that's the insanity to which many people tether their futures. And we wonder why so many relationships do not live up to our artificial expectations, which our psyches dream up.

Two artificial people with artificial dreams, trying to create a life together in an unpredictable and often artificial world – what could possibly go wrong?

Our hearts don't lie. If only we could let them freely express their loving truths! Yet illusions of love are so much easier to believe in, and are so dominantly represented in mainstream thinking, that it's hard to move away from our artificial psyches, and towards our true and authentic frequencies.

Truer versions of love are available to us all, but we need to learn how to attain them. It's not a simple process for most of us, but precious things in life are rarely easy to attain.

Our Version of Love is Creating Isolation

There is a powerful trend currently in the dating and relating world. Many people of both sexes are realising that the 'love game', in which they have been participating for decades, is not serving them well. The recurring disappointments that people are experiencing in romantic relationships, are building walls between the sexes, and these walls seem to be getting thicker and higher with every failing relationship. And from what I observe, many are simply giving up out of frustration and despair, and walking away to 'lick their wounds'.

Sadly, much trust seems to have been lost between the sexes, despite their intent as divine unions. We seem to have unions, but the divine aspect that deepens those unions into something more meaningful seems to be missing.

Catch cries heard with repetition on social media – like 'where have all the good men gone', and 'modern women want husbands, but refuse to be wives' – are indicative of the demeaning rhetoric that our egos, so willingly, entertain. Many people end up comparing their quite acceptable lives, to the highlight reels of others, and concluding that their partners are a problem. Surely this narrow-minded thinking needs to be replaced with higher wisdom that recognises the realities of love, and how to work with it.

It takes two to tango, as is often said, and both sexes need to carry equal responsibility for the raft of behaviours that are being directed at each other and making divine union so hard to attain. The blame game is a zero-sum game, and many of us have discovered this the hard way.

We need to realise that love is the prize in our love lives, not one sex or person. Our hearts want us to experience true fulfilment in love; not the illusions of love we have been subliminally taught we need to achieve.

I don't believe that most jilted lovers truly want to give up. At their core, every bone in their bodies, and impulse in their hearts, still hunger for satisfying love and deep intimacy. After all, this is what we were born to enjoy.

However, devoid of answers and saddened by the complexities that they have experienced in maintaining loving relationships, they are choosing peace and isolation, over the risk of getting it wrong again.

Many people are walking away from romantic relationships because they are witnessing how fragile they have become. They have 'chased the dragon', being their mind's fantasy of true love, and got burned along the way. They have been wise enough to see that, all too often, the love game has become a kind of auction process, in which many people have become accustomed to offering themselves to the highest bidder. The problem is that less people are deciding to bid, out of the fear of getting it wrong. And this is causing a massive disconnect to take shape.

A key question is, do both sexes want the privilege of being in a relationship, without the core responsibility of doing so in alignment with love, and the discomfort that this can bring forth. And is this confusing and uncomfortable state leading them to give up and walk away from relationships, or creating a kind of detached form of dating, called situationships, in which we protect our hearts from more pain, rather than act from a place of vulnerability. After all, once bitten twice shy!

I have been in their 'shoes' and walked the same lonely path. And I had to discover the answers to this dilemma for myself, for they were not readily apparent in the education system I attended, or in the words of those who I hoped would guide me forward to success.

There is a deep irony in this situation. We are ignoring, out of ignorance, the one powerful force that can bring us connection and unification, rather than isolation and separation. And that force is love, and the higher intelligence to which it connects us.

For centuries our minds have conquered our hearts and led us into relationships that do not really serve our happiness.

But these paradigms are now being challenged by a population that is shifting in its conscious awareness, away from co-dependency and compliance, into one of self-determination and greater sovereignty for all. And new rules are rightly supporting this shift.

After centuries of being the chattels of men, women now have the legal right to be free and to live the lives that they choose in western society. However, this new wave of positive self-centredness is causing confusion for many, as men and women, who for centuries have played by different rules, struggle to adapt to this purer opportunity to really love themselves and each other on equal terms.

And men now need to look at this situation and see that they too have the right to explore parts of themselves that society once said needed to be suppressed; and by that, I mean the more creative and nurturing aspects of themselves that they have every right to cultivate.

Old conditioning is clashing with newer, more conscious ways of living, and frankly our society did not see this battle coming, despite our extraordinary, combined intellects. Many people have been living in the fear that they will be the next to fail, in something they cherish so deeply, and in the process of trying to stay safe and in control, they are manifesting their fears into reality on a mass scale.

For as long as we are blind to what is really going on, the blame game will remain in full swing, our sense of isolation will grow, and our walls will only get stronger – whereas they really should be coming down, in the energies of compassion and care.

This book holds the answers to this dilemma, for those who are ready to open their hearts to its messages and transformative solutions. We do owe it to ourselves to discover more, rather than continue to suffer, because that is the only sustainable way out.

But beware, the advanced principles shared in this book require dedicated application, and an open mind. They are not a five-minute fix.

We Need to Rise, Not Fall, in Love

We are all familiar with the concept of falling in love, and we idolise the idea of finding true love, and yet very few of us know what this pure version of love really feels or looks like.

What we normally call falling in love has always been, in part, a kind of trance-like experience, highly based in the energies of fear and need. You meet someone and, almost without realising it, your ego begins to weave a fantasy story of security and completeness. It sees a future that it has merely imagined, soothing its own anxieties.

In this energy we create an image of love that is based on romance, passion, unrivalled joy and eternal promises, and this introduces fantasies and expectations into our love lives that are hard to live up to.

Indeed, when we look for completeness in another, what we are really saying to the world is that we need a companion, because to some degree we are lonely, and in need of validation. Then we enter various contracts and promises, to lock this illusion into our realities, without the required level of skill and self-awareness that would ensure both parties deliver on their part of the 'bargain'.

In many instances, the illusion of romance we ascribe to is a kind of silent pact that says, 'I will soothe your loneliness if you soothe mine'.

But when the first stages of ecstasy pass, many wonder whether they ever truly loved, or were loved, at all, or merely sought to satisfy their own needs through the attention of another.

This love is so often an impure one – formed out of a hunger for companionship, mutual attraction and a desire to fulfil whichever path we were taught to follow, and which we thought we needed to go down. But for many this is loneliness masquerading as love, and fragility disguised as security.

The type of love we can become obsessed with is like a flame burning in the breeze. It is susceptible to the changing winds that we are yet to see or feel, and the depth of 'fuel' that lies beneath it all. Yet this is the kind of impure love that many relationships are built around.

But our egos refuse to see this truth, falsely believing that they are the rightful owners and masters of love – whereas they can never be. Love can never be a concept we can contain in our minds. It is an energy we can only ever be a willing conduit for, as it flows through us and graces our lives.

Be the conduit of love, not the container, and let it flow.

We are in fact capable of so much more when we tame the very energies that separate us from the purer level of love that we are all capable of experiencing. In this place we can open our hearts to new possibilities and a version of love that – to most of us – is completely unfamiliar. It has no conditions, no desire to be captured, no interest in drama or chaos, no need to be based on promises, or the illusion that it needs to be rescued.

What this book offers to readers is the path to a truer love than the world currently understands collectively. It's a calm love, free of confusion and the need for theatre, based in simplicity, and strangely full of composure. The possibility that awaits you as a flame in this centred energy is the opportunity to meet and burn alongside another flame, that does not need you to complete it, for it is already complete. It simply desires to add to yours, for the sheer passion and joy that this can bring forth.

And once we enter this experience of love, our lives, and the society we are inhabiting, will also change for the better. After all, our habits always create our habitats.

This kind of love represents a form of freedom and bliss, expressed in a relationship that needs no lifetime promises, just the daily choice to stay together, because the mere thought of being anywhere else is unimaginable.

This ultimate relationship – based on two untethered but willing hearts in deep connection – is our birthright, and what nature intended for all of us. It is the miracle of true love in practice, devoid of the sense of lack that many of us currently carry, and that insidious need for external validation. This is the kind of love that fairytales try to represent but simply cannot deliver, because it is truly beyond story and thought… Until now!

It can take time to reach the level of self-awareness that supports this special kind of love, but every step we take towards it helps us to create better connections. The stepping stones to higher love await our fearless adventures.

In a world where we have lost sight of the fact that our romantic interactions are a mirror of our own selves – and give us license to grow in the energy of love and our own sense of accountability – we stand at the cross-roads and the opportunity is upon us to step forward into the types of connections about which we all dream, including our ultimate connection with another.

You do have the capacity to experience an unbreakable bond with another, when you release your chains of regret about your painful past, untether yourself from your fears of a painful future and admire the uniqueness of your own life, and that of others. Regret is the price we pay for failing to investigate what we are truly capable of, and to exit our propensity to see ourselves as victims, rather than the benefactors of love.

Love knows that now is all that matters, and it is urging us to forgive what was, and what is, and step into a new paradigm where higher versions of love await us.

This is not a fantasy.

This is a reality that the wisest amongst us already know about. Now it's your turn.

True Peace Must Start in Forgiveness

Collectively, we must face the reality that making romantic relationships work is proving to be extremely difficult, if not a very painful experience for many. The pattern can even repeat itself for generations, lifetime after lifetime.

But there is nothing constructive we can do about the past, except learn from it. We are where we are. What has taken place is what has taken place, and what is, just is. Now is the time to step forward into a greater place of peace, knowing that it all serves to help us evolve, individually and together.

If we are to draw a line in the sand and move forward in peace, however, we must accept and process our past pain, and learn to trust again, even in the presence of fear, so that we can allow new, peaceful possibilities to arise.

I invite all my readers to come on this journey from pain to possibility in their love lives. Forgive yourself for any failures you think you've experienced, realise that they were gifts to help you grow, appreciate the person you have now become, be grateful for the wisdom you have now, and be hopeful for the time when you can finally share the love that you are, with another with freedom of expression.

Let the stepping stones of your past relationship disappointments merge and form your pathway back to freedom.

It is time to learn, then return.

Balance and Harmony Are Critical

What I will share with you in this book is that balance and harmony hold the key to bringing masculine and feminine energies together in the way nature intended.

Only people who have high levels of personal harmony and balance within their own energies and ways of being can truly experience that with another person. And no one else can give it to them. They must find it for themselves.

And this is my area of expertise.

Those who are slaves to their subconscious beliefs and shadows will continue to struggle through relationships, particularly once the initial need for each other starts to wane. But once enough individuals find balance and harmony within themselves, this can ripple out across our world and through individual relationships.

Frankly, if you haven't tamed your own monsters within you, you could become a monster in your so-called loving relationships. And monsters can end up alone and avoided.

We have all witnessed those rare, loving relationships where people have been together in a loving embrace for many years, and still hold hands when they walk down the street. There is a purity that you can't help but notice in these exchanges, which deep down many of us also crave to experience.

My dream is to help make this possible for all, even if it will take time and commitment. Our lives together should no longer be squandered in the ignorance handed down through our lineage, not when bliss was the intention of our divine design.

It's time we embraced real love, and stopped chasing our dragons of desire, for we just keep getting burnt. But we can rise from these ashes, like the legendary Phoenix, if we choose to enjoy our love lives, rather than suffer in silence by choice.

Separation Consciousness is an Illusion

As I explained in my book *The Truth About Love*, in some detail, we have inherently come to believe that we are all separate beings, instead of one connected 'family'. And this belief in separation ensures that relationship breakdowns become a reality in our 3D world.

We have largely separated from our own hearts, and then this inner reality becomes our outer reality, at the expense of what we really desire: divine union with another.

For the sake of brevity, I won't repeat the detail of this wisdom in this book in any depth, other than to reiterate that when we start to understand, then believe in true union, we can create a world in which harmonious unions between partners is not only possible, but divinely supported and inevitable.

On this planet, we get what we put out, so what we receive is always for us to learn from. Or in other words, we receive what we have become. The day that two people take this wisdom into their romantic relationship is the day that true union becomes possible.

We need to believe in unification, not separation, and the purity of our relationships can lift to meet our dreams. What good is a desire for true connection between us, when in the depths of our unconscious minds we collectively believe that it is not truly possible, or sustainable, in the long term? We are what we believe after all.

We are meant to be all-one, not alone.

Chapter 2

How Our Separation Mindsets are Playing Out

The Current Landscape of Romantic Relationships

As I said, we live in a world where harmony and balance between masculine and feminine energies have seemingly become more destabilised and fragile than ever before. Separations are not only increasingly common, or at least seem that way, but social media has created a platform for problems and unresolved traumas to be aired for all to see, buy into and comment upon.

Our dirty laundry, once discrete and private, is now on constant show, and the battle of the sexes has morphed into a public war, in which thousands seem to participate every day on social media.

Frankly, this is not how things are naturally meant to be. Men and women are a force of nature when we come together with love and complement each other. When we act in union together, we have the capacity to create a situation that is rich in joy and happiness.

Alas, many current relationships seem to be more sad than sacred.

The recorded statistics are glaringly bad, suggesting that a new blueprint for the conduct of romantic relationships is well and truly overdue. Although divorce rates vary across the world, due to differing cultures and circumstances, if we use the rates in the major western nations in recent years as an indicator we get a view of the scale of despair. It is estimated that around 50% of marriages end in divorce.

Here are some statistics from 2023:

Russia: 72%
Sweden: 68%
United States: 45%
Australia: 43%
United Kingdom: 41%

But here are some other alarming statistics to consider.

According to *Psychology Today*, a US source, divorce rates rise for every subsequent marriage. The divorce rate for people getting married for the first time in the USA is 45%, but in second marriages it rises to an average of 67%, and for third marriages it rises even higher to 73% on average.

In addition, when two people get together because of an affair, only 1.5% to 3% of these relationships result in partnerships or marriages that last longer than two years.

What do these statistics tell us?

Of course, you may have your own views, but what they tell me is that people who remarry may not have done enough self-reflection and 'healing' to prevent their future relationships from also being fragile. And with every 'failed' relationship, they accumulate further wounds and fragilities, which can be triggered in subsequent relationships, making the later relationships even more risky and volatile.

So, are we doing enough self-development across the population to make us better lovers as our lives progress? Or do we just try again with blind hope and more scars on our backs after each failure?

I think the latter is often the case, which is why I took the advice of a learned expert in relationships, after my second divorce, and stayed single for years, whilst I deeply healed from my past experiences.

Now ponder this: if someone asked you to enter a business proposal that had these apparent chances of 'failure', would you invest your money in it?

Yet every day, more people get married, or remarried after a previous divorce, or jump into new relationships without properly exiting the last one in integrity and some semblance of self-reflection, as to how they contributed to the demise of their relationship, in turn allowing them to be more skilled at loving in the future.

Hope springs eternal! Probably because so many of the people in long-term enduring relationships argue that they have very joyful experiences, and if that is truly the case then I salute them for their apparent success.

However, psychologists also say that many ongoing relationships are not as happy as they appear to be, and could be more joyous if conducted more consciously. For example, although difficult to prove, relationship experts often refer to around 30% to 35% of enduring marriages as being unhappy or partially unfulfilled. And these are the ones that have not ended in divorce.

When you aggregate the divorce rates with these statistics pertaining to mediocre relationships, you get a staggering statistic that is in the order of 80% to 85% of relationships that are not really working.

Surely, we need to at least recognise that the probability of success is against us, within the current paradigms. When two people marry, or commit to be in lifetime union, irrespective of their sexual preferences, they are effectively signalling to the world that they have developed a deep connection with a single person, with whom they plan to spend the rest of their life. This means they've identified a single soul out of roughly eight billion as being 'the one' for them.

While marriage may be a beautiful concept, and one that we collectively grow up fantasising about, it's highly possible that the beauty of the concept will turn into regret, not because marriage is a bad idea, but because many of us are unskilled as to how to enter or conduct marriages. ***I know I once was.***

So why do we persist with marriage, when so many people struggle so much to make it work for them?

Perhaps when we enter marriage, or other forms of relationships that we intend to be permanent, we prefer to ignore statistics, such as those above, or perhaps we just don't care, because we wholeheartedly believe that our love or relationship is unique and will stand the test of time and change. I'm sure the latter is more often the case.

In a world where the art of conducting important relationships has been left to our unskilled minds and a desire to commit to each other on a 'wing and a prayer', pure hope without wisdom, is sometimes not enough to overcome the challenges that lie ahead.

In my book *The Truth About Love*, I speak about the need for more conscious relating in romantic relationships, so that egos don't dismantle them when issues arise. Love is a force directly linked to divine intelligence through our souls, so it will test us every step of the way in a romantic relationship, so we can grow both individually and together. We can thus evolve with love, rather than let it merely expose fatal wounds in our self-awareness and abilities to love.

But to accomplish this, we need to be well-armed in awareness and committed to our relationships, above our own egoic desires to personally 'win' from love.

This is not a fantasy. I have witnessed it in full swing between highly aware couples and have admired their outward expression of constantly expanding happiness. They will all tell you, however, that it took high levels of hard work, constant and deep self-reflection, and uncomfortable conversations to get to such a fresh place of relating to each other, at such a high level of love.

Of course, not all romantic relationships evolve into marriage or even proposed permanence. Dating is more prone to create more temporary relationships as people 'test the waters' with prospective partners. This is logical because such arrangements provide an opportunity to explore whether you are suited to another person or even love them sufficiently to commit to them.

But what if we approached the dating and relating games with a different mindset, and even higher awareness levels than we do now?

Could the outcomes be different and the rejections be less painful? ***I believe so!***

Fulfilled Relationships Make Our World Go Around

We are all different, but one of the key determinants of the quality of our lives is the strength and vitality of our human relationships with each other, and within ourselves.

True happiness comes from being uniquely ourselves and expressing that in harmonious union with people who we love and cherish. I called this the Code of Happiness in my book *Where Your Happiness Hides*.

But look around you, and witness where we are as a race, by virtue of our interactions with each other, particularly with respect to the relationships that matter most to us.

Consider these compelling questions…

Do many countries live in harmony with each other?

Are our corporate cultures full of love, and focussed on making our working lives a happy and fulfilling experience, given how much of our lives we spend contributing to our employers, and businesses so that we can pay for the things we need and want? Or do many of them create cultures of fear, as they focus on money as their primary intent?

And do we make the most of our romantic experiences by making sure that they represent deep explorations into what it means to be in love?

Collectively, are we in love with our lives, or do we deep down fear what our futures hold, because we are exhausted from living in a highly competitive world that demands so much of us just to, seemingly, survive?

For many years I endured stress in different forms, trying to be successful in different walks of life, and this eventually took a heavy toll on my nervous system that I needed to address. And romantic relationship uncertainty was the key source of my stress. I tried so

hard, but my consciousness was too low to align my relationship outcomes with my lofty, but normal, expectations.

The suites of relationships that we conduct have been impaired by imbalanced ways of looking at the world, primarily through the lens of masculine perspectives. And we have lost sight that this is even happening, for we are like the proverbial 'frog in the pot', getting gradually hotter, and more stressed out and confused. And this is the source of much stress and mental health issues in our world.

Relaxing into the peace and joy we all deserve is seemingly only possible for those who have wrestled through life's challenges, and come out the other side, bruised, but not beaten from the race.

In fact, let's consider how we call ourselves a race of people. This description is more apt than we ever truly recognise, for we all think we are racing towards some imaginary finishing line, which truly does not exist. And most people on their death beds seem to be the first to admit that, when all is said and done, the love they shared with others was what mattered most in their lives.

To a degree, we have become inherently competitive, cut off from our feelings and focussed on doing, rather than being, and enjoying our lives as a priority.

In Chapter 5, I provide a core list of masculine and feminine energies. When you witness them, the proverbial 'penny will drop' for many readers, because you will see what we have become by virtue of our core energies and beliefs in a patriarchal world. Descriptors like righteous, competitive, factual, impatient, biased to action and goal oriented, tend to reflect what our cultures in the western world have become biased towards for many decades.

Is this how we want to live, interact, date and relate?

I say no, and I have spent the last decade of my life unashamedly rebalancing the masculine and feminine energies within me to give me a greater opportunity to bring love and joy into my life, and my key relationships.

Success, as I have said, has seemingly become our mantra and has replaced the concept of fulfilment as our primary intent in life. And this subconscious persuasion has leaked into our romantic relationships and turned them into unhealthy battles that we must win, not loving exchanges within which we can find bliss. It's all seemingly about me, me, me without much we, we, we.

Is this what we really want from our exchanges with each other, in our many roles in life?

Do you think that our modern relationships are striving to be successful or fulfilling, as a rule?

I personally think that they have atrophied into the former, without us really understanding why. And perhaps they have been like this for many years, without us taking the time to honestly reflect upon the situation!

The Anomaly of Success and Fulfilment

One core paradigm that was baked into me growing up, was the belief that success was my 'ticket' to everything else I dreamt about, including true love. But I eventually realised the falsehood in this paradigm and reframed it. This is the formula I subconsciously, lived from growing up: Success, once achieved, gives me love, recognition, happiness, fun and peace.

Put differently, success leads to fulfilment. This unconscious belief turned out to be my greatest source of pain.

Life had a way of showing me otherwise, sometimes brutally. Dysfunction and fragility in my life showed me that the formula was truly the reverse, as follows.

Living fully filled with love (i.e. fulfilled) leads us to peace, and from here we can find true happiness, union, fun and, ultimately, the kind of success that is sustainable or recurring. When you live from love, you can create the life that you love from within, not based on some kind of external barometer.

Now most readers will probably say, 'I knew that'. But the bigger

question is, are you able to feel it, and do you embody this truth beyond your conscious thoughts? I believe this is rare, because of the success-obsessed incubator we all inhabit and with which we are programmed to comply

When you live from your heart, and embody its love and wisdom, success truly becomes a re-source – a recurring source of enrichment in your life.

Romantic relationships with love at their very core don't allow our dented egos to overwhelm them with fear and need, and tear them apart. They emerge and grow in an incubator of shared love and peace, which allows these beautiful energies to take them to new heights, full of happiness and shared success as a couple.

And this success is one that can be defined by both individuals, together, in harmony. It doesn't need to be defined in normal material ways, like money or having the biggest house in the street. In love, the possibilities are endless.

If you believe that your success, or the success of your partner, will bring you the happiness you crave, you have almost certainly bought into the false paradigm to which I once clung. And this is where so much distortion arises in relationships, because our happiness is being defined by an external definition of what our relationships need to look like to *make* us successful.

Fully fill your heart, and live in peace, and you can repaint your world with the most beautiful colours of life. And let's start with violet, because when we mix masculine blue with feminine pink, in equal measure, we get a beautiful violet colour, that represents the divine unions we all deserve.

Love has a blank canvass and awaits our artistry.

All in Life is a Choice

All in life is a choice, and our lives are determined by a series of decisions that add up to a lifetime. When you look at a headstone in a cemetery, we see two dates: the date of birth and the date of death, separated by a dash. We focus on the two dates, and celebrate the first one every year. But the true life we are remembering is found within the non-descript dash.

I wrote this book so that the dashes of my readers could also embody an uplifting story – in which love usurps value, and gives them the relationships that their hearts know are possible!

For many this will require a kind of rebirth in the way they witness themselves and engage in romantic relationships. ***But as I proved to myself, letting my past rest in peace, and starting again with new and fresh perspectives, was my best way forward.***

Finding the Love, We Deserve

Marcus Aurelius, the second century philosopher and Roman Emperor, famously said these words:

> "Never stop trying to deserve the life that you were given."

And the life that we were given is meant to be one of love and joy, not pain and despair.

Let me reiterate what I wrote in my book *The Truth About Love*. Love is a frequency, and what we call 'falling in love' occurs when our own frequency of love correlates with that of another who we meet. All souls love each other on some vibrational level, but intense love is essentially a close matching of frequencies between two people, because it activates the frequency of love that they share. It cannot be thought or controlled by their respective minds.

Love, in its infinite wisdom, is our eternal teacher, and it wants to rewrite our understanding of its very own force. It is here to make us, not break us, to guide and heal us through its presence, and bring peace where chaos once lived.

And it is patiently waiting for us to turn in its direction for guidance.

Love is not meant to drain us, be a sacrifice, confuse us, or make us question our worth. It is meant to be kind, loyal, caring, gentle, soft and help us feel like we are once again home in a place that we may have temporarily forgotten was possible. Ironically, we are all totally worthy because of the love that we are, yet we spend much of our lives trying to find that love.

But first we must understand it deeply, and allow it more fully into our relationships; because if we don't, love can turn brutal and ruthless in the face of our ignorance, and so often does.

If we trust love again, it can restore our desire for connection not righteousness, and for partnership not sponsorship. And our relationships can become what we deserve. Not transactions, but true partnerships that nourish our souls.

So, we need to open our hearts and trust in divine timing, and the reality that love may be preparing our hearts for a kind of love that does not look like the one our minds imagined, or which we were told to expect. And if we open our hearts and patiently trust in its intelligence, it will!

If you are reading this book, then I believe your heart is ready for more. It wants to experience a love that is sacred, not dramatic, painful, or conditional; just warm and free to express itself with pure passion. This is our collective birthright.

Not all relationships are meant to last forever, and this is a reality we must teach our minds to understand. But there is much hope for those who want to experience, honour and respect love and bring forth new beginnings where pain once lived.

Why Are So Many People Giving Up on Love?

It is apparent that many people – after repeated attempts to find love and create loving relationships – are simply giving up and deciding not to participate in dating and relating anymore. I'm sure they all have their own reasons, and to generalise can be unwise. But why is this the case when being in love is something so many of us deeply desire?

I have lived this experience myself, so I am speaking from my own experiences here. I believe I lost trust in myself to choose the right person to relate to, after repeated perceived failures. And I know that I also felt that there was no point in offering my love to women who did not seem to value it in return. My confidence in a world that had seemingly let me down in the past was simmering in my subconscious beliefs. Confusion reigned within me, and I admit that I had a bit of a victim mentality for a period.

My self-trust was also depleted by what my mind saw as repeated mismatches, and the belief that getting a romantic relationship right was just all too hard, at least for someone like me, who had given my all in the past and come out seemingly 'empty handed'.

My mind did a kind of logical assessment of the inherent risks of having another 'screw-up', and so I stayed well clear of the dating world for years, convincing myself that this was best for me and for my potential partners. I would just get hurt and so would they. Essentially, I saw myself as incompetent and incapable of getting relationships right. When you boil it all down, I felt somewhat unworthy and confused. I became both a victim and a martyr all in one.

Perhaps this was logical after multiple mishaps, but I came to see another core truth in the end. Essentially, my ego had a need for certainty and security that was not being met, and so it subconsciously told me to shut down my love life. My love life was fragile, to say the least, but the learnings and personal growth I finally attained from my past experiences became a great gift of awareness that I was failing to recognise, until I did. Eventually, I took full ownership for all my less-than-ideal outcomes and stopped blaming others.

I also witnessed, without judgement, but with compassionate discernment, the limitations of the partners with whom I had shared relationships. The relationships 'failed' not me, or them.

Perhaps this is what others are also going through? Only they will know. There is, however, peace in the avoidance of risk and potential pain. But is there adventure, learning and fulfilment in playing safe?

To come out of my fear of trying again, I had to embrace the reality that expecting any relationship to have certain outcomes that met my mental constructs of security was an illusion. Love carves its own path, and relationships are intrinsically uncertain, particularly when we enter them in an unconscious way.

Our minds simply cannot lock in a future that they need to feel safe and secure, despite their grandest attempts to do so. The future cannot be foreseen by the human mind, no matter how hard we try. What we need to see is that love is leading us home to a better place, but sometimes we must trust in its wisdom, and be prepared to face our fears, as scary as that may seem at times. Nothing in this world is certain when it comes to relationships, but our hearts have higher intelligence than our minds.

Courage requires us to trust our hearts and ignore the safety-first protestations of our minds. But first we must come to terms with the insidious and often subconscious chains within which our egos have us constrained.

I believe that through deep soul-searching others can find their way back to a better love life, for this is their heart's desire. Our desire for romantic connection is not a problem, but our fears that they will not meet our expectations are. After all, expectations are the enemy of fun and fulfilment!

Ditching the Current Blame Game

Most of us try hard to find love and keep it. But this is one of the key issues that prevent us from being at peace in our lives.

So many of us try to keep loving someone, even when a matching level of love is not present. Or we love with shadows in our hearts after past disappointments without trying to remove them. Try as we may, these situations often set us up for even more disappointments, which add to the ones we are already carrying in our minds. The result can be debilitating, and lead us to abandon relationships all together, and eventually close our hearts as our trust in love diminishes. The irony is that love is the one thing in life we can trust!

When past relationships end, we often carry guilt, or choose to carry shame or blame, into our futures – which is not truly ours to carry. These energies can block the flow of love that is possible in our current or future relationships.

This is not our fault, but it is our opportunity, once witnessed.

Our egos are normally the source of hope when new relationships arise; but can swiftly become the source of pain when we fail to meet our original expectations. It's a kind of 'Jekyll and Hyde' situation, creating a recurring story of union and separation all in the one script. And this is a learned way of being that can deny us the love that we deserve, until we witness it, in integrity, and learn to release it.

Ascribing blame to relationship problems is a form of ignorant judgement, because in doing so we are failing to accept that all in life happens for purpose.

Sitting in the shadows of any relationship disappointment or problem is a chance for us to grow, individually and collectively. Relationships do not usually fall apart if they are happy, so we need to learn how to keep them happy.

When people enter relationships, it is fair to say, that most people are trying to make them work. But when we need to try too hard, it is a fair sign that love is not flowing naturally, or fully within the relationship.

We must learn to accept that, try as we might, our hearts and/or minds may not be fully matched in a relationship, and we just need to separate, with kindness and regret in our hearts, knowing that each partner did their best.

We also need to ensure that we have not imposed unrealistic expectations on the people we were originally attracted to and decided we loved enough to form a relationship with. It can be quite normal to place higher expectations on those people we say we love or desire, then measure them against our unrealistic plans and expectations, whereas we would never treat others in this uncompassionate way.

Sheeting home blame, rather than forgiving, and, if need be, putting up loving boundaries, is a common practice we need to question in this age, where we credit ourselves for being more educated than any generation that came before us.

This book gives us the chance to turn this misconception into reality!

Love is What Really Matters

It is often said that to be fulfilled in our lives we need to follow our hearts. We speak of passion, and passion can only be derived from the love in our hearts. It does not originate in our minds, contrary to the teachings of some.

I contend that for someone to be fully in flow and happy in their life, they need to love what they are doing and feel the joy in the expression of this.

The combination of self-worth, self-love and self-expression is a powerful combination capable of taking us forward to a life of great joy. And this clearly applies to our love lives.

The natural way we are meant to live is to feel from our hearts what would make us happy. From here, our minds orchestrate this reality, for they are our inbuilt, logical orchestrators and coordinators. Our bodies then step forward as the vehicle that physically allows us to implement what we aspire to do.

But how do so many of us live this way? Most people *think* their way forward and implementing what they *think* is the best alternative for them. But in this process the messages of the heart get ignored and deprioritised. Obligation takes over, as does our sense of needing to be successful, based on external measures of what 'should' make us happy, and not what really can.

This was my modus-operandi in my life for over 50 years, until I saw how fundamentally unhappy and fragile my life had become, all because I was ignoring my heart in most things I did.

When our hearts, minds and bodies are in sync, in the way nature intended, passion will grace our lives, and life will become addictive in its beauty for us. Not because we are meeting some external measure of success, which purports to signal how well we are doing, but because we are feeling the fulfillment and joy of life rising from within us.

My new catchcry is therefore this: 'nothing is worth doing unless my heart is in it'. Or to put it another way, 'these days I only do what I love, with people I love'.

Our Love Has Become Disposable

Many people think that finding love means achieving a life with little pain, because the right partner will take away our bruises and problems. But this is a fantasy on a grand scale for most people. And this is why so many relationships with unlimited potential end in separation or apathy, or are thrown away before they even got to be fully explored.

We are all human, and there will be times when we will let each other down, in ways neither partner saw coming. The question, as this book explores, is not about how we can just preserve our love through the tough times, but how we can use adversity and pain to bring us closer together, and deeper into the magic of love.

Can we stay calm when things get tough? Can we forgive rather than hang onto resentments for months and even years? And can we choose to prioritise our relationships if possible?

Perhaps the partner worth being with is not the one with the flash car, the public profile or the perfect body, but the one who will not walk away when things get tough, preferring to be loyal, heal and grow alongside you?

Finding someone you can share love with, who will continue to choose you again and again, even on the days when it would have been easier to walk away and start again, is a special kind of love.

This is the kind of love that our hearts want us to experience: a love so deep that it just keeps getting deeper, like walking into a sparkling ocean, regardless of what goes wrong or right in your life.

This is what is possible when we learn to become more loving, and love in an advanced way. And this is our opportunity, together, to start with a fresh canvas and repaint our romantic relationships with a new kind of colour, until they're the ones we were always meant to have.

Can you stop for a moment and just imagine this in your life? If you already have it, I honour you more than you know. If not, give me the opportunity to inspire you through the wisdom in this book.

Chapter 3

What Price Are We Paying for 'Love'?

Our Current Romantic Confusion

Most people enter adulthood full of hope about the prospects of meeting the love of their life and living happily ever after. We are all 'sold' this dream.

However, the dream is sold at different prices to different people, many of whom do not know what they truly deserve, and some are now refusing to pay the ever-inflating price it costs to play and compete.

Unfortunately, the contemporary dating world has created a sense of disposability for many people, particularly those who we unfairly judge as average, or even below average. It is highly transactional and many people are being made to feel like they are just disposable options, in a market where transactions are plentiful, and where many people date multiple people at once, because they can. And all this is occurring against a backdrop of conditioned mindsets that silently set us up for failure.

I don't want to buy into the frailties of the relationship world too heavily with too much judgement, because I know that the mess is the result of bad habits, and limited ways of thinking by both men and women. ***And I once was a part of it all unknowingly.*** But it doesn't hurt to witness some of these conditioned ways of thinking and acting, so that we can build a baseline for change. If we want to change what I call the 'system', we need to be able to see it for what it is first.

Pain is one of the most powerful teachers we have at our disposal, so it can help to feel into its wisdom as we strive to grow and evolve. None of us like pain, but it is truly a messenger of love that we can learn to respect. And this can mean seeing and dismantling our old habits with intent.

Let's take a brief yet high-level look at some of the junk we are buying into, which we have become mesmerised by – these will be considered in more detail in later chapters.

Most 'men' are brought up in western societies to believe that, to be deeply loved, they need to be successful in their chosen career. They need to make money, be strong inside and out, and win to be loved. It becomes their subconscious mantra. They believe that they are in competition with other men for the best 'toys', and the person who dies with the best toys wins. This includes their wife, who can often be a status symbol for men – hence the term 'trophy wife'.

Once in a couple, they then fear that they need to make and keep their woman financially happy to be retained in that relationship, which can be a constant source of stress. And in this often-illusory state, they may disconnect emotionally from themselves, and their partner, as they focus on making money at all costs. And one big cost of this can be losing the partner they are working so hard to impress.

Like me, they may earn the money they thought was needed, then pay the price for this unconscious obsession in divorce.

At the same time, most 'women' are taught by societal expectations that they must attain impossible beauty standards just to get a man to look in their direction, for without beauty they may not be lovable.

They need to laser off every hair on their bodies, bleach the parts that lasers can't reach, wear strings on the beach, but then be humble and motherly should a man show interest in them. If they later fail to upkeep such time-consuming and expensive beauty standards, they then fear their man will become unhappy and leave the relationship or temporarily stray towards a younger or more beautifully presented woman, which can also be a constant source of stress.

For centuries, women have also been expected to work as 'homemakers' in their families, then judged by society for the outcomes they achieve in this regard. And while many excel at this type of role, compared to men, others do not, as it is not within their skillset or passion. Yet they endure pointed criticism and societal disapproval when failing to reach the same level of achievement as those who embrace the acts of motherhood and homemaking, even though they did not choose the role for themselves. In the same way the patriarchal world forced men to compete in the office, it forced women to compete in the home, and with other women for husbands. Same role, different location.

It is also apparent that men are not approaching women as frequently as they once did, because they not only fear rejection, but they fear devoting their time and money to a woman who will walk away if a 'better' man comes along, and who may even be dating multiple men. The same fear also applies to women, of course, who must cope with the seemingly endless possibilities that internet dating has placed at the feet of both sexes.

Even if a date eventuates, expectations are increasingly high on both sides. Men feel pressured to shower women with gifts and compliments, all the while wanting a return on their so-called 'investment', as they apply transactional principles to an emotional encounter. Women can feel pressured to perform sexually without attaining actual fulfilment, only to be 'dropped' or 'ghosted' afterwards.

In fact, there seems to be a strange 'dance' that goes on now these days, where both sexes respond to messages slowly, or not at all, to give some strange perception that they are in hot demand, even if they remain interested in the other person. More illusion, lots of confusion. And the worst part is that this show of disrespect seems to work.

Thus, the dating and relating world is seemingly grinding to a screaming halt, and a massive gulf is distancing men and women, particularly among our young and impressionable adolescents.

Men and women are closer than ever before to enjoying equal rights. There is still a lot of work to be done here, but we will get closer as the years go by. Meanwhile, we're failing to adapt to the new dynamics that result from such societal changes.

For example, following on from the greater financial and career success women have achieved, many women now desire a different kind of man – one who can offer them a safe domestic environment with emotional connection, free of ego and violence, while also contributing a variety of masculine qualities to the relationship. They have essentially shifted their base standards, as they themselves have evolved, which men must learn to respect.

Equally, many men now need a different type of woman – one who can contribute healthily to the domestic income (because it takes a dual income just to run a household these days) yet still offer feminine qualities to the relationship.

And there are many quirks that fly in the face of equality and make no sense.

Men are still predominantly seen as the initiators of dates and marriages, despite this being an old-fashioned concept, and are still largely expected to pay for dates that they must initiate.

Many women now engage in the business world, an arena once dominated by men, whereas 50 years ago most were homemakers. This realignment has altered the dynamics that once existed, in businesses and in homes. It's not better or worse, it's just different, and we have failed to adapt in many cases to this change.

Greater financial and career success has been achieved by women, but this has altered the kind of men that they desire and, in the process, made many of them less attractive to men, who are still caught up in old fashioned ways of valuing women.

The kind of women who men desire has not significantly altered since the advent of feminism, because softness, youth, femininity and good looks seemingly remain at the top of their preferences. Many men do not fully value a woman's career or financial success, because old programming remains in men's belief structures from yesteryear – that they should be the providers and 'saviours' of women. And if less women need saving or providing for, where does that leave their egos, or sense of self-worth?

Some women are said to still want men who are more successful financially than them, which has become a higher bar for men to clear. This also has its roots in out-of-date conditioning, but it is a valid choice.

Societal paradigms tell us that women are more in touch with love and understand it better than men. However, this is another fairytale that we have swallowed. We both want love for we both have hearts – we just approach it in different ways.

It is a documented fact that more women are now filing for divorce than men in marriages, as their freedom to choose rises. For many years this option of choice was not open to them, but now it is.

Overall, in many ways, men have failed to change within the shifting sands of feminism and equality, as much as women have – possibly because, after centuries of suppression, women are now more able to choose their own lives and partners. In short, their needs, as they perceive them to be, have shifted. Men can either complain about this shift, adapt to it, or just self-select out of the dating market. Many are seemingly doing the latter.

The dating market has always been highly focused on value-driven needs and wants that are highly superficial and material in nature, simply because it is more likely to be attraction based, with participants (typically in younger age-cohorts) searching so specifically for compatibility. Internet dating has, reportedly, also exaggerated the transactional nature of dating and given sex a greater level of availability than it once had, in eras where virtue was more highly regarded, rightly or wrongly.

Women are, in a sense, broadening their masculine energies, as they embrace arenas of life once dominated by men. The rise of the single mother as a societal norm has probably added to this situation, because single mothers (like single fathers) need to have broad skills to survive, and raise a family.

But how many men feel comfortable embracing their feminine energies and more traditional female roles, like caring for a home, children and frail parents, unless they are forced to do so?

Another expression of inequality is how women who take multiple sexual partners are subjected to increasing levels of criticism in society, which men seemingly escape, and always have. This makes no sense in an equal world.

Many men, rightly or wrongly, feel like they are no longer needed to be the leaders in families and relationships, despite holding this level of 'office' for many centuries, because of societal norms and rules. Again, are men failing to adapt to the new world of equality, or are couples not proactively designing their individual relationships because of old habits?

Many women are reportedly struggling to find the men they now need, such as men able to take care of themselves, who can meet their partners in an emotionally open state, who are unlikely to ask a woman to nurse or mother them, yet who can offer companionship for mutual growth. One of the main battles contemporary women face, is achieving the right work/life balance for them, but since many men have not evolved into this perspective, such women remain fearful that they will not have the circumstances they need in place to create their family dynamics of choice.

In all this change, and in the face of rising financial pressures, birthrates are falling across the western world. On the one hand, this could be due to the rising cost of living and the housing crisis, or because of women's desire to enjoy an increasingly independent life before committing to child-rising. But, on the other hand, it could also be because both sexes are really struggling to find a partner with whom to start that commitment together. With ageing populations becoming an increasing issue across the world, this may have negative implications for the world economy, though positive implications for the planet itself.

The net effect of all this change is a potential loneliness epidemic whilst we adapt to this inherent, but hopefully temporary, dislocation in relationship dynamics.

It seems that we need to create the new modern-day man and woman, who can cope with the wave of change that is taking place. I address this opportunity further in this book, because it matters.

My sense is that we need to speed this adaption process up through higher awareness of what is taking place, plus new ways of thinking, so that we can find a better place of equilibrium. Some of the age-old conditioned mindsets that are holding us back, need to be identified, rethought and restated with haste.

Put simply, it is a sad story that flies in the face of the Hollywood movies and fairy tales with which we grew up, and yet has been partially created by us. And the mainstream media and community rhetoric has yet to pull together the threads of a quite serious epidemic of relationship disappointment and despair. But when you talk to people in the streets, they all seem very aware of the difficult circumstances playing out before their very eyes. They just don't know how to solve it.

Governments are doing their best to provide essential services to assist with societal dislocations, like mental health services, building more homes and childcare services; but this seems to be primarily treating the disease, rather than being a cure for what is unfolding.

Unfortunately, young men and women are both becoming brutally aware of this growing dysfunction, and one wonders how they will behave in a future where their dreams of love have been crushed under the pressures of changing expectations from the opposite sex. The behaviour of young men is a particularly major concern here, because when young men lose purpose and intent, they are more prone than women to become violent and destructive, even resorting to self-harm.

Many children are increasingly having to grow up in split and broken families, living in two homes and trying to love stepparents they never expected to meet, let alone live with. This is a tragedy unfolding on a mass scale, ***and one experience, my own children were forced to endure unfortunately.***

No-fault divorce is a positive concept, but it has also made many marriages disposable if we feel that our needs are no longer being fully met, or we feel prolonged disharmony with our partner. But is this disharmony being created by our relationship, or was it always caused by our sense of incompleteness resurfacing and simply getting too hard to face, so we blame our partner, and leave in search of new validations, rather than face our own demons.

This is the price of unconscious relating, and it's a price that can be very hefty.

All up, there is a series of changes taking place in male/female dynamics, which we either did not see coming or we failed to adapt to over the last 50 years. Without judging either men or women, I truly believe that we can address these issues in a positive and wise way through collaboration, education and higher awareness, which would enable new and better-informed choices to be made.

And I'm sure there are some very learned psychologists and mental health experts who could and already try to add, great wisdom to a societal level debate.

Read on to discover more.

Chapter 4

The Confusion Between Love and Attraction

What Are We Calling Love?

In my book *The Truth About Love* I describe the complex array of factors that must align to create a really fulfilling relationship for both participants. In short, an alignment of mind, body and spirit is ideal to support a great relationship.

In practice, romantic relationships are normally based, to differing degrees, on love and attraction.

Love is metaphysical, so is beyond the power of the mind to initiate, or regulate.

Attraction, be it based on physical appeal or other forms of admiration, is largely based around conscious or subconscious mental constructs and physical impulses.

Both matter in the formulation of relationships, but both are sourced from our different operating systems, our hearts and our minds.

Still, we often confuse love with attraction. When we become highly attracted to another person, and the thought of being in relationship with them excites us, we often refer to this as love, even when a close frequency match, may not be present. Unfortunately, love cannot be thought, so this low frequency or 'thought love' is temporary at best, and often tagged incorrectly.

Ironically, I believe the hierarchy of the attributes driving romantic connection within us, is inverse to our ability to control these attributes within a relationship. There are three aspects of a loving connection with another through which we seek to connect: mind, body and spirit; and the last two are the most potent, important and natural, in my view.

By spirit I mean love, and our minds have zero control over this. Our souls determine who we love, and how intensely we can experience this love. Our bodies were manifested by our souls, and we can but alter them marginally in our lives, through self-care, surgery or otherwise. Our minds, however, can be fully reminded of who and what we are, when we make the effort to connect to our truths, and turn the subconscious into the conscious.

In other words, we can change our minds if we seek to, to elevate the kind of love lives we can experience. We are constantly changing our minds, and this is a threat or ally of sexual polarity, if we are not conscious of its workings.

We, therefore, have much more control over our minds, than the other aspects that determine whether we can take part in a fulfilling relationship with another person.

This is the dichotomy that puts our hearts and minds into conflict when relationships take shape, and that brings us back to the truth that there is no love in control. And unless we are deeply connected to our hearts and bodies, we will be prone to make decisions about connection from the ficklest part of our being.

Love, and its expression through passionate sexual and intimate connection, is the most natural part of our connection with another in romantic relationships, which is why the universe took it substantially away from the control of our human egos. Our minds can never be pure consciousness, like our souls, without massive personal expansion. This gap is one we are substantially ignorant to, unfortunately.

You could read hundreds of books about love, including this one, but only the fleeting moment when two souls meet will ever show you what it truly is. It is pure consciousness at work, for both souls are aware of the presence of the other.

There are additional energetic forces that can influence relationships too, such as karmic and other metaphysical forces. Such energies feed into our conditioned ways of being. These are advanced concepts, and for the purposes of this book I will largely harness them as part of my references to intergenerational conditioning. There is more detail on this metaphysical phenomenon in my book *The Truth About Love*, should a reader wish to understand it further.

Our normal level of consciousness is based around limited belief structures that are encapsulated in my first book, *Where Your Happiness Hides*. These beliefs play out within many of us, but also project into the dating and relating world that we witness.

Much of the human experience involves a battle between our hearts and minds for control of the decisions and actions we make in life. And the battlefield of love is no exception.

The answer is to move our beliefs from illusion to truth, from separation to a sense of unity, from scarcity to abundance, from success to fulfilment, from co-dependency to shared sovereignty, and learn that we are all lovable no matter what we do or achieve. This movement involves a constant evolution out of our egos and into our hearts, as our platform for making decisions and overcoming our fears.

It is not our fault, and we should not carry any guilt for our fears, for we are all the victims of social conditioning. But it is our responsibility to remove the shackles and get free of the cage of conditioning that we are imprisoned within, so that we can radiate love into our lives.

Higher awareness is the key to opening the locks on the cage of conditioning that we share, and to finally setting us free.

If confusion always precedes clarity, isn't it time we got clear on what love really is?

Exploring the Amazing Qualities of Love

Love has certain qualities that our egos rarely embody, because of the conditioning most of us carry.

Love has incredible qualities, because it is linked to pure consciousness. Below are some examples. Love:

- Never judges, although it witnesses
- Is pure presence and keeps us in the now
- Is compassionate
- Has infinite intelligence at its disposal
- Is always light and happy
- Refuses to suffer
- Forgives and is grateful to simply be alive
- Wants us to learn and have fun
- Is aligned with truth and supports transparency in our lives
- Is eternal and patient
- Brings forth powerful self-esteem for it knows what we stand for and want out of life
- Does not require validation and does not attach to any specific outcomes
- Knows no limitations, only infinite possibilities to achieve what we desire
- Is our true protection in life, for it gives us what we need in life, then what we want, and always has our best interests at heart

When we relate and date outside of this incredible energy – or, on the other hand, swamp it with negative beliefs – we limit what is possible in our own lives, and in our relationships. And we can turn infinite possibilities into finite frailties.

Chapter 5

Our Polarity Is Shifting

The Importance of Masculine and Feminine Energies

We all possess masculine and feminine energies, which we each hold as a mix in varying degrees. The soul is the perfect balance of masculine and feminine energies and seeks to embody this experience on Earth within the human form it has manifested within and as. The human body and mind, however, are rarely in this special place after absorbing the conditioning that we are all subjected to by life on this planet. We typically identify as male or female, and this concept limits our thinking, and opportunities in life, significantly. This is a great challenge we can all embark upon, should we choose to, and the more people who do so, the more balanced our world will be. I cover all this in more detail in my book *Where Your Happiness Hides*.

Below are some common masculine and feminine energies:

Common Masculine Energies	Common Feminine Energies
Righteous	Compassionate/caring
Competitive	Collaborative
Protective	Nurturing
Goal-orientated	Empathetic
Factual	Intuitive
Monotasking	Multitasking
Impatient	Patient
Assertive	Forgiving

Bias for action	Express emotions
Independent	Understand interconnectivity
Individual success	Collective success

These energy categorisations were not derived by me, but by the psychology profession, after much in-depth analysis.

We each have a different mix of these energies, regardless of what kind of body we exist within. However, as a rule, you can see that cisgender women generally have a predominance of feminine energies, and cisgender men generally have a predominance of masculine energies.

The more self-aware we become, the more centred we can also become in these energies. In other words, the masculine and feminine energies will move closer together in terms of becoming more balanced.

The diagram below shows how polarity, and the associated attraction, operates in principle, as the sexual energies of a man or woman change:

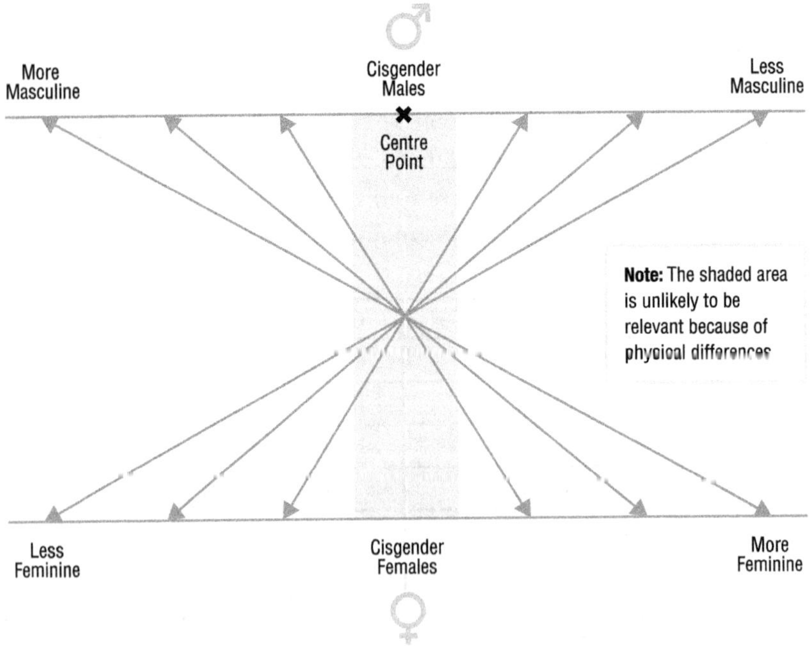

Figure 1: A Graphic Depiction of the Polarity of Sexual Energies

Of course, our bodies don't change their sexual predominance as we become more self-aware, although our cellular structures will alter to reflect our overall energy mix.

We live in a world where polarity is an inescapable reality in all that we encounter, not just in terms of sexual energies. Opposites are an essential part of life on Earth. Consider light versus dark, intelligence versus ignorance, impulse versus loyalty, love versus hate, fear versus courage, night versus day, and so on. Essentially, we need some extremes to witness the other end of the spectrum, and to some extent the choices we make determine the experiences that we can have on this spectrum.

Fundamentally, men and women have the potential to be the same in many ways, except for their physical bodies. This is possibly a controversial statement, but one I believe in. Centuries of conditioned beliefs have laid the groundwork for most of the differences we perceive. However, they are largely illusory or expected of us. For example, why do more women than men have long hair and wear make-up? Is it just a human habit?

The patriarchal world that we have witnessed for many years have created a bias towards masculine energies in our world, as I have outlined. But meeting the needs of this paradigm has also impacted on the beliefs and mannerisms of men and women, who are simply trying to adapt to what is seemingly expected of them in society.

When you view these energies, you can see why relatively unconscious men and women, who are the norm in our society, do struggle so much to connect fully once the differences between them start to cause friction in a relationship. Put simply, the less conscious or self-connected someone is, the less likely they are to really know themselves intimately and be able to adapt within a relationship to achieve a balanced level of compromise with a partner.

Resolving Conflict Through Energetic Alignment

No matter whether a person identifies as being a man or woman, when a person is more in their feminine energies they will often have more emotional awareness than someone who is more in their masculine energies. This is partly due to social conditioning, which has cheated so many men of the ability to identify and thus become aware of their own emotional language, and how they experience just as many emotions as women, just different ones.

People with dominant masculine energies and mindsets, on the other hand, may often be more aware of the structure of a relationship or dynamic, and whether it is aligning with their mental expectations.

Early in my life, my tendencies were skewed towards masculine ways of being in my life, including relationships. So when my relationships had issues or ended, I was always needing to understand why it was the case, and how I had contributed to the outcomes. I found it hard to accept anything, and even forgive myself, until I made sense of it. And I was not open enough to awareness of my feelings, or therefore those of my partner. My mind was all too ready to make me the victim of relationship issues.

My female partners were arguably more aware of their emotions with regards to those same relationship issues, and less interested in understanding what had factually gone wrong. Bridging this gap in perspectives was particularly difficult in counselling and conflict resolution situations, when my factual mindset was confronted by more emotionally aware ways of responding.

All this ultimately made sense to me when I learned about the polarity created by sexual energies.

After contemplating all this deeply, my view is that for effective resolution of issues in any walk of life, including romantic relationships, a healthy combination of both masculine and feminine energies is ideally required to fully resolve and overcome something. If feelings are present and expressed without the filter of understanding,

or vice versa, you have the makings of a disconnection and adverse judgement of one another.

In everything we do in life, feelings supported by factual interpretations and implementations gives us the best way forward to resolve concerns. Our hearts, bodies and minds are a powerful team when in sync. Alone they are less effective and can result in less-than-ideal outcomes.

We just need to remember this if we want to evolve together in love. In my book *From Pain To Possibility* I described to path to higher intelligence as moving from understanding (thinking), to knowing (feeling), to becoming (embodiment through physical and energetic alignment).

A couple would do well in any conflict situation to be compassionate to the way the other party processes information and pain, and try and meet somewhere in the middle. This is how advanced relationships unfold and grow stronger, and I think it is a rare trait in most romantic relationships, particularly if winning not resolving issues is the key subconscious objective of one or both parties.

In affair situations, I contend that effective resolutions can become extremely difficult to attain, because the feeling side of the connection may have become infiltrated or corrupted by the energy of a third party. This can make reconnection extremely difficult.

The Power to Shift the Reality of Polarity

But there is hope that all this can change with a dose of higher consciousness, and a rebalancing back to a place in which masculine and feminine energies are more equally valued and rewarded within us all.

These polarised forces are not fixed, however, with the masculine and feminine energies within all of us altering as we go through life, and as we grow through new experiences that bring forth new opportunities for higher doses of self-awareness. The constant interaction of masculine and feminine energies, within and between us all, is more akin to a 'dance' between the active presence of these forces.

For example, if a person does deep inner work to enhance his or her self-awareness, that person can't help but bring their masculine and feminine energies into greater balance, and even strengthen both. And this can alter the way they connect to themselves, and the kind of partner who will be of interest to them.

Similarly, the more conscious or self-connected a person becomes, the higher their sense of self-love also tends to become, which can alter the type of match they want and make one or both partners feel like they are 'falling out of love'.

And I'm not referring to spiritual practices here. Spirituality is just one way to attain connection within oneself. Some people are just naturally connected to their true selves and have been highly skilled at maintaining this during their lives. The more connected we are to our true selves, the more we can connect to the true essence of another.

Physical attraction doesn't just drive polarity. Our energy balance and mindsets drives this magnetism just as much.

As I write this book, I have just completed over 10 years of deep self-awareness work that has significantly altered my energy structures and self-connection levels. I can evidence this shift, so I know that it is true. This is explained in my book From Pain to Possibility.

But there is one inescapable fact when it comes to finding a loving relationship that we must take account of, and that is how finding the right partner for a deeply romantic relationship requires us to open our hearts to soul-based connections, then apply our bodies and minds to detect whether physical chemistry and lifestyle compatibilities are also present and can drive sufficient levels of polarity.

Of course, the way in which we consider and prioritise each of these respective forces is a matter of personal choice. I consider soul connection to be first base in my relationship choices and measures of matching, but each reader is, of course, entitled to their own basis of choosing.

But I ask you this: can we fall in love and have a loving relationship, without love being present?

Polarity Across Our Society

The last 50 years of human societal shifts have caused some disruption for masculine and feminine energies, compared to traditional paradigms. Quite frankly, this is a wonderful shift and, as I outlined above, well overdue.

When you consider the key masculine energies listed in the table above and reflect on the characteristics of the societies that we have been inhabiting for centuries, you can see how the dominance of masculine energies over feminine energies has created social habits and structures that largely reflect these core masculine traits.

Ask yourself a few of the following questions:

- Is our world excessively competitive, and diminishing our happiness as a result?
- Do we value doing, over simply being alive?
- Do we fully value people's emotions, or encourage them to be kept controlled and private?
- Do we value people more on their independent success, rather than our collective achievements together?
- Have our work and home experiences become highly goal-oriented, and somewhat intolerant of people missing superficial deadlines?
- Have we become progressively obsessed with earning money, and becoming wealthy, so that we 'keep up with the Jones's', rather than becoming genuinely fulfilled?
- Are our key leaders typically men who can be very self-righteous and assertive, rather than compassionate and caring for the common good?

- Are our education systems heavily focussed on factual or intellectual types of subjects, rather than on creative subjects that are seen as being more heart-based in nature?
- Are our corrective services more about punishment, than reformation and restorative justice?

This list could be much more extensive, but my point is that a shift away from masculine energies towards feminine energies is a positive, and once we get further into this shift I believe we will have a far more harmonious society with greater levels of care and collaboration on show.

Men and women may criticise each other, but we are on the same team. We have all been born into a male-dominated society, and it has affected almost everything we do and experience, including the way that we love and interact with each other.

As relationships have broken down and modern forces have shifted, many women have been forced, or have chosen to, apply their masculine energies to a world that values this more so than feminine energy. But greater feminine energy is the gift that our world needs more of because it is naturally slated towards care, compassion and kindness.

Now that we are heading in the direction of greater balance, however, we have much to be hopeful about. The feminine energies that we have suppressed for centuries can only make our lives better once we all embrace them more fully in key walks of life.

And when more men and women embrace a more balanced set of energies within themselves, and actively cultivate them, we will see happier individuals, couples and communities, richer in fulfilment, because the excess levels of competition we have endured will be supplemented by more fun and compassion in a society that finds fulfilment and beauty in a different kind of way.

Magnetism is Natural

Polarity is a form of balance. We live in a physical world in which all must be constantly rebalanced to find equilibrium. Night always follows day, and spring follows the winter. Our world is suffering from imbalances on many fronts at present, and many of these are becoming more pronounced. Consider the imbalances in economic, environmental and military power across the world at present. These imbalances cause much unhappiness for those in scarcity.

One of my aims is to help men and women find a batter sexual energy balance within themselves, such that it can enhance their ability to love each other romantically with a purer level of connection, should they choose this.

This is a good thing. Though, on the flip side, it is also likely to cause increased relationship instability, at least temporarily – unless two lovers commit to growing together – because the polarity between them is likely to shift as energies change. This can, of course, result in enhanced upsides for both parties in the relationship, once they confront the issues that arise.

Let's consider polarity in nature.

The Earth itself has a north and a south pole, and between those two poles electromagnetic fields actively influence the world. Human beings are essentially surrounded by their own electromagnetic fields, which magnetise or repel people to, or away, from us. Most of us are ignorant of this invisible force, but it explains why another person's energy can be so attractive, or otherwise, to us for no apparent or logical reason.

And the same goes for our physical bodies. Highly masculine people are generally attracted to highly feminine people, and vice versa. If you view couples, you will generally notice that the more attractive a person is aesthetically, the more attractive their partner is likely to be. This is natural selection (i.e. polarity) at work, supported by the forces of conditioned choice.

Both sexes are drawn to each other physicality, for we are all essentially programmed to procreate the species. And the physicality of a person is invariably the first thing we notice about them.

We live in a physical world of density, and therefore physicality matters to all of us. It is partially what we are. We are both human beings and light beings, combined in one dual form, with sexuality being the most powerful 'glue' that holds the masculine and feminine together. No matter how many emotional differences we encounter, or how much faith we lose in romantic relationships, this will rarely disrupt our desire to be intimately connected to others who are the sexual persuasion that we prefer.

But one thing we all need to understand is that physical attraction is a personal preference, not a fixed point of reference. One person may find you attractive and another may not. It can be easy to feel invalidated when someone indicates that you are not attractive to them, particularly if you are not used to rejection in this way. But this is just a function of life that we must all accept.

Self-awareness work and the process of going inward to process rejection can assist us in this area, because just intellectualising this kind of belief change is never enough. We must feel and embody the changes we are striving to make, and this can take time.

Rejection, on a physical or emotional level, is one of the hardest things for a human being to accept and fully process, particularly if we believe that a loving connection is present. ***I know this pain all too well – after multiple rejections from women I loved and with whom I shared relationships and deep attraction.***

There are times in a person's life when being in a relationship suits them; but there are also times when being single better suits their personal growth and ambitions.

I have chosen both experiences as a mature adult and benefited from both situations. However, I always found that I desired intimate connection no matter what my relationship status was at the time.

But need and want are very different experiences. Our need for intimacy is one of the most difficult needs to overcome and our fear of sexual irrelevance is up there with the fear of death, as the top two fears to overcome in human form.

Both fears can be overcome, but our desires to live and procreate are primal aspects of the human beings that we are. And our design to love and be loved is a key aspect of our soul's divine blueprint. So, both aspects of attraction and love matter to the dual realities that we all are in our current paradigms.

This reality keeps masculine and feminine energies constantly aware of each other's presences in our 3D realities. It's hypnotic for those who are unaware of its impacts upon them.

The polarity between two people is never static. It can change over time, just like the way that the poles of the Earth are in constant flux. It can be influenced by multiple factors, but there is some truth in the phase 'opposites attract'. A person's individual circumstances, attributes, wounds and preferences can and do influence their level of attractiveness to others, particularly those to which they are sexually drawn. And many of these forces can be subconscious within us.

Societal mindsets and collective forces can also exert an influence on relative polarities, for they influence the way we think and process the forces of attractiveness. In short, they influence our conditioned beliefs about ourselves and others.

Need can dampen the magnetism between two people, unless it is shared on a reciprocal basis, because need is derived from our egoic fears and our cravings for validation.

Want, on the other hand, is linked more closely to desire. It is a soul-based energy sourced from natural passions and impulses and the force of love. In the body we often refer to it as chemistry. Want is purer than the energy of need, for it is usually soul-based.

In the general population where self-awareness is normally low, neediness can't help but be a common force creating polarity in romantic relationships, because deciphering love from attraction, and consciously allowing love to be the 'glitch' in the normal machine, that we call our love lives, is so often improbable.

Need can be an attractor, or a repellent, depending on the relative awareness levels of potential partners, and can shift in longer term relationships.

Chapter 6

The Most Important Relationship of All

Loving Yourself is the Key

In my book *The Truth About Love,* I explain in detail how you cannot feel the love for, or of, another person beyond that which you can feel for yourself. This is simple physics, although it contradicts what we have collectively been taught.

But since we feel through our bodies only, and not through the body of another, all feelings are capped by our capability to feel within ourselves – and the sad truth is that most people do not love themselves strongly, for their hearts are somewhat closed through the pain of past experiences. This is why returning to self-love is such a core element of human evolution, and the process of recovering from relationship pain.

Love is love, so when I say self-love it is just the love we acknowledge and feel within our own hearts.

We often speak of our beloveds being a person outside of ourselves. But the truth is that it all always starts on the inside of ourselves. When we open to embrace and love the beloved inside of ourselves, meaning our own hearts, we can open the door to other would-be lovers, who can come into our lives and be-loved by us. Be in love with you and you can't help but be the love of another.

The experiences we have in life shape our ability to love. Each time we think that our hearts are 'broken' by the behaviours or actions of others, our minds can start to lose trust in relationships. Our bodies and minds hold onto physical and emotional pain, and our subconscious psyches can store debilitating fears for very long times.

Our ego-centric minds tell us to avoid situations that may have hurt us before, because the mind's role is to protect and project us, in the endless pursuit of success without failure. It's akin to encountering an electric fence. Get electrified once and, from then on, we will be wary about the prospects of touching whatever electrified us.

But the more closely a person connects to their true self, the closer they become to their soul energy. Higher self-awareness is the doorway to higher levels of self-love. We are all pure love at our core, yet after centuries of life on this planet we have essentially forgotten this undeniable truth.

The fastest way to love is therefore to find your own frequency of love within you. Love is a vibrational or frequency match, so the higher your frequency becomes the higher the purity of love will be that you can share with another at that same level. We must take this path to ever experience 'true love'. It is not available to those who have not 'done the work' to make it possible, unless they were born with a high vibrational state, and their conditioning has not disrupted this energetic gift.

For the rest of us, romantic relationships give us the opportunity to grow, as they are vehicles of higher awareness, providing us with extraordinary circumstances in which to test and develop our awareness. It is a source of learning on steroids!

Again, this is not an awareness that many of us possess, for we have been taught to see romance as a pink and fluffy experience that should be predominantly positive and emotionally supportive. While relationships usually start out this way, they invariably end up in a very different place because of our lack of awareness and skill in how to embrace romantic experiences and growth opportunities.

In many western societies, people typically lack high levels of self-love such that 'true love' rarely features strongly in romantic relationships, only attraction and versions of love, based on different levels of desire and need. But this represents our pathway to evolution in love, when we learn to grow through it.

When high levels of self-esteem, self-love and self-expression combine with cohesion, we have the necessary attributes to experience advanced levels of love. But it can take inner work to get to this place within us. This book outlines this opportunity.

In the absence of much self-love, and in a world where ego-centric human minds are so in-charge of our every move, is it then any wonder that so many relationships are grounded in attraction, and not the more enduring force of love, and thus fail?

The relationship you have with yourself is the most important relationship that you can ever cultivate and grow. Yet how many of us are taught this reality?

Most of us are taught that giving to others is what brings love into our lives. Yet the strength of the relationship with ourselves essentially determines the extent to which we can be loved by another human being.

Learn to love yourself and the love you are ready to receive will be magnetised towards you. From here, you can choose how you react. This is a universal reality.

Some people will never be happy in relationships because their heart truly yearns for something another person can never give them: themselves. In this way, trying to satisfy a partner who can't satisfy themselves is a zero-sum game in which we should not too readily participate, once this pattern becomes clear.

Choose to be love, don't chase love, is my best advice. In this energy you attract.

This is why connecting to our hearts is so important. At present, most of us falsely 'think love', and believe that we are relating from a place of love, when often we are not, we are just using the presence of another to fill the holes in our own hearts.

The Power of Soul Connection

Soul connection is the key ingredient in any loving relationship. The extent to which a person can connect to another person is a mirror image of the connection that they have with their true selves. By this, I do not mean their image or personality, which has been created by their ego over the course of their life; instead, I am referring to their soul, their source of love and truth, which is found within them and is ever-present.

If you want an amazing romantic relationship, value and develop the connection you have to your own heart as a priority, and trust that it will lead you either to someone with whom you can connect, or to be closer to your existing partner.

And if this connection is substantially free of egoic distortions – because both people have accessed the love in their hearts – what I refer to as an ultimate connection is possible. Such a connection is available to all who seek to do the work to make it possible, together and individually.

But beware, it is not easy.

Chapter 7

Our Ignorant Power Plays

Seeking Power Over Each Other

Masculine and feminine energies, and in turn people, essentially exist in a massive power-play, which is influenced by a diversity of factors – some seen, but others not seen.

These energies naturally offset each other, but they are meant to complement each other and come together to assist our evolution, rather than try and overwhelm each other.

Yet, with so many egos in charge of the dating world and the long-term relationship landscape, many people try to assert power over their partners to get what they need, or think they want. This coercion is now influenced by the information age we now so readily embrace, which speeds up the adoption of collective ideas across the population – not all of them positive!

Historically, women have been able to use their beauty and sexuality to exert influence men, whereas men have been able to use their wealth, status and physical strength to control women. Some of these types of power-plays still exist today, even in more egalitarian societies, though are at least diminishing.

But relationships are meant to be a true partnership – particularly marriages and relationships that are intended to be permanent. Those romantic relationships that are more transactional interactions invariably atrophy over time, as conditioned mindsets come to the fore. Love in its purest form does not seek to exert power over another soul. It doesn't need to, for it needs nothing to be joyous and has no fear. It knows its own worth and gives us empowerment, and this power is felt within.

The battlefield we call our contemporary love lives is essentially lacking in true, or unconditional, love. True love does not judge or compete within a relationship – it is complete within itself, and knows that it stands ready to infuse itself with the love of another for the benefit of both parties. Two people who are in love, with limited fear and need, add to each other's lives. They do not subtract from them, and they stand ready to support their partner through 'thick and thin', in sickness and in health, in good times and bad. This is why many traditional marriage vows, in the Christian faith at least, spell out these kinds of principles. In true love, there are no questions around their commitment to each other and equality is truly honoured. Neither partner is seen as an option, for no other options are wanted.

Unconditional love itself is rare, and I have heard psychologists say that we are only likely to fall in love two to three times in a lifetime – although this is up to the discernment of our souls, of course. Contrast this with the number of dates most people go on, enhanced by the power of the internet, and you can start to get a sense of how many relationships are likely to be based on love, as opposed to the more fragile forces of attraction.

We are in a world in which 'connection' through digital means has never been easier, yet we seem to be experiencing record levels of loneliness and disconnection. We would be well served to understand this anomaly. What it shows me is that a true connection is only able to be detected in the energetic presence of another, not through a computer screen. Without true presence we get interactions, not connections.

The Potent Power of Energetic Resonance

Our world is full of situations in which negative events impact on human relationships. This occurs on all levels, even between warring and competing nations, which fail to fully resolve their differences in the face of truth and forgiveness.

Energetic resonance, whether positive or negative, does not leave us just because we think it should or could. It requires truthful expression and real forgiveness to be liberated. Energy is different to thought, and love is an energy beyond the control of our minds.

But nowhere is this limiting resonance more toxic, and sometimes more subtle, than it is between two fractured lovers. In their attempts to maintain peace and evade conflict, they can avoid the truth for days, months or even years; and turn negative feelings into full blown resentments that threaten their happiness. In this way, connection can be overwhelmed by the presence of unnecessary pain, and mental confusion.

I once experienced a long-term relationship where both of us were unskilled at expressing truths, which could have helped us turn our pain into new possibilities. Many of the resentments that had accumulated during the relationship, did not surface until it was too late to effectively resolve them. Instead of becoming opportunities for growth between us, they were ultimately used as reasons to justify a separation.

If enough irritants go unresolved between lovers, and are allowed to aggregate over time, relationships can atrophy and implode. Red flags have a way of going unnoticed, you might say, if we fail to wave or spot them.

This is a learned behaviour in some cultures, because we are taught not to hurt those we love, by creating conflict or hurting another's feelings. In the long run, however, the practice of avoiding conflict and harbouring grudges, without full expression of truth, is a core reason why so many relationships fail to meet their full potential.

Anyone can be good at having fun with their lover, but it's how you resolve your differences in the dark times that determines the longevity and level of happiness possible in a relationship. The pathway to higher versions of love is about turning this darkness into light, and the subconscious into the conscious.

The continued resonance of love requires the purity of truth to be possible between two individuals on an ongoing basis. It's time we modelled this for the next generation of lovers who are watching our every move and feel the misalignment between our words, moods, and actions.

Our focus on getting attention, and on how our relationships look, needs to be replaced by a focus on true connection, and the resonances that we feel.

Fulfilling romantic relationships unfold when both participants are empowered by the full expression of love, not by the practice of withholding it from each other, out of ignorance or resentment.

The Negative Power of Stories

One of the forces that egos use to control their partners and the narrative of their relationship revolves around stories. Stories can be positive or negative, but we are all prone to cling to interpretations of the past that often do not serve the truth, but do block the connections that we desire. They often serve to protect our own precious images.

Similarly, we can create stories about the future of our relationship that merely create expectations that may have no basis in reality, and just serve to put undue pressure on our relationships.

As hard as it can be to do, we need to drop the stories and be in the moment and our feelings when we are relating to a lover. This is easy in the good times, but can be hard in the bad times.

Experiences come and go, and they always have meaning for us to enjoy or from which we can learn. Hanging onto them to prove that we are superior or right in some way, is a great avenue for the stimulation of negative resonance to be created and maintained with your partner.

Our predictions of the future, and our interpretations of the past to achieve control in love, are truly irrelevant when the energy of love is present, for it only knows one thing – presence in the now moment. It cares less about the past or the future.

Overcoming These Power Plays

Readers who are already in relationships may ask, how do we as a couple overcome these inherent power-plays for the good of our relationship?

The only true solution lies in the power of higher awareness, which opens the door to love being truly felt. Once we become aware of patterns of control in our relationships, those patterns lose their power over us when we witness them, or perhaps even laugh at them and openly accept that they are a destructive force we can change in the now and in our futures, together.

This will take commitment and a willingness to drop our egoic patterns of behaviour, which are holding us back from what we want.

When we allow love to empower our relationships from the inside, we can't help but find greater joy on the outside.

Chapter 8

Filling the Holes in Our Hearts

Our Need for Romantic Relationships

Despite the power plays we often endure, many people are conditioned to seek a relationship to meet the general societal belief that a relationship will make them feel more complete, and to fill holes in their self-esteem.

This can prompt people to seek relationships with urgency once they are single, rather than learning from their past endeavours and being patient until the right person enters their life, for whom they will feel a greater love and with whom they will be highly compatible.

Many relationships spring from a need to avoid the perception of loneliness. However, great peace and self-love can be discovered in solitude or single life, and this period, if used wisely to help you grow, can prepare you for the loving experiences that are beyond your previous experiences and expectations.

When you are connected to your own heart, you are never alone, because your feelings and conscious awareness are truly ever-present. In this place, neediness can be replaced with the gift of knowing a truer you.

After my second divorce, I spent several years being single, and at times in partial isolation. I was driven to face my inner pain and 'demons'. This helped me to more fully understand myself, and also I

learned to become much more sovereign within myself. In distancing myself from other egos, with whom I might have felt a need to align, I gave myself license to become the truer me in an unfiltered way. My deeper self-love was born in this chrysalis of self-reflection.

Our Battle to be Whole Again

Few people believe or feel that they are whole, or in other words, complete. And this is a key reason why we so often fail to create happy relationships with others, in all walks of life.

We are all born innocent and ready to explore a world that fascinates our curious minds, and our desire to have fun and learn. This is our natural state. As babies and toddlers, we wait to be loved with a smile on our faces, and the light of love in our eyes, until the reality of life so often sets in.

Growing up, we are normally separated from our true loving selves – and our true ability to love unconditionally – because the world teaches us that, to be enough, we need to prove our worth. We need to win, not fail and fit in, and if we do all will be okay. Our spirit of exploration fades as we compete for things that we already are and focus on our self-image.

This separation grows as we age and get further away from the little boy or girl who entered the world, bright-eyed and pure, and so ready to love and unite in harmony with a new world that we so wanted to love.

Later in life, we carry this sense of incompleteness into our romantic relationships, looking for another to help us feel complete and safe again. Our inner child is still inside us, wanting to feel his or her full force of joy once again, but we ignore this and seek completeness from others, not from within ourselves.

Some lovers predominantly give to their partner in a relationship in the hope of receiving love and validation from them, whereas others mainly seek to receive. Both are subconscious strategies that we adopt to prove to the world that we are enough.

The balanced ones – either raised by wise parents or just naturally wise – already know that they are enough, and stand ready to give and receive love in equal measure.

Where two people in a relationship are not balanced and operate in this energy of fear, it is only a matter of time before this tenuous relationship will be tested by life, then potentially detonate under the pressure of perceived incompleteness. Our souls can choose to make sure of this, as they attempt to help us grow in wisdom. The reality is that no person can complete another, because it is not possible. Love is a frequency and we must generate our own frequency to feel love in our hearts, by removing the illusions that stop us connecting to this truth. Every person has a unique frequency, which only they can bring forth from within.

It can take much soul-searching to close this gap between the illusion that you are not lovable, or enough, and the inescapable truth that you are, and always were.

If there is one thing that people need to be taught in life, it is this truth. You are already love and always were. Another person can add to your life in wonderful ways but can never complete your own inner sense of wholeness. So, we must stop trying to be loved, and accept that we already are lovable, no matter what happens – no matter what we achieve or what we don't achieve.

To do this, though, is often easier said than done, because to feel truly whole someone must remove the illusions and negative energy blocks that keep their destructive egos in command. And this can take much self-reflection. It is ultimately an unlearning process, not a learning one, and this goes against the grain in a society focussed on intellectual learning.

True peace comes from not trying to find what you already have, or competing for what others are trying to find in all the wrong places. True happiness and love cannot truly come to you, until they arise from within you.

Romantic relationships should be the icing on top of our otherwise happy life; they should not be the cake itself. Another person's happiness should not so readily dictate our own. The commonly used catchcry 'happy wife, happy life' is a myth we must crush, as is its less-used mirror image 'happy spouse, happy house'. This is discussed in a later chapter.

Two people who exist in a place of no need can, however, achieve true love together, as my book *The Truth About Love* explains.

Consider the following diagram to show the high-level overview of the path, back to truer frequencies of love, within your own heart. Your rebirth as the true you, capable of true love, truly awaits. It is your birthright, and the only real entitlement your heart wants you to remember. In a later chapter I break this path down further into its core steps.

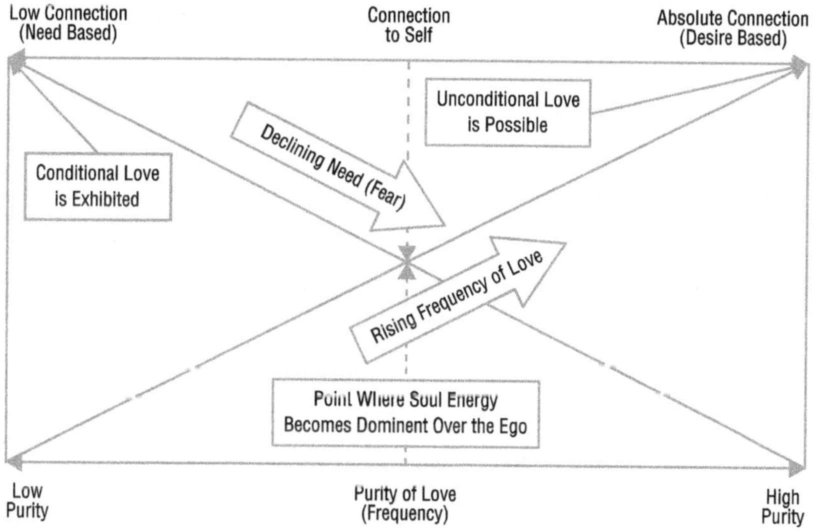

Figure 2: The Human Path to Unconditional Love

The path to higher frequency is shown as a straight line for simplicity only. The path is different for all of us, though it is more likely to look like a lightning bolt, with flat spots and then advances. Conscious awareness never goes backwards permanently, because once you become more self-aware, you cannot put the 'genie back in the bottle'.

Overcoming the Burden of Betrayal

One of the things that can keep us trapped in pain is the experience of a perceived betrayal in a relationship, which we once valued. This is particularly powerful when the betrayal is executed by the 'offending partner' with deceit.

Psychologists say that being badly let down in a loving relationship, such as being the victim of an affair, can create a powerful form of Post Traumatic Stress Disorder, which is akin to fighting in a war.

Unfortunately, I know this experience all too well. In my life I felt 'betrayed' by three partners, despite being committed to their welfare and happiness. I ended up doing deep inner work to overcome these experiences, and I admit that this kind of experience was one of the hardest things of my life to overcome. I also left a marriage and other relationships, which I know greatly hurt my partners at the time. I could have handled these exits better in hindsight.

However, I know that I was meant to experience these events to grow my own awareness and restore my self-love. I essentially, became aware that relationships give us what we need, so that we can grow, and I took these lessons from my experiences. In the end I stopped letting my pain and fears speak more loudly than my love, as I reset my openness to love again. But this took years.

What we need to understand is that the emotional scarring of what we call betrayal, particularly when it is sexual, is hard enough; but when your partner's ongoing lies get added to the lie that you were to blame for their actions, it is a bitter pill to swallow. And these kinds of emotions can last a lifetime, unless you do the inner work to overcome them.

Remaining in a victim mentality is not helpful, and forgiveness is always critical, for it is primarily for the person giving the forgiveness, not the person being forgiven.

Regardless of what your partner does, it is important to know that you are always enough, and if someone acts without integrity that is their karma to carry. But again, this must be felt, and not just thought, before it can become embodied into our realities.

In addition, people are what they do, not what they say they do, or say they will do. Accordingly, trusting my intuition and own observations in relationships, over what I was told, was a key lesson for me to take forward.

Social media and internet dating have of course intensified the level of temptation to which people can be subjected, and have made it increasingly hard to maintain trust in some relationships. The commoditised nature of many modern relationships has also added to the stress that a partner might be lost to such temptations. But this is where your partner's values and sense of commitment is so important. If they hold the same values and sense of commitment that you do, temptation isn't even on their radar, ever – no matter how beautiful or successful they may be.

In a world where truth is in short supply compared to the volume of opinions, in so many walks of life, it is sad that we so often hold back our true feelings from the person that we supposedly love and are closest to, until it's too late for them to take the action necessary to rectify underlying relationship insecurities or problems, or even come to terms with the reality that someone does not want to be our partner anymore, and therefore wants to exit.

When any relationship ends, it is difficult for both partners. But when integrity and truth are seemingly absent during, and when such a relationship then ends, the potential damage to a person's self-esteem is likely to be much higher.

As I outlined in my book *The Truth About Love*, love cannot be created, destroyed or even enhanced by what we think. It is a feeling originating in our hearts.

What does this mean?

It means you have little control over who you fall in love with. If you genuinely find love in the presence of another, your mind cannot erase it no matter how hard you try. Only your soul can if it chooses to.

A war between your heart and mind is likely to occur if you do try, and this is not a war your mind can ever win. Love lets go when it is ready, not when the mind orders it to.

Sometimes people meet someone new who is a better love match (i.e. frequency) than their current partner, and this is just life. And this may spell the end of your existing relationship. Though it might also end up making it stronger, if you both recommit to grow together!

Love has an intelligence and a force beyond our comprehension. And once fully expressed between two lovers it can become unstoppable, and this can be painful for a person who is left or discarded in a relationship.

One aspect of betrayal and abandonment that helped me to finally overcome my pain associated with both, came after understanding its possible link to death.

When we are very young, we can often believe that if we become unloved by our parents, we might die, because they will stop sustaining our life. And this fear can remain with us through our lives and find a new form of expression with a person who we love romantically as an adult. Our subconscious reaction, which makes no sense, can be to perceive the end of a loving relationship as a threat to our lives.

This is primitive conditioning on steroids, but none the less it exists according to psychology, and was subconsciously present within me.

I believe that deep love demands that both partners choose their relationship every day, not just on their wedding day! So, if this choice is becoming more difficult to sustain, then they should be honest about that choice and their feelings as soon as possible.

Truth is a flame that great romantic relationships need to be forged within.

I learned this wisdom the hard way!

Unconditional Love is Supposed to Be Us

As I said, when we feel incomplete, we cannot love ourselves unconditionally, and so we often turn this sense of not being enough into a quest to find completeness through a romantic relationship. But we can stop this pattern, once we see it for what it is.

Consider this: for centuries, women have inhabited a world in which they were treated as second-class citizens, and essentially required to create their lives through a man, rather than through their own endeavours. What damage could that have done to their psyches, and their sense of selves? Could it have created a giant subconscious belief that they are not enough on their own? Could this idea then have been handed down from generation to generation, such that it still subconsciously lives on today? And is feminism and the push to greater equality slowly reversing this concern?

And after centuries of being subjected to physical abuse from men, is it any wonder that some women might struggle to trust men anew and seek a partner they believe can physically protect them.

Not only that, but after centuries of being restricted financially, with marrying up being a woman's primary career move, could women still subconsciously believe in the benefits of being hypergamous (the practice or tendency of dating or marrying a spouse with a higher social, economic, or mating status than oneself)? Despite having greater equality in life, do women still therefore seek men who they perceive to be more secure and advanced than them? And if they do, can we compassionately see the source of this behaviour?

And on the flipside, let's consider how men have held the upper hand for centuries over women, because they had the ability, in ignorant patriarchal societies, to create their own lives and were told that a woman's role was to support them and give them sexual expression and a family. Is it possible then that this mistaken identity lives on today in men's subconscious belief structures? Can it explain why some men are still obsessed by a woman's beauty and sexuality, and feel the need to constantly ensure that the woman with whom they partner desires them, and can bear their children? And does this explain why so many men are not turned on by a woman's career success, when it is no less impressive than their own achievements?

Men were for centuries the primary 'breadwinners' for their families and saw their career success as a key way to secure a woman's love and admiration. Does this live on today, even in an age of supposed career equality? And does it explain why, after courtship or even marriage, men may overfocus on their careers rather than on being emotionally connected to their partners, in the misguided belief that this is essentially their best path to being loved and receiving intimacy.

For centuries men were also required to go to war, should that need arise, to defend their nations and families. Has this willingness to give up their lives influenced their inbuilt propensity to be of service and to sacrifice for the good of all, including their partners and children?

Do both sexes now want to be worshipped by the other, such that they feel validated, and essentially use external aspects of themselves to attain elements of control in their romantic relationships? Perhaps they just use different things in their power to attain this, without consciously understanding why they, and the opposite 'sex', are behaving as they behave?

And do men today truly understand that they are prone to factually think their way through life, whilst women are more likely to feel their way through life? It may be an evolutionary reality or habit, but higher consciousness can change all that, in my view

Other authors have written about this, but what have we done to address it through education or mass communication?

Not much, if my experiences are any guide, because I painstakingly did it for myself. The education systems which guided me while growing up offered little to no assistance in this regard.

To me, the answers appear obvious. If we truly believe in equality and put it into practice in our societies, we must let go of all the subconscious junk that our psyches have embodied, biologically and emotionally.

But first we need to witness them, to be able to let them go.

I discuss these conditioned anomalies in greater detail in later chapters.

Chapter 9

Our Obsession with Value and Interest

Seeking Self-Worth from Relationships

Self-worth cannot truly be measured because we are all priceless and cannot be valued. We are all equal at our core. We may try to measure ourselves against each other in terms of artificial factors like wealth and looks, but these are illusions that we have been taught to accept when judging each other. Greater personal freedom lies in understanding this truth.

We are unfortunately conditioned to constantly judge and rate each other with our minds, in everything we do, until we become conscious enough to witness this charade. And this system can stop us from creating more meaningful relationships, because first impressions can so often become the last.

As I said in the Introduction, we often seek success in relationships at the expense of true fulfilment, and this drives us to chase value and interest, over love.

In a society where self-love is at a premium, our sense of self-worth is also proportionately scarce. How many of us command the inner rhetoric that we are not enough, particularly in the face of what we classify with our minds as romantic betrayal, abandonment, or unfair rejection?

Our tendency to see ourselves as not enough leaks into our romantic relationships. Again, our inner reality cascades into our outer reality, as we battle with our own self-inflicted demons and insecurities.

Essentially, attachment is driven by our inbuilt sense of lack, which creates a need within our psyches. If our egos believe we lack something in life, we can become validated or even obsessed by its attainment. This sense of lack is not derived from our hearts, for our hearts know that we truly have all we need in life to be loved. But it's this sense of lack that makes us vulnerable to attach to the 'right, wrong' people and to be prone to manipulation away from the love we really deserve. Need can drive attachment, but can never form the basis of real love-based connection.

In the modern dating world, this makes us prone to be attracted to people who we think add the most value to our lives and who are the most interesting. These people, we subconsciously believe, will diminish our odds of failure, and enhance our prospects of appearing to be a success.

There is a quote I read – which has been attributed on the internet to Rumi, the 13th century Persian mystic, but which is more likely just inspired by him – that says a lot about loving relationships:

> "Don't chase the ones that run, like shadows from the sun,
> The soul that truly belongs with you, will never need to be won,
> For love is not a battlefield where wounded hearts compete,
> It is two quiet destinies, finally learning how to meet."

This advice, is steeped in the truth of love, for we tend to diminish the importance of finding soul-to-soul connections, around which we can build a relationship.

But what if we all took the sovereign view that we are responsible for our own life, and our own levels of fulfilment, and do not expect another person to be the source of our own happiness or security, even in a relationship? How do you think that our lives would shift, and how do we think the dynamics between men and women could change for the better?

Collective realities also stand in our way, however, impacting our assessment of value and interest, which varies according to our intergenerational perspective. While some generations value financial security and conventional sexual attractiveness, others place a higher value on image enhancement, the ability to enhance social opportunities or provide offspring. The listing is extensive.

Value may also be perceived in different ways depending on people's levels of self-awareness and their conditioned mindsets.

The biggest issue is that, as our needs change, the value we ascribe to our partners also changes, particularly as we evolve through life's many experiences and our interests shift. In different phases of our lives, we may seek fun, connection, recovery, meaning or perhaps just support and respect. What we find interesting may be mystery or certainty. But either way, the more we see something as scarce, the higher the value we're likely to ascribe to it, much like humans do with precious metals, like gold.

Love is not steeped in the energies of value or interest, however. Love just is – no matter what we are doing or achieving. There is little to no superficiality in purer forms of love.

Yet, when we are not using love as an essential criterion on which to base a relationship, value and interest becomes a core ingredient of our needs and wants. And if we are basing our choice primarily on value and not referencing love, our selections and preferences run the risk of being more temporary.

This can cause us great harm, as any truly great romantic relationship is of course based on mind, body and spirit connections. If only we could all accept that we do get to choose the extent to which each of these cornerstones influences our partner selection, and retention.

Of course, if we try hard enough, we will always be able to find alternate potential partners of higher value than our existing ones, because none of us are perfect. We all also age, change shape, lose jobs, and have health concerns, just to name a few factors that can fluctuate over time.

Our resilience and levels of commitment to our chosen partner can be fragile, especially in a society where it can be unexciting to wait for love, or even difficult to feel it. The thrill of a new relationship can often feel exhilarating and present itself as more valuable than an existing lover.

But is this really the case, or are we just jumping for the 'new shiny toy' in the bar, or on a website, which we perceive as a novelty, and an escape from our own pain that we are reluctant to face?

The reality is that resilience is not found in comfort. It is found in the confronting process of discovering our own truths and removing our own illusions. But how often do we see it this way, and run towards the fire of discomfort, rather than run away from it in search of safety and security?

Have we redefined peace, availability and familiarity as boring, and now chase novelty rather than commitment, given how easy it is to find someone new in this modern world? And in a world of more instant gratification, with 24/7 online services, is this trend translating into the way we date and relate? Why would we do the hard work to fix an existing relationship, if we can just move past the issues of the past and find somebody new in a few keystrokes?

Despite what we consciously know to be true, our egos are often programmed to chase perfection in all that we do. Why? Because when we perceive that we have done something perfectly, we also perceive that our lovability is beyond challenge, even temporarily. A person who applies perfectionism to their romantic partner is likely to be impossible to please. And their partner is likely to feel that they are just not enough on many occasions and suffer great stress along the way.

Love, when expressed in purity, does not expect perfection of anyone or anything on this planet. Imagine romantic relationships where neither partner, consciously or subconsciously, expects their partner to be perfect, and in fact also loves their partner's imperfections. This is pure acceptance, and acceptance is one of the core ingredients of advanced romantic relationships.

But is this becoming harder to do in a world where social media and dating apps project so many images and stories about other people, and their lives, based on the illusion of perfection? Are we prone to compare ourselves to the endless stream of illusion that is on offer, and judge our own situations harshly?

We are subconsciously programmed to seek the perfect partner for us, yet in this process we are prone to hide our own imperfections to achieve our goal. How can this process possibly go wrong, I ask you?

If only we were taught how to relate consciously and without high doses of judgement, we would surely be better equipped to grow relationships, rather than end them so readily.

Romantic relationships are supposed to be structures that humans create to honour love and attraction, and facilitate the evolution of human society through the creation of families. But have we set them up to in a very different way?

Are Our Love Lives Becoming Too Machiavellian?

The 16th century Italian diplomat and psychologist Niccolo Machiavelli lost favour with conventional thinkers of his time, when he published views that many humans relate to others through the dark lens of self-interest, and will take whatever steps needed to achieve a goal that is important to them, even if that means they have to act without empathy, honestly or high moral values. This is the source of the expression, describing someone as 'Machiavellian' in nature.

Most of us want to believe in the goodness of humanity, and there is a part of us that will resist Machiavelli's theories. We are all unique of course, but what his book *The Prince* essentially puts forward is the view that – because we commonly relate to each other through conditioned egos that are needy, and are often in pursuit of success in relationships, not love – our relationships are inherently unstable. There is an uncomfortable reality in what Machiavelli suggested, based on modern relationship paradigms.

Polarity is present in everything on this planet, so we must take the good with the bad, if we choose not to address it. Nothing is completely black or white, and most areas of our lives have benefits and drawbacks to consider when we take part in an activity, no matter what we choose. And so it is with dating and relating, when we do so out of need and in a transactional way.

What Machiavelli was essentially saying was that in a relating world so heavily based on self-interest, when you lose the traits that once made you attractive to another person, or the other person's needs change significantly, you may no longer be seen as appealing. Lose your money, your job, your looks, your status or, perhaps, your abilities that made you special to another, and you may be seen as a burden, not a benefit, and go from what I call 'hero to zero' in rapid time.

It is hard to argue that most human relationships are not based on an element of self-interest, particularly in our modern world, in which there are so many options available to us if we become unhappy in our love lives. It's not that people are evil, they have just been conditioned to seek value in a partner, and if they think they have 'fallen out of love' with their partner, they may seek to 'upgrade' that relationship with another person, even if they consider themselves to be a loyal and committed partner.

I believe that we need to accept the reality that in a world where conscious awareness is often quite low and truth is rare, this kind of behaviour is not uncommon, and many of us will subconsciously participate in this transactional way of relating, and even blame a relationship downfall on our partner, despite their loving intent.

When a relationship is fundamentally transactional and it loses its balance, because one partner believes the value of what they were receiving has changed, they will probably not put up with this change indefinitely. And if we are honest with ourselves, some readers may have witnessed this in their own behaviour.

In a world where minds dominate hearts because masculine energies are dominant, many of us rate relationships on a cost/benefit basis, usually unknowingly. If the cost of being with you exceeds the benefit you provide to a partner, you may be replaced. This is the cost many of us bear when sufficient love is not present in a relationship, or perhaps never was.

Another proposition Machiavelli put forward in his book was that respect is distinct from love. Someone you are in relationship with can respect you even if they don't love you, if you establish sound boundaries with the way you interact with them, and are prepared to follow through on those boundaries, by making people accountable to your non-negotiables. In the absence of appropriate boundaries, you can become potentially disposable, because what you are prepared to accept is seen as unlimited, and able to be exploited.

You could be the most giving lover in a relationship, but unless you demand respect from a partner, they are likely to lose respect for you, because they see you as weak and too available. Neediness does not breed respect but often leads you to disrespect yourself. And this is one reason why couples who end up in co-dependent arrangements – where they give up on their own individual needs – end up losing polarity to each other.

There is no mystery apparent to the human mind when a person you know everything about is always present in your life. Some level of genuine independence is needed to maintain attractiveness to another in a relationship and reinforce your sense of intrigue. This is likely where the 'nice guy' narrative, taught to many men, fails in its ability to maintain polarity with some women, who subconsciously align generosity with a lack of excitement and self confidence

So, what does this all mean for modern-day dating and relating? It means that every one of us has two core alternatives, and a combination of the two.

If we continue to relate from a 'normal' level of consciousness – without a focus on finding genuine love, rather than just value – we must accept the reality that, once we are no longer seen as providing enough value to our partner, we stand a good chance of being replaced, sometimes coldly. This means we need to be constantly aware of what our partner's needs are, so that we can continue to meet them sufficiently, as well as we can within the confines of natural ageing.

And in the process of relating in this way, we need to be clear on our personal boundaries so that we continue to be sufficiently honoured or respected as the relationship unfolds. We also need to maintain sufficient independence to avoid becoming seen as boring, and unexciting.

True love is never available in the kind of relationship based on need and value, and this is the norm, unfortunately, at least to some degree. It can also be difficult for your nervous system to be involved in a relationship like this because you must be constantly vigilant about your partner's needs, and whether you are meeting them. And this can be even harder when your partner is either subconscious of their own needs or fails to articulate them to you.

The reality is that our relationship needs are likely to change as we move through the different stages of life, and this is something few people consider, let alone discuss.

The second alternative to overcome this problematic way of relating is to take the path to higher awareness in love, which this book puts forward for a reader's consideration. I appreciate that following this path is not for everyone, because it requires a more advanced way of relating to both yourself, and a real lover. But it can eventually bring forth the ultimate connection that is truly unbreakable.

Our Egos Reject Accountability in Relationships

The human ego does not like accountability. Because of this, a dominant ego can treat guidance received from a partner like a personal attack, and uncomfortable truths like insults. A person who is primarily living from their ego usually wants validation and comfort as a priority, even when this defies the truth and limits growth. And the moment that you hold them accountable for inappropriate behaviour, you can become their enemy.

It is very hard to build a meaningful relationship with someone like this, who does not want to hear or face the truth. They see your concerns as a form of control, and your advice as accusations. They can become defensive, not because you have been disrespectful, but because their ego just can't handle the truth.

I have lived this experience in a relationship with a partner, who would not take any responsibility for the issues in our relationship. She would shut down whenever issues arose and ultimately blamed me for every issue that required our attention. This made the effective resolution of problems very difficult and, essentially, one-sided.

Communication can be used to attain camouflage and control when a person is in their ego. But sadly, the victim is normally the relationship itself.

Without the opportunity for redirection, a relationship can start to lack clarity and authenticity. If one or more of the participants cannot welcome truth into their relationship a genuine partnership is not possible, and it will eventually suffocate, until there is nothing left but resentment.

Fear is the enemy of accountability and growth in relationships.

Are we better off being honest and happy with our partner, or righteous and miserable? Ask yourself, what do you value? Then ask them!

Have We Forgotten How to Have Fun?

We live in a world where obligations are high, and there is pressure on most people to make ends meet financially. When much of our validation comes from societal versions of success and not fulfilment, we can lose balance and attractiveness to our current or prospective partners.

Optimism can be high at the start of new relationships, because we offer each other excitement, fun and new possibilities. But when we 'settle down' into long-term relationships, and even have children, we eventually create new phases that can become more repetitious, and perhaps less exciting. We accept this begrudgingly, but does it need to be this way?

Many modern relationships can become entrenched in the process of accumulating assets, raising children, meeting the needs of our jobs and families, and eventually, we can feel like our lives have become somewhat predictable, and perhaps even boring.

I had this experience. With five children, a senior corporate career, multiple properties to care for and a multitude of perceived responsibilities, including trying to stay fit – I know I lost my sense of fun in a sea of commitments. Out of ignorance, and with a strong sense of commitment to my work and family, I abandoned many of my own passions in life.

My sense of obligation and sacrifice essentially overwhelmed my joy. And this impacted to a significant degree on my relationships. After all, if I was successful and busy all the time, didn't this make me more attractive? The answer turned out to be an emphatic 'no'.

In a world where we often define a person's value by reference to their material or external achievements, is it any wonder that some people overcommit to achievement and lose their sense of fun, and their openness to love.

Getting the balance right between fun and achievement is a critical element of creating wonderful and sustainable relationships.

I wonder how many relationships break down because the fun part gets lost in the need to be financially successful and create comfortable lifestyles?

Where do you sit on the continuum between fun and being serious in your relationships?

Often when I hear people talk about being ready to embark on a serious relationship I cringe, because I know that seriousness, without enough real fun, is a wonderful pathway to eventual separation or unhappiness.

Fun is attractive, and we need to allow this energy to remain in our lives, even after we 'settle down' with someone we love.

To keep the love growing, keep the fun flowing!

There is Really No Such Thing as Average

In a world where value seemingly matters more than love and loyalty, spare a thought for those in the dating and relating world, who are likely to be passed by more often. By that, I mean women who aren't deemed to be beautiful, men who aren't deemed to be successful, and older people who may feel like their best years are behind them, at least physically. ***I have had to confront the latter one in recent years.***

And yet beyond all this the reality remains. We are all pure love, and therefore all worthy of love, not because we have superficial qualities, but because we all matter, and are where we are meant to be. We all have hearts of gold if we let them shine. This we must learn to trust in.

Our individual journeys may all differ, for all are unique, but in this world where the intelligence of our souls is our silent guide, there remains the real prospect of love for all who are patient and ready to open to it. No one is excluded, unless they choose to be, or refuse to trust in this divine force.

But are we open to love, and are we patient that it will arise when it's meant to?

Trust is the key to it all. The power of love awaits those who believe in it.

Chapter 10

Our Greatest Obsession of All

Who's Hot and Who's Not?

We live in a physical realm and therefore our physical appearances and experiences do matter. But, from a relationship perspective, looks have for centuries been elevated beyond their ideal significance, out of our ego-centric ways of thinking. The reality is that it is normally the first impression we make of a new partner, and often it is the spark that creates our initial interaction with a potential partner. But interaction is different to connection.

Rumi, the 13th century mystic, said this about beauty:

> "A beautiful person is not always good,
> but a good person is always beautiful."

Our conscious minds understand this, but do our subconscious beliefs resist it?

When we enter a romantic relationship, the level of our partner's physical attractiveness matters. It is a falsehood to say otherwise. This is the person we probably desire to have an intimate sexual relationship with, so it is probably the only person in the world who we have rightfully valid grounds to consider from a physical perspective. But do they need to be Mr. or Mrs. Universe to meet our needs and wants?

Chemistry matters in sexual relations, but chemistry can be created by more than just physical beauty. It can be generated by the alignment of other factors, including emotional and mental constructs. Beauty is truly in the eye of the beholder, and therefore it can be temporary, and even fleeting.

All in life is a choice, whether it is conscious or unconscious. Even the physical bodies we possess were chosen by our souls before birth, and the way we choose to look after them during our lives determines to some extent how attractive they continue to remain.

As I have said, powerful romantic relationships are grounded in the alignment of mind, body and spiritual energies. But has the relative weighting of these core factors become distorted, because of the way we process our thoughts and make life's many decisions?

There is no doubt that, on a collective level, this is the case. As humans we are drawn to and accepting of the physical, rather than the metaphysical aspects of life, because we can see them and touch them. Yet what really matters in life most, is rarely matter. And this anomaly also applies to romantic relationships.

Sexual validation and relevance are key components of this egoic paradigm most of us share. Many relationships commence based on physical attraction. We meet someone we think is physically desirable and, in modern society, sexual activity can commence relatively quickly. Most people no longer expect to marry a virgin. And we often confuse the physical and emotional heights we get from these interactions as love, despite love being a completely different energy.

This confusion may convince our minds that we have found the love of our lives, when it may just be the best sex of our lives so far. But if we learn to access our hearts, clarity can replace the confusion in which we unknowingly exist.

A relationship that is based primarily on sexual attraction, and devoid of love, is incomplete; and anyone who is in their heart energy will most likely feel the nagging pain of this at some point in the relationship. A relationship based on sex alone, and not love, is not in alignment with the natural order of our soul's desires.

We are programmed to want lust by the physical components of our bodies and our instinct to promulgate the species, but at a far deeper level we want to love and be loved. If at any stage we tap into this truth in our souls, we can't help but feel the misalignment that we have introduced into our lives if we are just with someone for sex.

I have had several relationships that were primarily based on sexual chemistry and lust, and ultimately, I had to end them, because they were simply not enough for me to fully be blissful within. My heart told me in no uncertain terms that I had to end them, despite the intimacy and physical closeness being wonderful.

I also felt that my sexual relations were more fulfilling when I felt that the exchange of energy was more equal with my partner. The less balanced the flow of energy, the lower the satisfaction and meaning I felt in the exchange.

Compatibility can also create this same distortion in our romantic relationships. We meet someone and our propensity to enjoy the same activities, values, hopes and dreams can create the mistaken belief that we are in love.

Women are the primary beneficiaries and victims of our collective obsession with physical appearances. Societal pressures have taught many women that the main value they can bring to this world, and to a partner, is through their looks. And unless a woman is exposed to wise parenting, they are likely to grow up thinking this way.

This message is both subliminal and obvious. Ask anyone to describe a woman and the first thing that they will normally comment on is their relative beauty, particularly if they have above-average beauty. It is programmed into our societal norms and distorts the foundations of our romantic relationships. Listen for it. You'll hear it frequently.

Men have historically had power over women in society because of inequality, which was supported by laws that enabled men to select the most attractive woman available to them to be their wife or partner. Men cared about a woman's looks so much that the value a woman may offer, such as a woman's career, was largely irrelevant to many men.

We have all heard that age-old expression that behind every successful man stands a strong woman. Outdated ideas like this prevail and continue to contradict our conscious belief that we stand for equality.

To this day, the average woman's sense of self-worth can still be highly correlated with her looks. If you see a woman exercising or working out in a gym, remember she is partially working on her health and fitness, but she may also be subconsciously working on her perceived value to the world. Society has imposed this ridiculous consciousness upon her.

If we are looking for a person who gives us a great match on a mind, body and spirit level, and all they offer is one or two of these matches – like beauty – the future of that relationship is likely to be shaky in the long run, because the glue that holds the relationship together is superficial to some degree.

Physical attraction matters: but on its own, it is not love, and never can be.

Chapter 11

The Continuum from Independence to Connection

Balancing Connection with Freedom

There is a fine line between connecting with a lover, and becoming too attached to them, which can cause many relationships, and individuals, unnecessary challenges.

The human soul seeks connection with others, but it also knows the power of freedom or independence, which it needs in order to express itself fully. Deep in our hearts, we all crave a degree of independence; yet at the same time, we also want to be loved, and experience deep intimacy with others. But how many of us are aware of this contradiction, which love itself can solve.

To put it another way, we all want intimacy without losing 'me'!

It is healthy to be self-centred – which means being neither selfish nor selfless, both of which essentially represent forms of personal imbalance. If we are overly obsessed with giving or receiving in love we are embracing need, just from different angles.

For centuries, there was a kind of co-dependency in the way men and women related to one another. And to some extent this still exists today out of habit. Traditionally men went out into the world to earn money, and women cared for a home and children. This was a very needs-based way of relating to one another, and it fostered a system that demanded compliance with normal ways of behaving and committing to each other. As we grow up, we are all then conditioned to want to fit in and be part of our communities, so we embrace this compliance, at first. But when this compliance stops us from being what we want to be, it can destroy our sense of joy.

In fact, the whole world has a kind of 'system' that indirectly demands certain levels of compliance and sacrifice, in order for us to be held in high esteem by others. And for the most part, many people do their best to become a part of this way of being. But are more people waking up to the costs of living this way and turning away from relationships, so that they can enjoy a level of freedom that their relationships can't deliver to them? And does it really matter what others think of you, or is what you think of yourself more valuable?

Many of us still want to be needed of course, so that we can feel safe and secure. But the more self-aware we become, the more our hearts are likely to want higher levels of freedom than we once had, more adventure, greater choice, more peace and less attachment to traditional ways of relating.

This explains why so many people are giving up on relationships that have not previously served them, and are embracing the single life more readily. They simply don't want the old paradigms any longer, or the pain that comes with them.

Deep within us there is a desire to be whole, and relationships that are too enmeshed in need, and in our normal egoic patterns of seeking to be completed by another soul, are unnatural and can, quite frankly, be soul-destroying.

I have had this experience myself. I found that, after several romantic relationships that were not fulfilling to me, I craved a period of being single, to live without obligation to another, and essentially found myself in the 'rubble' of what had ended. That's not a criticism of past partners, but an awareness that my nervous system needed a reset, away from the need to satisfy another person.

I had never had total freedom in my life before, and finally I

was having this experience in a kind of bubble, which protected me from my old habits of people-pleasing in relationships. Finally, I was only committed to pleasing myself and my children, and doing some meaningful self-discovery that really brought me to life.

This may sound selfish, but I was able to see myself more clearly in this bubble and step forth in search of greater relationship balance. I was alone, but not lonely, for I was meeting the real me, and I loved who I finally met!

What I see now is that, for a relationship to be truly natural, there needs to be love and commitment between two lovers, whilst also still allowing each of the partners to express themselves as sovereign people, to a certain degree, within that relationship.

Of course, this expression is best considered alongside honouring and respecting the sacred aspects of romantic connection.

Accordingly, both people in a union need connection, with a degree of space to be themselves, and to be able to interact and connect without following any predetermined script that might otherwise lead them to contraction and control. And this means doing away with any unnecessary reliance on each other for our personal happiness.

But this does require high levels of trust.

Indeed, the formula for true happiness in any relationship – be it in business or love – is to get the right balance between being uniquely yourself, whilst being in union with another who accepts you as you are, and trusts in the love that you share. The relationship matters, but so does your own life as an independent person.

Essentially, for centuries our society has underestimated the power of freedom and overplayed the importance of self-sacrifice and the commitment to others. But we enter this world alone (unless we are born as some kind of multiple birth, like twins or triplets), and we will exit alone. As adults, we are led to believe that our value is best expressed by being loved by another soul; but what if we can find both the value that we are within ourselves, and the value that we can express with that other, who also wants to be uniquely themselves, in a wonderful union?

This is one of the key tenets of true love, and thus true happiness – union and uniqueness experienced in fullness by both partners, together. The two U's, felt by a more natural you.

Conversely, when we believe that our happiness is dependent on another person and the way they interact with us, we risk creating unhealthy paradigms – like obsession, clinginess and controlling behaviours. And, without a healthy balance between uniqueness and union, you have a high probability of disharmony in any romantic relationship, over time. This is the result of fears coming true, which they probably will, thanks to the intelligence of love itself, which will want us to face and overcome those fears.

But if we can get this balance right, we can limit the push/pull that we might otherwise witness between couples – as they struggle to have their needs met, out of fear – and fulfilment is more likely to arise.

Finding equality and complete connection in a relationship can, however, only occur when we are uniquely ourselves and express that with another, who is also in this same identity of self. Equality is not about being the same, it is about being unique but knowing that we are of equal value to the world. And this is a lesson that needs to be embraced by the dating and relating world as a while.

Men and women are different yet equal in every way, and when we come together in a complimentary way to love, there are no limits to what we can achieve and feel together. Whether we work or look after a home, are married or single, or choose to adopt different models of relationship that suit both partners, it doesn't make a difference to our worth to this world or to ourselves. Happiness is the end game we all hope to experience and must embrace.

Relationships based on love are rich in connection and interaction, and low in attachment.

Know thyself, and then you can truly know another.

Chapter 12

Returning to the Unity and Harmony We Deserve

Equilibrium is Natural, Not Normal

Reversing the pain that relationship problems bring forth is a big ask. However, it is a must do. The disharmony and imbalances in relationships that we currently witness, and have done for centuries now, are simply not serving our individual or collective happiness, or our ability to inspire future generations to enjoy their lives. Again, this does not apply to everyone, but I'm sure it would apply to many.

We must take responsibility for this dilemma and not put our heads in the sand any longer. We are choosing this suffering ourselves and must turn to face the issues head on.

Our acceptance of suffering as a race and our victim mentalities are a massive contributor to the current levels of misery we endure, sometimes in silence, but always out of the self-induced crisis of consciousness that we call normality.

Our collective suffering in relationships is both a loud and silent killer. We must take this on together, for each other and with each other, hand in hand. Collective bickering and finger pointing between the sexes about the current state of romance, both on social media and in real life, is not helping us to move forward constructively.

Currently most relationship dilemmas are faced on a micro couple-by-couple level, and of course this is helpful. But who is pulling together the common threads of our problems to inform our future levels of conscious awareness about romantic relationships, and taking it into mass media and education? The macrocosm must morph from the experiences of the microcosm by joining the many dots.

At present, we are spending billions of dollars on space exploration, yet do we have enough resources focused on exploring why so many relationships fall apart, and why lovers stop loving each other on this planet. Is it time we worked on the intuitive intelligence that we should be deploying in relationships, rather than throwing billions of dollars at developing artificial intelligence, and perhaps speeding up our current issues?

We have millions of smart psychologists and relationship advisers. Why have we failed to consolidate their wisdom for all to see, from which we can all benefit? Wouldn't happy homes serve us greater than a human civilisation on Mars?

There are whole industries that have been created to address the symptoms of our ignorance about love, and to some extent, this is a waste of our precious money and energy – because prevention is better than cure.

It's clearly time we address the issues and end centuries of intergenerational self-abuse and heartache. How many hearts must break before we take a stand together in the name of love?

We came to Earth to live a life of love, so I urge us to now remember this, and really choose it, and actively pursue it in a state of awareness, not just blind hope. This is a quantum leap that we can take at a time when quantum energies are on our side.

From Separation to Reunion

In my book *The Truth About Love* I wrote about the endless cycle we seem to be caught up in – of being in separation, then in union, and back again in separation, with partners who we often say we love. And for some people, this cycle can take place with multiple partners on multiple occasions. ***This was my unhappy experience.***

This pattern mirrors the inner experiences we often go through within ourselves, as it must. We come into this life alone (call it as one), then as we grow up many of us lose touch with our true selves as we strive to fit in and belong. Essentially our hearts and minds separate into what some call the 'duality of living'. And in our modern society, our minds so often rule our lives in a world that encourages thinking over feeling.

Then, if we find our way back to our true selves later in life, we are said to come back to oneness, or wholeness. If this last step does not take place whilst we are still alive, it does after we die as we return purely to our soul energy. I think of this pattern numerically as a journey from one (1), to two (2), and back to one (1).

And so this same pattern often takes place in our love lives, because our inner beliefs always reflect in the realities we create in the 3D world. So, if we believe in separation, and not in the unbreakable bond – guess what relationship reality we so readily create to our own detriments?

One of the most powerful things we can remember in our lives is that we are all united through love. Our hearts and minds can also be unified when we remember that we are all an expression of love, living a human experience. And if we do our best to live from our infinitely intelligent hearts, and not our intellectual minds, our inner realities will be one of unity.

As I said in the Introduction, we can probably all remember the feeling of love in our lives even if it's been fleeting for some, for it is our natural state to be in this energy, if we allow ourselves to be. As humans we have largely been taught to think our way through life and not feel. Yet feeling is the only way to be present with the energy of love.

How often do we think about love, and not simply remember the feeling of it? And if millions of people are merely thinking love, how many different versions and representations of love are being created by our minds every day on a mass scale? And if we are not used to feeling into the energy of love, how might we react to it when it is bestowed upon us, in the presence of another? Could we become overwhelmed, or perhaps just avoid it all together because it feels unfamiliar or threatening in some way?

If two lovers meet, predominantly in the thought of love, and don't share love's undeniable feeling with each other, what are the chances of a disconnection of the two different interpretations of love taking place?

When we remember the love within ourselves by feeling into it, then offering it to another, with little or no conditions, who is also feeling into it, we can find a wonderful union with a partner who is also able to experience this blessed togetherness. After all love is love; and it has, in its purest form, just a natural frequency or feeling. The important thing is to feel for love and be committed to the thought of union.

When we consciously relate to another, this is another way of recognising that both partners are home in their hearts, and on one level are kind of forming 'one heart' together.

We can experience being all-one in loving relationships, when we drop the belief that we are alone and separate in this world. We are not – we are individuals, connected through the force of one source, and that source is love.

Isn't it time we remembered this truth and came together to honour it. This can only occur when hearts and minds become truly one, both within us and with another.

So, to bring us all back to closer more loving relationships, I urge us all that, when faced with any kind of painful separation or conflict, we should bring ourselves back to the feeling of love, and resolve any issues from there.

Let's remember the feeling of love, and allow it to be the catalyst for our many unions, through connection in the present moment.

It may help a reader to stop in their now, and feel into the words you have just read, for the feeling of love within you has the potential to change your life 'forever' in a magical way.

We Must Start Within Ourselves

It is easy to speak about balancing the masculine and feminine energies of the world, but truly this must start with individuals doing it within themselves first, preferably en masse.

Only authentic people can have truly authentic relationships.

But how many people have done the inner work required to balance the masculine and feminine energies within themselves? The answer is not many – yet.

Thankfully, more people are starting to follow this path to higher self-knowing. ***I have done so, and I know others who are also actively on this path, so I speak with some authority here.***

I cover this in more detail in a later chapter.

Chapter 13

Honouring True Equality in Love

Do We Really Believe in Equality?

For centuries mankind has struggled with the concept of equality. Most people would say they believe in equality, but have some kind of subconscious or conscious bias with regard to certain types of people. We often resist the full acceptance of those people who are not like us, whether that includes their religious orientation, skin colour, race, sexuality, ideology, and so on.

It is quite normal for people to hold subconscious prejudices against people who don't meet our version of the norm, and to judge them harshly. But make no mistake, comparison and judgement are the great separators in this world.

Lawmakers, in many countries, have tried to overcome the human tendency to be inequitable by creating rules and regulations to enforce the concept of equality, including punishing those who don't align with these rules through their actions. However, this has limited effect if belief structures are not in alignment with these rules.

The truth is that we are all truly equal, no matter what we think or say. We are all part of the same universe, and although it is not commonly understood we are all connected through our hearts, to the light and love that we share. When we meet someone, we should remind ourselves that they are, first and foremost, a loving soul experiencing life on this planet, just like us. Perhaps we can look to witness the light within them, not just their physical attributes. They are not perfect as a human being, but they deserve our respect as a fellow soul, having a human experience just like us.

But in a world where many people select romantic partners primarily on the basis of their mental and physical attributes and compatibilities , as opposed to the connections that they feel in their hearts, is it any wonder that people end up polarised and in relationship with people who look, think and conduct their lives like they do. In the dating and relating world, this severely limits the possibilities that love could bring forth.

As I have mentioned, this propensity to predetermine the characteristics of our ideal partner tend to limit who we could fall in love with. Contrary to what we may believe, love does not care about the colour of a person's skin, or the job they do, and it certainly does not check birth certificates before it is activated.

There is another dimension to this, and it relates to the human tendency to compare people, particularly potential romantic partners, and place certain people on a pedestal above and below us. Pedestals unfortunately create obsessions with those people we perceive to be above us, and unfair criticisms of those we perceive to be below us. And our hearts are never involved in this judgement process, for they see the light in all. That is the handy work of our separating minds.

We are best placed – whenever we witness ourselves building a pedestal for someone, or placing them in a dungeon beneath us – to remember that we all have different strengths and weaknesses, because none of us are perfect. Our tendency when we fall in love with someone, or find them very attractive, is to ignore their less-than-ideal features that are not compatible with us, and revere them completely. This is why people say that love is blind.

How often have you heard someone describe their new lover as perfect, yet at some stage in the future, they seemingly go from 'hero to zero' when their initial gloss wears off, or when their lover finally allows themselves to witness their not-so-perfect traits? They were always present, but one party was probably trying to hide them, and the other party was trying not to see them, to keep their fantasy intact.

When we put somebody above or below us in a relationship, we can create a distortion in that relationship in terms of energy flows. To be equal there should be an evenly balanced flow of energy between both partners. If this is not present and one gives much more than the other, the relationship is probably on borrowed time, either in terms of its survival, or its level of shared happiness.

PART B

CONQUERING OUR HISTORIC CONDITIONING

Chapter 14

Are We Clear on What We Want and Need?

We 'Love' from Fear

When it comes to finding our next partner, we are so often in a seeking energy. However, seeking arises from need. Opening to love and allowing it to overwhelm us, rather than chasing it, is always the more natural option, for in this energy we trust that our hearts will help us connect with the partner who is the right match at the time.

When we lose our need to be validated by material things, we open ourselves up to fully value the one thing we already are and deeply desire to feel: love. To arrive in this place, however we must tame or, if possible, dissolve the human ego.

Fear plays out heavily in our relationships because it is normal for our egos to fear being rejected and/or losing the attention of a lover, with whom we once felt safe and secure. Our egos are constantly thinking about the future, or the past, rather than focusing on where they are right now. As a result, they struggle to keep us in the energy of presence.

This creates a tendency to enter and stay in relationships in a state of fear, leading us into inauthentic interactions. To stay safe, we often withhold our truths, only give to others to receive from them, act overly nicely, avoid important conversations that we think may upset our partners, and sacrifice our own desires to keep the peace. Yet together these 'fake' behaviours will inevitably threaten our relationships in the medium to long term, because – although they may come across as acquiescent – they are not conducive to maintaining high quality relationships that will continue to expand in the interests of both parties. They block the passage of reciprocity.

In general, we interact with other human beings on two levels: at a soul level in our energetic fields (which also manifests or mirrors into the cellular structures in our bodies) and in our bodies and minds. Needy, fearful behaviour in romantic connections is not something that our souls tolerate, even if our egos can for extended periods of time. Relationships need peace to thrive and, when we are not bringing peace to a relationship, we are setting it up to fail, in line with the universal law of attraction or energetic resonance. Our souls will make this a reality, depending upon the agendas they are here on Earth to pursue.

When we delay discussing issues for fear of hurting another person in any relationship, we are likely to hurt them and ourselves more in the long run, because truths have a way of eventually coming to light. The universe makes sure of this in its own divine timing.

And one of our greatest shortcomings in relationships is to put up with the behaviour of others who treat us with disrespect for far too long, without addressing it, or even putting up suitable boundaries.

Excess people-pleasing, contrary to what we may have been taught, is not a virtue in relationships. It is just a different way of getting our needs met.

Replacing Our Needs with Wants

One of the most positive shifts that we can make in life, in anything we do, is to move from the energy of need to that of want. Neediness is a by-product of fear; but the energy of want in its purest form arises from love, and the passion in our hearts.

The movement away from need can, however, be harder to achieve than we think. We can think that we are in the energy of want, but until we remove all the subconscious elements of need that our minds hold, we are probably not.

And this requires us to consciously feel into, understand and eliminate our needs, so that we can truly replace them with our wants.

And to know what our wants are is another process that takes a similar path. We must access our hearts, feel for our desires, and consciously articulate them to a universe that stands ready to co-create them with us, and for us.

Our pure wants could be looked at as a kind of reward for eliminating our ego-centric needs.

Imagine a dating and relating world that understands this elementary, yet precious wisdom, and is willing to apply it to their relationship experiences!

What is My Love Life Supposed to Look Like?

One of the core issues we all face as we reach adulthood and begin the quest to find our 'forever' partner, is that we invariably have preconceived views on what that person is meant to be like, and look like. We are subconsciously programmed to think that we must partner with a certain type of person, who meets the expectations of our family, friends, society and own egos. Perhaps there are religious or racial needs we are expected to meet, or expectations that surround our physical looks? In my first book *Where Your Happiness Hides*, I called this 'checklist love'.

But how do we know that such a person will complement who we are in terms of the love in our hearts, and the balance of masculine and feminine energies we possess?

At a young age, I was told by my parents that – because I was born into a relatively poor family – I should not partner with a woman whose family was of higher economic standing, unless I became rich on my own accord. This comment shocked me, and I know I subconsciously

absorbed it into my psyche. Such women, I was told, were clearly out of my league, as were incredibly good-looking women.

Indeed, our propensity to predetermine what our partner should look and be like, can't help but prevent our lives from unfolding through the natural power of love. Our preconditioned beliefs limit what is possible.

I'm not saying that compatibility doesn't count, or that individuals don't have the right to choose who they enter relationships with based on their own set of priorities, because they clearly do. But we can essentially prevent destined lovers from adding to our lives, because our minds tell us before we even explore possible connections that they are not right for us – which is sad.

The key is to feel for love and attraction before assessing its apparent value, because perhaps the gift of love will arrive wrapped in packaging that you did not expect. And perhaps that packaging will be even more attractive than we ever imagined.

This might challenge us, but perhaps that's what we need to go through to find the love we always dreamt about feeling! And perhaps what you ultimately experience will surprise you in a wonderful way.

Chapter 15

Understanding the Competing Players

Judgement is Futile

There are many convoluted behaviours that men and women have adopted in the dating and relating world. And many psychologists who work more directly with human minds are better able to enunciate them in detail to a reader. I focus more on consciousness in my work, and consider the mind to be the primary issue we need to overcome to become more evolved, not our closest ally.

In this, evolution back to one's true self is principally an unlearning, rather than a learning process. When we eliminate the illusions that we have been taught to live by, we can become the truth of who we are, and that is a loving human being.

Many of our relationships are based on our illusions of happiness, and therefore the happiness we hope they will give us can be somewhat illusive.

It is not overly constructive to dwell on any criticisms levelled at men and women. In fact, it is arguably destructive to focus upon them, for it simply brings forth the energy of blame. I will leave most of this commentary to podcasts and so-called experts seemingly trying to enunciate our relationship gaps, rather than solve them with higher levels of consciousness and love.

There is little to gain from expecting human egos, which are busy creating problems, to then actively solve them in the same level of conscious awareness in which they were creating them. Accountability and facing change are not the ego's greatest strengths.

Accordingly, I will not do so, other than to record some of my high-level observations gleaned from my research, and from watching internet and social media posts, to illustrate in high-level terms that we have a problem that we need to address together. Many readers will already know and feel these, but we all have our own experiences that colour our observations.

Our way out of the mess we are in, is not to dwell on the negatives too much, but to move to creating the solutions we can all naturally embrace, should we choose to do so. Not everyone will choose to take this journey into higher awareness, but for those who do a new paradigm of love awaits them. And higher conscious awareness will naturally remedy the problems that cracks in our relationships bring forth for each other.

In this part of the book, I will thus consider some high-level observations of the different ways men and women are said to relate. These are not meant to offend any reader, for they may not apply to them, but are designed to just kick off a more useful discussion around some of the conditioned thinking we may then choose to address once aware of them.

The Core Paradigm

There is a core paradigm that paints the picture of the traditional masculine/feminine dynamic that is now being challenged, against the forces of much resistance and confusion. Frankly, it is overdue for a total restatement, for it proposes that men are the saviours of women.

In return for money and better lifestyles, women therein give men their beauty, intimacy and nurturing capabilities. They are the homemakers who control the family home. Men are the doers who have traditionally held society's most senior leadership roles, done the dangerous jobs, and driven progress through their more competitive minds.

Further, a primary belief structure was that behind every successful man was a strong woman helping him to take on the world, while creating a family and a legacy for them both to share.

This paradigm has thankfully had its day, as a *fait accompli*, although some couples or cultures may continue to choose it.

I grew up in this model in the 1960s, and I witness how much it is all changing, but under some duress. In my childhood there seemed to be unwritten rules with which every family seemed to comply. It was very standard. The mothers stayed home, and the fathers went to work. Divorce seemed to be rare, at least in my community.

The co-dependent model, in which men and women supposedly complete each other, is now being questioned by a new paradigm that recognises that, except for their physical bodies, men and women are equal in every way, and should be able to choose their own way of living and relating.

We are all sovereign beings, here to live our own lives, not make others happy. And moving to this new paradigm is likely to need us to face up to some illusions we once held up as true.

Let's consider some differences between men and women.

Male and Female Common Stereotypes

Here are some traits I have noted in men relative to women, and women relative to men, which reflect their predominance of masculine and feminine energies respectively:

Most men are:	Most women are:
Less in touch with their emotions	More in touch with their emotions
More focused on doing rather than being, though this should change	More focused on being and feeling than doing, though this is changing
Often less intuitive	Often more intuitive
Often more factual	Often less factual
Often more success-focused than women	Often more relationship-focused than men
Prone to enjoy activities with strong physical contact	Less physically strong than men, but do compete with vigour against other women
More protective, righteous, impatient and autonomous by nature	More caring, empathic, patient and collaborative by nature
Less likely to do self-awareness work to develop their senses and 'spiritual' understandings	More attuned to doing self-awareness work to develop their senses and 'spiritual' understandings

The important thing to understand in this comparison is that all these traits can shift with higher awareness. They are not fixed and can be changed.

We can alter the strengths and mix of our masculine and feminine energies, and these can alter the polarity that we experience with a prospective partner. ***I know this because I have done it.***

More conscious men and women are better able to support equality in their relationships because they understand that both partners deserve to have the right to be true to themselves in the relationship. And this means possessing their own:

- Boundaries and barriers

- A sense of sovereignty and self-determination
- Financial freedom, should they choose it
- Self-determined careers
- Spiritual beliefs and practices
- Differing forms of sexual connection, and
- Hobbies and personal ways of self-expression.

A more conscious, or self-connected, partner, be they male or female, operates from a higher place of authenticity when interacting with their partner.

But how can this show itself in relationships and polarity?

Well, historically, the average man (i.e. probably of normal levels of conscious awareness) who identifies with age-old paradigms of relationships, tends to seek the following in their romantic relationships, as a priority, because they are less likely to challenge societal norms:

- Respect
- Physical attractiveness
- Intimacy
- Loyalty, and
- Softness/nurturing capacities (i.e. high levels of traditional femininity)

However, a more self-connected man is more likely to be drawn to women who:

- Possess above-average intelligence and conversation skills
- Believe in true equality between both partners
- Can give love as well as receive it in a balanced way
- Can support them in their purpose or career, even share that journey with them without any form of resentment
- Are capable of unconditional love, and won't leave him if he has a difficult period in his life

- Can grow with him on a spiritual/awareness level
- Are attractive without needing to be excessively so, for such a man is not beholden to beauty as much as more unconscious men
- Are emotionally balanced and value their partner's emotions as well as their own
- Can feel into their emotions and understand them before projecting them onto their partner
- Are loyal and unlikely to leave or disrespect him, because they are in the energy of a truer form of love
- Are not co-dependent, and
- Have their own career intentions and levels of success.

A highly conscious man is not likely to be as intimidated by beauty as less-aware men, because he knows that a woman's beauty does not define her, him, or their conscious way of relating between their hearts. He will simply enjoy being in her presence and radiance when she wants him to be.

Less-evolved or normal women, on the other hand, who are living more in their egos, tend to seek the following in their romantic relationships from men:

- Respect
- Fun and confidence
- Physically attractiveness and strength, including height (preferably over six feet tall seems to be the attribute most articulated)
- Emotional availability, but not too emotional
- Loyalty, and
- High-earning individuals with above-average wealth, powerful positions, or jobs that give them profile and make them strong providers.

I have heard this crudely referred to in podcasts as the rule of the sixes – a man must be over six foot tall, earn six figures, have a six pack, and have a certain appendage over six inches long to be the kind of man that most women seek.

However, as a woman grows in self-awareness, she is more likely to be drawn to men who:

- Are loyal, gentle, kind, respectful of their opinions, possess above-average intelligence, who don't try to limit their freedom
- Believe in true equality between both partners
- Can give love as well as receive it in a balanced way
- Can support them in their purpose or career, even share that journey with them without any form of resentment
- Are capable of unconditional love, and won't leave them if they have a difficult period in their lives
- Can grow with her on a spiritual/awareness level
- Are physically capable without needing to be excessively attractive, for their overall energy and confidence matters more than their looks
- Are committed and unlikely to leave her, because they are in the energy of a truer form of love
- Are not co-dependent
- Have their own career intentions
- Don't break under pressure because of deep inner strength
- Have deep purpose and know where they are going, regardless of who goes forward with him
- Doesn't need her in his life but wants her; he does not need her guidance but will accept it if on offer
- She cannot manipulate, for he will not tolerate disrespect to himself no matter how physically attractive a woman may be
- Are fun, but even in the energy of fun they remain composed and mature
- Are free of addictions

- Feel deeply and can express these emotions, though are not unstable or in need of emotional validation or rescue
- Is strong but would never violate or physically harm her
- Can hold her emotions, because she can have the propensity to be more reactive to changes in the relationship dynamics, if she has a greater propensity to feel, and
- Is someone she doesn't need to lead, because he will co-create a life with her in the manner they mutually agreed upon.

In short, a more evolved woman doesn't need perfection, but instead desires a man with presence, discipline, wisdom and confidence, above all else.

The more conscious men and woman become, the more-evolved traits listed above become their conscious, rather than subconscious desires. In high-conscious awareness, a person knows that this is what he or she wants, and they can detect it in the prospective partners they meet. And they connect to their intuition consciously to make these choices. They are more likely to feel for love and attraction, not just think it.

They are not drawn to superficial qualities that may approximate these ideal descriptors and will more actively respond to red flags that they spot. Less-aware people are more likely to follow the accepted societal script that tells them what they are meant to seek.

All is energy and, when a man or a woman is highly present, they can love without being co-dependent or requiring male or female validation. They are authentic and know what they stand for. This kind of person is highly attractive to both men and women alike because of the absence of neediness and relational fears.

One common stereotype that women get labelled with is that they are essentially hypergamous. But the reality is that both sexes are hypergamous to some degree, because of inherited paradigms of success.

This term refers to the propensity for men and women to upgrade to higher value people if their partner disappoints them, or if an opportunity to upgrade presents itself, when their relationship is not overly satisfying.

Men, by reputation, tend to go after younger more attractive women as they age, whereas the stereotype is for women to upgrade to more successful men as their relationships atrophy to mediocrity.

But we must bear in mind that people do not normally leave relationships if they are happy, fulfilled, or in love. And the more evolved and integrated a person is within themselves, the more capable they are to truly loving their partner.

Our Unconscious Confusion

There are so many ridiculous and outdated habits in the way we interact with each other in romantic relationships, because that's 'how it has always been done around here'. But many of these conditioned beliefs and behaviours no longer need to be relevant in a world where we are supposedly embracing equality, and the freedom to choose in our own lives.

More people are beginning to question these conditioned mannerisms and reject them as a threat to their sovereignty. Social media is full of individuals calling them out, but still blaming the opposite sex, rather than understanding that they are just learned behaviours, which can be met with compassion, not vitriol. And of course, any negatives you can witness in another are only visible to you because you hold that potential characteristic within yourself, under the mirroring principles discussed earlier in this book.

Carl Yung, the well-known psychologist said these famous words:

> "Until you make the unconscious conscious, it will direct your life, and you will call it fate"

How many of us are relating in an unconscious way and calling our experiences fate or destiny?

The Distorted Beliefs of Men and Women – Let's Get Specific

The beliefs we have inherited from our human lineage are one of the core reasons why we struggle to have successful relationships. That and our individual experiences and karmas.

Here are some of the commonly held mannerisms and beliefs that distort our lives together, which we could change with higher levels of awareness.

Let's start with men.

Below are some examples of outdated belief structures and fears that contradict our so-called world of equality and distort the behaviours of men.

- They need to look after and protect women, even if it costs them their lives, because they must be the heroes.
- They must provide for women to be loved, which includes paying for dates, ongoing lifestyles and courting activities.
- It is a man's responsibility to initiate a relationship with women, and to provide romantic experiences for women. In other words, men do the choosing, and women get chosen.
- They should always respect women, even if they do not return the same energy.
- Romance is expected of a man to win the heart of a woman and get respected in return. This is their stoic duty.
- The more money men earn, the more they win and the stronger they are, the more lovable they become.
- Women are the key nurturers of family members and men are the providers to this 'ecosystem' that it operates within, such as housing.

- A man should not date a woman who is beyond his league looks-wise.
- Men are essentially the saviours of women, like knights in shining armour. If he saves her, she will be forever in his debt.
- By saying "yes, dear" all will be okay – a happy life, requires a happy wife (or partner). His own happiness is less critical than hers, and he must sacrifice to make her happiness a reality.

Perhaps some male readers can find some of these distorted beliefs within their own psyches. ***I know I was prey to all of them, until I saw them in my unconscious belief structures.***

Now let's look at the flip side and consider some examples of the negative conditioning and fears with which many women must cope. Again, please keep in mind that these are not criticisms of women, but distorted perspectives imposed upon them by centuries of human ignorance. Most of these were put forward to me by women.

- Women need to ensure they are always financially independent, because even if a man promises to take care of you when you're off work with child-raising, they could either leave or abuse you, and you need to be ready to become independent at a moment's notice.
- The main things men want from a woman are sex and intimacy.
- A woman should be attractive, soft and feminine so that her and her partner can build a happy home together.
- Men are predators, so the way you dress, how you walk, what time of day you walk, who you're with and the expression on your face can all make you a target, signalling vulnerability and putting you in danger.
- Sometimes it's easier to say 'yes' to a man, rather than risk his displeasure, because you never know when that displeasure will turn to anger and violence.
- Women need to be careful when they do say 'no' to a man or challenge him, because men can become violent and oppressive.

- Women need to be careful about their safety, and stay away from angry men as they are dangerous (although, two clear facts here are that every day 140 women *are* killed by a man in their own family across the world, and 60% of all women murdered are killed by men who supposedly loved them).
- The more attractive you are as a woman, the more men are likely to pretend to fall in love with you just to 'win' you as their prize 'status symbol'.
- Women need to be careful expressing their emotions, because some men can't handle issues without feeling criticised, and they will be tagged as a nagger.
- •As a woman I am expected to do most of the housework and child raising activities.
- To have your opinion heard by a man, women must first massage the man's ego, so he doesn't feel threatened by you.
- If I am to succeed in my career I will need to be better than most of the men, because of the glass ceiling.
- A woman's key value in life is her beauty, and it determines the quality of the man that she can attract, and whether she has the right relationship and/or lifestyle.
- A woman's role is to be the nurturer of the extended family and create a 'nest' for the family to enjoy.
- It is a man's responsibility to initiate a relationship with me, to court me and to pay for our dates if he wants me to commit to him.

Many of the subconscious attributes listed above are generalisations, and I accept that they will not apply universally to all men and women, particularly those who have intentionally established their own conscious beliefs.

There is obviously so much junk and distrust between the sexes, so these lists above could have been much longer.

As a man I was somewhat taken aback by the responses I got from

some women. I had not fully appreciated the fear that some men put into the hearts and minds of women, particularly on a physical level.

I have witnessed it to some extent in my life, but not in my family. Men are generally physically stronger than women, but the misuse of this strength over the centuries has diminished the way some men are perceived by the opposite sex.

Isn't it time we addressed these fears and inequalities and brought modern dating and relating into the era of real equality, respect and reciprocal admiration? We are in denial about how we are really living, and this absence of consciousness is ripping our relationships apart and destroying many lives, including the lives of children.

We are essentially dating to win and not to lose. Yet in the process many people are losing and not winning. Love, in its wisdom, and our ignorance, makes sure of this, at our expense.

A rebalancing to higher intelligence would help us address many of the anomalies discussed in this book, and more.

A Final Word

Any reader could add or subtract from this chapter, for we have all had different experiences in relationships. I recognise this. But this just magnifies the point that we have a complex situation mired in new desires and old conditioned thinking.

I repeat that we are all equal, but without a stronger dose of acceptance and compassion, and a willingness to evolve together, we will never solve this mess, which is without doubt repairable. Every new way of life started out as a thought, backed by conviction. Perhaps it's time we gave more thought to our relationship malaise, and acted upon it with a new force of conviction, directed at transformation.

So, if our conditioned and karmic pasts are influencing our chaotic now-moments, let's consider what is shaping some of our present-day problems in relationships.

Chapter 16

The Perennial Power of Fairy Tales and Generational Patterns

Our Childhood Stories

Since the dawn of time, stories have been a big part of the way we live and remember. Our egos are also constantly filling our heads with their own stories, to support the false identities that we think we are. Cultures are cultivated out of stories, because they create societal expectations, learnings and memories.

Some stories are highly positive and help us learn. Others can be destructive because they merely serve to support our need to be right or superior in some way. We see these in all walks of life. History is normally written by those who win, not by those who lose. And many stories are baked into our conditioned thoughts from childhood, then handed down to the next generation.

Consider, for example, cartoons as early as Disney's Mickey and Minnie Mouse, and how it portrays women (Minnie) as being a support act to men (Mickey), having a caring support role to the man's more central stage role in society. Minnie was always depicted as the woman behind the front man. Although Disney have now created a stream of female lead characters who are their own central character – such as Mulan, who saved China from the Huns, Moana who sailed across the ocean to save her island and tribe, and Raya, a fierce warrior who saved her country – the depiction of Minne not only reflected, but perpetuated, the limited role of women in society at that time.

Also take the fairy tales that we enjoy but silently absorb into our psyches. A common one tells of a beautiful damsel in distress saved by a brave and handsome prince or warrior, who is greatly revered by the community. In this, the hero saves the damsel from physical harm or poverty, then the damsel becomes forever in his debt. She then gives him the love and support that he had always dreamt about, saving him from a life of loneliness. And, of course, they live happily ever after with great riches in a castle, and deeply in love. Picture Disney's version of *Snow White* (1937), Cinderella (1950), and *Sleeping Beauty* (1959) as examples.

Many of these old-fashioned fairytales are being or have been remade, with the stories being updated so that the damsel is not saved by the prince. However, there are some common and quite damaging paradigms in those stories that have already impacted the way that those currently over 45s relate, since the stories have been infused into the artificial identities of Baby Boomers and Generation X alike, and these do tend to be handed down by osmosis to younger generations.

Luckily, younger generations such as Millennials and Generation Z have had more diverse paradigms craft their conditioning, such as Disney's *The Little Mermaid* (1989), *Beauty and the Beast* (1991), and *Tangled* (2010), which promote mutual rescue. Ariel, Belle and Rapunzel are all saved by their relative princes but also save the princes themselves.

The adult fairytale *Pretty Woman* (1990) follows suit, with the beautiful woman saving herself – after refusing to become Edward's mistress, Vivian instead decides to finance her own return to college – and the elite man Edward overcoming his fear of heights to apologise to Vivian in a faux 'rescue' wherein they both save each other emotionally.

Disney's *Frozen* (2013) was then a breakthrough story, as neither Elsa nor Anna were saved by their respective princes but rather save each other through the power of self-esteem and the bonds of sisterhood

– inspiring Generation Alpha (and hopefully Beta) to appreciate the broader sovereignty of love.

Regardless of whether it's the vulnerable, beautiful and loyal woman being saved by the elite, brave and high-value man – most fairytales do end with a relationship commitment that suggests the couple will become a force in society, and never separate, because their relationship is perfect, being built on rarest of all loves: true love.

Let's consider other influences on male and female mindsets and conditioned paradigms.

The Conditioning Embodied in Movies and Other Stories

It's not just the fairy tales and movies that we are exposed to as children, which alter our conditioned minds and dating expectations – this conditioning is built upon as we mature in life, through other forms of media like books and television shows.

In most Hollywood movies – at least up until very recent times – it is the aloof man of high masculinity who couples up with the most beautiful fellow actress. He is often adept at violence, is emotionally unavailable, and has an important purpose or mission from which he cannot be swayed. He may even be a 'Bad Boy' with a license to thrill and even kill, and she is the beautiful light that helps him discover love and happiness.

These good-looking co-stars often experience a kind of power struggle that depicts a love/hate relationship dynamic. Eventually, however, this hard man who is intelligent but of few words, wins over the beautiful girl and gets her full admiration and attention. The feeling becomes mutual, as the hero's heart starts to connect with hers.

This is particularly so in thrillers such as *James Bond, Top Gun* and *Mission Impossible*, all of which obviously depict this kind of macho masculine image.

In *Superman*, Louis Lane was not attracted to the superhero's alter ego known as Clark Kent but fell in love with Superman once she witnessed his powerful abilities. Same person, different image, different levels of interest and perceived value.

Is love present in these depictions? Not likely, just attraction on steroids, along with a certain illusion of love based on external qualities of success and being elite.

I have never read Mills and Boon romance books, but I understand that these books are heavily read by women. They depict a very traditional style of love in which elite men save beautiful women, and they live happily ever after with lots of passion.

However, are you seeing the pattern of attraction that can play out so readily in our experiences and influences our choices in 'love'?

Music Also Sets the Tone

Most musical songs we hear are usually about finding love or losing it. Not much else seems to be sung about.

But next time you are listening to a love song, pay close attention to the words and phrases that are so often used, because they reflect many of the falsehoods that we consciously and subconsciously cling to about love.

You'll hear phrases like:

- 'Love breaks your heart'
- 'Let me be your hero'
- 'I'll love you forever more'
- 'I can't live without you'
- 'You're my only one', and
- 'You are mine'.

You get the picture. Is it any wonder that we are so delusional about love? We are essentially brainwashed into these misconceptions every time we put our headphones on!

The one I always laugh at is the first one. Why would love break your heart, when our hearts are the only true source of love in the first place? That's akin to our hearts committing suicide. Hearts don't break, and they don't lie. Only our egos do these things to us.

Further, the concept of owning another person and relying on them to sustain your life is clearly delusional, and aligns with the saviour or hero concept with which we often love to align ourselves.

Chapter 17

The Many Victims of War and Societal Conflict

Violence Damages All Souls

One of the worst aspects of human life on Earth, since the dawn of time, has been the regularity of wars and human violence. Violence has been a common thread of many civilisations with which we have all had to contend, and it has its roots in masculine energies and ignorant patriarchy.

In modern western society, we have many laws and authorities that attempt to prevent and punish unnecessary violence. But in the past, this was clearly not the case. For many centuries, life on Earth was brutal and dangerous, and although this has no doubt diminished in modern times, in some countries, we still see evidence of violence, including domestic violence in the news every day.

In Australia where I live at present, approximately one woman per week is killed by her partner, the person she should be able to trust the most. And countless more are abused or physically assaulted by men.

Is it any wonder that women have trust issues with men with respect to their physical safety? It's mainly women that get raped in society too, not men. And these situations have been going on for generations to the detriment of the male/female dynamic.

Frankly, men need to take more responsibility for this diabolical situation.

Firstly, let's consider wars more closely for I believe they have left a deep shadow in human psyches that still play out today, even in 'peacetime'.

For centuries, we have tried to take power over other tribes and nations by killing people. This is the greatest atrocity we have ignorantly bought into, as an acceptable way to settle differences, and to take the resources of others that we want or need, or to merely settle ideological differences. But beyond this awful reality, wars, in addition to physical violence, have done long-term energetic and psychological damage to our societal ways of living. Put simply, we struggle to forget when someone trespasses against us, and it can sometimes take generations to resolve.

I was born not long after the end of World War II, and although I never experienced conflict directly, my family was heavily influenced by the need for men in the family to be involved in fighting overseas. It also changed the lives of the women in our family significantly.

My mother suffered from heavy abandonment issues, during and after the war in her father's absence, and constantly spoke of it in my childhood. One of my grandmothers lost her marriage because of the war, and as a result I never met one of my grandfathers. I am totally compassionate to these forces in my family lineage, as they left deep scars upon the family dynamics, some of which impacted upon me, and others in the family, decades later.

For centuries, men have been required to leave their families and tribes to fight in battles. Many have been killed, injured or emotionally stained by the need to kill as an act of duty. This is a horrendous way to be forced to live and is totally contradictory to the true nature of our souls.

In military forces, men are valued for their warrior-like characteristics, including their ability to kill, handle pain, bury their fears and emotions, and to honour the collective for the good of all, putting their lives on the line in the names of gallantry and sheer sacrifice.

Involvement in war is often glorified as the ultimate act of masculinity, yet it leaves many men buried in emotional pain for the rest of their lives, sometimes without sufficient compassion, and with families destroyed. And it creates intense negative energetic resonance for the human souls involved, directly or indirectly, and sometimes the generations that follow.

The experience of women in war has also been horrendous through the centuries. Although historically they were not on the front lines of battle, except in support roles, they were required to forfeit their normal lives to support the war efforts, supporting and raising their families alone, and taking up roles traditionally done by men. While the traditional providers and protectors in the family were absent, women would be under immense financial strain, which they otherwise need not have faced. They would also be vulnerable to predatory men, even on unoccupied homeland soil, with their own countrymen subjecting them to physical and sexual abuse.

For those living in occupied territories, whether they still had the protection of their partners or not, women were killed, raped, or became chattels of the conquering army.

My point around the influence of war is this: war, on top of more normal societal violence, has hardened both men and women through the centuries, demanding men be warriors and the protectors of their families from, ironically, other men. And women have had to survive these ordeals, which collectively they did not start, with some men being their predators, and some being their protectors.

This glorification of war and the warrior-like image of men have been passed down through societal lineages for thousands of years. We have learned to value hard men with the ability to physically protect and inflict pain, and who hide their emotions; not loving men, who can express their emotions or nurture others.

Wars still occur on a regular basis across the world, but the last world war was many years ago. However, whether it's in sports, business or other walks of life, we still tend to glorify the alpha male who wins and has power over other men. He is sometimes ruthless and assertive. He is subconsciously desired by women. But how creative is he really for the common good? Often not.

The male propensity to seek power over others physically has no doubt led to the declaration and conduct of many wars and even civilian-based conflicts. One wonders how many wars and cases of violent crime would have been perpetrated across the world had matriarchal, or at least more balanced leadership structures been more common, rather than patriarchal ones? ***I suspect very few.***

The perceived ability of a man to protect their partner seems to be a core desire of women. Obviously, as a rule, women are less physically able to defend themselves than men, so they seek the warrior who can protect them, in peace and war time alike.

Most women prefer tall men too. Does this have a link to some subconscious belief that they are better able to protect a woman than short men?

History has taught women to want the man who will come home to them once a battle is over, meaning they won't have to go in search of a new partner, or provider for their children. They have also sought to partner with a strong man who can protect them and their children from violence, which is typically perpetrated by other men.

War and violence are unnatural acts of mankind, and I believe that it has shaped us in ways that we don't fully understand, including energetically. I honour those who sacrificed themselves to a wartime cause in which they believed, but I do not honour the patriarchal leaders who created these abominations, and the energetic distortions that we have been forced to face for centuries as a result.

The use of the term 'mankind' does not rightfully describe many of the aggressive men we have witnessed over the centuries. Several of them clearly were not kind, as their egos strived to create their legacy as a winner, for the world to remember.

As for violence in normal daily life, we must remember that only hurt people, hurt people. The subconscious belief that many men (and some women) hold – that violence is a valid way to settle differences and even get revenge – has shaped the way we relate, if only because it has shaped the way women and men attach to and interact with one another.

I believe women may hold back their issues for fear of provoking men to become defensive, shutting down, or even becoming violent in relationships. Dating men who they don't really know well, can also be a risk for women, which does add an extra layer of risk to internet dating, which few men probably have had to contemplate.

But some of the discussions I have had with women have shown me that women do get criticised for nagging, or giving men the silent treatment, at times.

Everything has an equal and opposite reaction, of course, so it is likely that the if men and women cannot fully express their feelings with each other, and feel safe doing it, this must be a shared issue and is not something either sex can distance themselves from – we must address such issues together and not 'point the finger' at each other, for that is naivety at play.

We must be able to express our feelings with the truth, and be confident that they will be met with care and compassion, not violence or disrespect; otherwise, conflict resolution is not likely to improve between the sexes, and fear is likely to remain a problem.

But we need to be blunt here. Men may be seen as the protectors of women, but they are also the main physical threat to women. And I don't believe many men comprehend how much damage their aggressive behaviour has impacted on the historic conditioning of women to not trust men, until they get to know them well.

Perhaps the man in uniform is a man that many women idolise and want, because he is perceived as the protector, who can keep her safe from harm, and look good at the same time!

Men need to get more adept at controlling their tempers, and never becoming violent or distant, to give women, who are often more emotional in relationships, more licence to express their feelings with comfort and safety.

I was taught this as a boy growing up, but clearly many men were not.

Chapter 18

The Nice Guy Paradigm

Nice Guys Finish Last

There is an old saying that 'nice guys finish last'. Unfortunately, there is some truth in this narrative, and it needs to be addressed, because it is closely related to the principles of polarity.

Male niceness, when excessive, is truly perceived as a form of weakness, to which many women are not attracted. This contradiction is often demonised and seen as female unfairness of men, but on deeper enquiry it is not.

I know this paradigm all too well, for I was the nice guy who disguised my subconscious fears in relationships with excess giving. But being discarded in relationships, after being a totally devoted partner, taught me a set of core truths about myself that I am now thankful to know. My tendency to be excessively nice, and to people please, was a form of neediness in disguise.

In western cultures of the past, including my own, men were traditionally raised by mothers, more so than fathers. Historically, women took on the role of homemaker and accordingly were more active with their children than men. Many men believed that they were less equipped to handle the role as the nurturer of children, so were more focused on providing. Most men also shirked away from any nurturing role because it carried social image implications that positioned them as overly feminine, and so less attractive and less valuable to women and society.

Modern society has fortunately now shifted to a degree, thanks to greater gender equality and higher levels of general awareness, such that many couples now choose to have both partners working in employment, or running their own businesses, while raising children together. High competition for housing has been a major force, necessitating this choice for many.

However, most mothers still bear the brunt of childbearing responsibilities and probably remain the dominant influence on the beliefs of young children in western society where the extended family concept has been partially abandoned, and single-parent families have become more common.

Put simply, boys and girls were historically more likely to be conditioned to align with the belief structures of their mothers, particularly in my generation. Boys thus grow up primarily subjected to the influences and controls imposed on them by their mothers. Even their schoolteachers have historically been women. Most men learn to be obedient to women as children, and this often does not change unless they are taught otherwise as they mature. In addition, their fathers are also conditioned in this way, so the male role models that they see and emulate may also be somewhat subservient to women in the home.

If we have historically positioned women as homemakers, and therefore given them the role of controlling the family home, is it any wonder that they tend to be more dominant than men in domestic environments, and 'wear the pants' at home.

Many men in my generation were taught to always be the nice guy to women, be giving and respectful. There are many men who were not taught to be this nice guy, and may even have been taught the opposite and to treat their partners with disrespect, emotionally and physically. This probably reflects the fact that they were exposed to a totally different dynamic growing up.

Not all men become the 'nice guy', some become the 'bad boy' (or something in between); but this seems to be less common, particularly among highly educated communities.

Many men who enter a romantic relationship are subconsciously programmed to be committed to the needs of their partners and often they lose themselves in their process of over giving and pleasing. This is a learned behaviour from childhood. But this can ultimately 'crush' their attractiveness to many women, and cause them great confusion.

Many women say they admire nice, caring men, but can lose attractiveness to a man who is too nice, possibly because if a man is too nice, he is ultimately acting out of fear and not love. Love does not people-please, nor does it give without expecting to receive in return. Men thus deceive themselves if they think that wearing the nice guy tag will give them an advantage over other men – they clearly do not understand the impact this tag has on feminine psychology, nor that this behaviour, once over-played, is a sign of fear, capable of being detected by a woman's intuition.

The reality is that when a man disrespects or fails to honour himself sufficiently by over-giving to his partner, he opens himself up to be disrespected and dishonoured back.

The same is true in reverse of course, though a submissive woman is less likely to diminish the polarity with her man, for he is more likely to be drawn to feminine submissiveness.

The 'happy wife, happy life' distortion is likely to occur when a man feels that he cannot readily receive, or stand up, for his own needs in a relationship. Out of self-preservation he wears the badge of honour of a devoted partner, and his ego mistakenly takes credit for this despite it truly putting him into the position of being emotionally weak – an anxious lover you might say. He may then fail to be a leader in the home, like he would be in the office, leaving the woman to make most of the family decisions.

Deep down, all men and women want partners with self-esteem, authentic and psychological 'backbone' and strength, and not ones who are emotionally weak. This strength is an energy we admire and are programmed to trust, and its absence is one of the key reasons why many relationships begin to lose sexual chemistry and polarity. Men must own this junk and move away from it.

The modern, slang description of an overly submissive person who gives their partner excessive attention and affords them excessive compliance is known as a 'simp' – a submissive wimp. And there are too many male simps thinking they are what women want, when in fact biology and psychology alike would say otherwise. Many women say that want a nice guy, but can become confused when they start to lose interest in their partner who fits this description. Avoidance is better than repair.

Many of the men in my era, who I know and have observed, grew up to become simps. One factor in generations past that contributed to this form of anxious behaviour, was the partial segregation of boys and girls in schools, sports, and so on. Many younger people in my generation were denied regular access to people of the opposite sex, which made them more prone to be anxious with the opposite sex on a social level. This anxiety translated into unnatural displays of behaviour to get noticed.

The growth in co-education structures in recent decades has no doubt diminished the awkward social environment that I endured.

I carried the nice guy trait into both my marriages, until my self awareness work helped me to see it with clarity. And I witness it with many men. I have since forgiven myself for being a 'simp' for much of my life, because all I was being was what I was taught to be, and witnessed in my father's behaviour. And I'm sure he was similarly programmed to be what he became.

But we need to defuse any unhealthy dynamic in any equal relationship, because the lack of polarity in that relationship – and particularly in marriages formed to raise children – will eventually ruin any home or family that results.

The nice guy who over-gives out of fear of rejection need never wonder why he is rejected by women in favour of less fearful men.

The latter simply has traits that make him seem more masculine and confident, and this drives polarity that the 'nice guy' often struggles to create or maintain.

The solution to this oddity starts with men observing this dynamic and doing the inner work to overcome their fear. Men can become more centred in both their masculine and feminine energies, and make more conscious choices about how they wish to interact with their partners and children. They need to build their confidence with women, so that they do not become submissive over-givers, who are more likely than not to end up in relationships that lack polarity and passion.

Men need to stop being fearful nice guys, and become loving wise guys, with more emotional composure. Men – stop being simps, it is simply not working! Become fearless!

Be the nice guy to a degree because you care and respect your partner, but don't let yourselves become too fearful to a partner who also needs you to carry yourself, have the masculine strengths she desires, and a backbone to go with it. It's all about balance.

I witness many women on social media saying that they left their very supportive and nice partner because something was missing. And some seem to be struggling to put their finger on this reality. What might have been missing was self-autonomy and thus polarity, in my view, so a subconscious reaction of rejection took place.

Of course there may be other reasons for this diminished attraction. There is rarely one cause for human behaviour. The women may have been in a phase of life where they were seeking better communication from their partners, more fun, or simply a desire to develop self-awareness as they were developing.

The key is to be considerate and kind, but learn to admire yourself, have confidence in yourself, and be autonomous to a healthy degree.

The Sexless Relationship Paradigm

Many long and medium-term relationships atrophy such that sexual activity dies off significantly. Many relationships that start out with intense passion end up largely devoid of sexual closeness. We don't need statistics to prove this, because it is a well-known but silent epidemic, impacting millions of couples.

And this can be particularly shocking for men because they often start out innocently assuming that if a woman loves them, they will always want to express this love for them in the bedroom.

Sexual desire is largely linked to the strength of polarity between a man and a woman. And so, if polarity diminishes or dies, so will the sexual passion in a relationship.

Men and women both want to have satisfied sex lives, so when sex dies off between two people, it's often because some other source of resentment or disharmony is driving the problem, not the sex act itself.

We can all have periods in our lives when circumstances can lower our libidos temporarily, but many men complain about their partners eventually losing sexual desire towards them for extended periods of time. And this can be a difficult experience for anyone as they struggle to comprehend and cope with it.

According to some psychologists I have researched, most sex-less long-term relationships involve a man who has lost the attraction of his partner. Perhaps he is the excessively nice guy, or perhaps he is not emotionally connected enough to his partner. No one warns you of these phenomena when you get married, and our fantasies tell us that marriage will bring us a lifetime of intimacy, eliminating the need to go out to find it. But we must all work on polarity, as well as our love connections to keep them healthy.

In the past, many people married to attain a sex life. But these days are gone, and sex before long-term commitment is now the norm.

Psychologists say that, what is always available is rarely seen as valuable by the human ego, because it lacks mystery and excitement.

Put simply, it gets boring. Familiarity breeds contempt and can kill magnetism, and sexual polarity.

If two people in a relationship are unable to properly resolve areas of conflict, or resentment, the sexual closeness they once shared is likely to be collateral damage. And this is when honest and compassionate conversations need to take place to determine why polarity has been diminished within a relationship.

We cannot blame men or women for this relationship anomaly, it simply is a function of passion being lost for various reasons between two partners, and not being truthfully addressed on a timely basis, because neither party wants to hurt the other.

But as well as an honest and compassionate sharing of feelings, couples will need a dose of the acceptance that what was once present, has been somewhat impaired. ***Avoiding the issue is not a winning strategy, as I learned the hard way.***

Honour yourself and you will be honoured back. This is the magic mirror of life that we all need to understand and apply. Honouring yourself may require you to leave or terminate an existing relationship, after having the difficult conversations, but if you want peace, intimacy and respect in your life this may be the only way to attain it.

I believe that when sexual intimacy is not forthcoming in your life or relationship, there is a deeper message being sent to you. And that message, which I encountered in certain relationships, is that you are worthy of intimacy even if you are not perfect. But your behaviours, beliefs or attitudes may need to change in some meaningful way to reestablish sexual polarity with your current or future partners, including exiting a situation that is diminishing your sense of self.

Remember, there is no love in control, and any form of over-giving or excessive taking is always a form of control, delivered out of fear, not love.

Chapter 19

The Fearless Woman

Balanced Expectations

Diminishing polarity comes from both sides of the partnership, and missteps are normally traceable back to limited belief structures created by long-held societal norms.

Let's consider how women have been consciously and subconsciously programmed to select their partners in life, other than through love.

For centuries, men have been the leaders and primary participants in most societies. This patriarchy was supported by laws, rules and mindsets that effectively deprived women of their natural right to be equals.

The physical bodies of men and women are different. Historically, men have always been generally stronger at lifting, carrying, fighting and hunting; while women had the divine gift of being able to create new people from their anatomies after impregnation, surviving the dangers of childbirth, and enduring long days of menial labour. These factors have tended to influence their respective roles. Even where a man and a woman were both present in the home, women thus still performed most of the housework, while men went out to work. There was an accepted reciprocity in this arrangement, even if it was a conditioned habit.

But, apart from physical differences, men and women are essentially equals in every way, and this reality is now being enshrined in new ways of life.

Still, there are many 'hangovers' from our previous ways of living.

One of these is that women are the nurturers in society, with a primary focus on raising children and managing family homes. Another is that women must be chosen by men, rather than being the choosers – something that surely isn't necessary anymore.

Women no longer require a man to create their lives for them and to fund their children. Previously, women were not encouraged, or in some cases allowed, to express their own masculine energies. But that too has changed.

In the past, the status and wealth of a woman's partner determined both her quality of life and that of her children, and this was the case for so long that it's possible women still carry a subconscious tendency to look for a man who can give them safety and security, and thus a certain lifestyle for them and their children.

The move to greater equality in society has clearly altered this. Feminism has been a major force behind this shift. However, how a person chooses to express themselves in life, in their careers and hobbies, naturally has an impact on their romantic relationships.

Everything has benefits and drawbacks, and women who work in formerly masculine roles are likely to acknowledge that this alters the way they can be perceived by men in a relationship sense. Unless both parties are more fully conscious in tandem, then the more masculine women become – by virtue of doing things that men traditionally did – the less attractive they are likely be to less-conscious men following normal patterns of behaviour. But then, do such women want to be attractive to those types of men anyway?

Awareness of choice is clearly key here, as well as expectation. Thus, even though some men and psychologists repeatedly ask on social media: what can modern women give in return for the provisions and protection offered by more traditional, but perhaps less-conscious men, the answer is for each individual woman to determine their own modern narrative with balanced expectations. And this is best done by being willing to explore the interplay of their conscious and subconscious beliefs.

Does she want to offer a less-advanced man her beauty and nurturing abilities in return for him providing for her? Or would she rather offer her heart to a more-advanced man who then wouldn't provide for her in that old-fashioned sense? If the latter, then… women, be fearless! Embrace your new equality and meet the men in your lives as equals, not providers! They are waiting to be your companions in life, journeying through all its ups and downs with you as a partner – not just a provider! For a man cannot be both less-conscious and more-conscious at the same time.

And in this, who cares what others are doing, or what social norms suggest? We should all choose what's right for us as individuals, then offer up our loving authentic selves to others for join with in a highly conscious connection!

The less we need and expect from each other, the purer our shared love can be!

Chapter 20

Debunking the 'Happy Spouse, Happy House' Narrative

Do our Stories of Sacrifice Need Rewriting?

The 'Happy Wife, Happy Life' and the less gendered 'Happy Spouse, Happy House' narratives are mentioned throughout this book, in various chapters, because it is a sad myth destroying the fabric of the relating world by creating imbalances, which ultimately erode many promising relationships.

I grew up soaked in this narrative and heard it many times to my detriment. Frankly it had a major role in destroying my love life, and now I admit that I despise it!

As I have said, when someone is not happy within themselves – which is synonymous with a lack of emotional security and an inability to feel good about who they are, independent of a relationship – there is nothing another person can do to make them happy. No relationship can fill this void, and whether it's a man or a woman, we have been falsely led to believe that the right partner has this capability to complete another to 'make' them happy. This is a falsehood we must smash.

Some of the collective conditioning mentioned in earlier chapters plays into this destabilising and fear-based narrative.

So, how did it arise, and what damage is it doing to our love lives?

As a more traditional man, I certainly found this subconscious belief within me after deep personal enquiry. I had a programmed propensity to put the women that I loved on a pedestal and totally commit to their happiness, and also put the happiness of my children above my own. This included an extreme willingness to die for the woman I loved, as crazy as that may sound.

I also put up with behaviour at times that clearly dishonoured me, because of my focus on her welfare, above my own.

And I didn't get caught in this paradigm just once; I was guilty of applying it multiple times, until I saw the damage that it was doing to me, and the polarity in my relationships.

I kept deprioritising myself for many years to ensure my partners were happy, because this aligned with the 'hero' story I was immersed within while growing up. Effectively, I subconsciously believed that my happiness didn't matter as much as that of my partner. My job, as the 'knight in shining armour', was to provide money to keep her safe and happy, not necessarily give her love. In return she would love me and be forever in my debt. Money and lifestyle became a surrogate for love, which I now see is completely naive. The whole dynamic was completely screwed up.

Is this linked to a societal belief that men within a relationship are more valuable and desirable than one who is single? If so, who wrote that rubbish? And is it a function of the history of war and conflict, in which men were taught for centuries to sacrifice their lives for their countries, partners and children?

Let's face it, on a sinking ship, it's the women and children who get the first seats on the lifeboats. Men have the physical strength, so must swim when the spots are filled. But in a modern world, should there be other criteria to determine who swims with the sharks, like age or stage?

I suspect that many men never do the work to question the happy wife, happy life psychobabble, and therefore do not do the inner work to find their own centre; the centre that would probably improve the polarity with their partner, and allow them to consider their own welfare more in relationships. From this centre they could naturally offer love, not just money and provisions.

Unless we are self-centred, we will always love out of need and fear. And in this narrative, we believe we need to over-give out of fear to be loved.

Of course, there are men who would be far more self-centred or selfish, and accordingly this narrative would not apply to them.

So now let's look at the female context of sacrifice in this paradigm. I accept that I am not a woman, so here are some points to ponder.

As I have said, for centuries, women essentially learned that their happiness and lifestyles were determined by the men they were paired with. This was an economic necessity that some women were forced to comply with to survive, let alone thrive. The more successful her man was the less she suffered in material terms. Pursuing love didn't necessarily get her protection, a house, a family or even a meal.

How many women were forced into relationships out of sheer necessity, because they were essentially programmed to seek value over love to survive? And if so, it is most likely that this subconscious paradigm is still playing out in the lives of some women, because it is a collective consciousness at play, within the screwed-up 'system'?

How many women were coerced by societal norms to find, and commit to, the most impressive man they can find, not the one they love. And does this explain why so many women today are initiating between 70% and 80% of divorces, because there comes a time in their lives when they see this paradigm, no longer need to prioritise security, and go in search of greater happiness, which they do not feel in their current relationship?

In other words, do they tire of being in a relationship that is successful, but not fulfilling, and go search of something which makes them feel more alive?

Or perhaps they have not been as happy in their long-term relationship or marriage, and instead of searching inside themselves first to find happiness, they walk away, and espouse the rhetoric that they fell out of love? Maybe they were never deeply in love in the first place, they just thought they were? They were in need. Again, each relationship has its own identity.

A further example to ponder is the situation of domestic abuse. According to estimates published by WHO in 2023, 1 in 3 (31.6%) of women worldwide (840 million women and girls) have been subjected to either physical and/or sexual IPV (intimate partner violence) or non-partner sexual violence in their lifetime. In Australia, roughly 1 in 4 women (23% to 27%) have experienced violence from an intimate partner since the age of 15 (Australian Bureau of Statistics Personal Safety Survey 2021-2022).

Among the many reasons women commonly remain in such horrifying relationships, would surely include how they fear disrupting the 'happy house' they've built with their spouse, often for their children. The Institute of Family Studies cites how many abusive partners also convince women that the abuse was their fault, such that they come to believe that they can stop the abuse happening if they can just alter their behaviour and keep their spouse happy – they believe they can 'love the abuse out of them'.

Abusers can also devalue their partners so much that woman can feel worthless, such that their personal happiness has no value compared to their partner's. Abusers can also threaten to escalate their abuse of course, and that terrifying threat keeps such women trapped in the relationship. Fear for their children or other loved ones will easily have them sacrificing their personal safety. Financial restraints and isolation are also cited as reasons.

Ultimately, whether our drive to make our spouses happy comes from putting them on a pedestal or from fearing for our safety, the result is the same: we come to believe we are less important, of less value. This is of course a fast ticket to misery and imbalance, because every option minimises your own sense of self, and puts a limit on your relationship.

Trying to Make a Wounded Person Happy

With so many people dating and relating out of a place of fear and need – and not through pure connection and being inherently controlled by their subconscious beliefs and wounds – is it any wonder that these disconnecting forces derail our relationships so readily, and can make people somewhat subservient to their partner's needs over theirs?

When we carry emotional wounds into relationships, they invariably turn into needs. Similarly, if we do not confront our needs as they arise, they will often add to our existing library of wounds. It's a cycle we need to diffuse.

If two people are not feeling into the energy of the love that they share, but instead are committed to their respective ideas of it, this can add another layer to our shared unhappiness, and the fears of rejection that we hold.

'Happy wife, happy life' and 'happy spouse, happy house' are both simply dumb ideas, which fly in the face of equality.

The Fear of Emotions in Relationships

People with a predominance of masculine energies do tend to look at relationships in a factual and structured way, as noted in an earlier chapter. And when a person is more in their feminine energies, they can be more emotionally aware, and this can add weight to the 'happy spouse, happy house' impulse.

If one partner essentially fears the emotions of another, or fears that they may negatively shift, and has not been taught how to stay composed when they are being expressed with force, they can become subservient to their partner, particularly if they are more inclined to try and compassionately see things through their partner's eyes .

I grew up with a mother who was emotionally erratic, and it led me to essentially fear strong emotions from women in my earlier years, until I grew through it.

We need to teach people to honour their feelings, but stay in control of their emotions, because the expression of feelings without filters can be a confronting place to be for some, and lead to self-deprecation and the creation of pedestals just to keep the peace.

Go inward, before you go outwards with your emotions, I always say, to preserve connections.

PART C

MODERN FORCES WE ARE YET TO MASTER

Chapter 21

Coming to Terms with Changes in Social Dynamics

Potent and Powerful Innovations

Modern relationships have shifted under the influence of significant societal forces and innovations in recent decades. A number of these changes are, in themselves, very powerful, potentially potent and meaningful. However, our response to most of them has been somewhat ignorant and naïve in many cases.

Our egos, in their usual style, have used these modern innovations to promote and protect the participants, not with malice, but in somewhat selfish and inauthentic ways.

Let's consider six of them.

1. Feminism

In the patriarchal world in which we have been existing in for centuries, another way of framing the word feminism is that we are now more fully respecting matriarchal energies. And this is long overdue change that can only make our world a better place once it all restabilises into a new equilibrium.

Western society, unlike some others, has been moving slowly

towards greater equality for men and women over an extended period; but in the last 50 years this shift has been accelerating and profound.

This is a shift that I have lived long enough to actively witness.

Feminism, or more precisely greater equality, is now enshrined in many laws, rules and customs in the western world.

However, the substance of the feminist movement, in terms of true acceptance, has been slower in its adoption than is ideal. The impact of feminism on relationships between men and women has been profound, and akin to an earthquake in our love lives. Equality is so desirable in romantic relationships, yet it needs to be consciously created between men and women, because it has the potential to disturb our shared polarity.

A key impact has been through a shift in the way money impacts on attraction. In societies where men were traditionally the 'breadwinners' and providers, and women were the stay-at-home nurturers, or worked in lesser paid roles, the transfer of wealth stemming from feminism has seemingly reset this paradigm; yet it has still not led to the relationship harmonies that many expected it would.

Many women now earn similar incomes or more money than their male counterparts, yet still desire a man to be the primary funder of the relationship. This makes no sense. If we are collectively questioning the continuity of the age-old arrangement of men providing for women, then we need to question all aspects of it, especially given many women no longer need this assistance.

With greater opportunity for higher levels of self-determination, many women are altering the kinds of men that they want to be in relationship with, and this is their sovereign right. But more men then need to adapt to this new world and do the work to become the kind of man that women want, not complain about it, and just give up.

One wonders what the medium or long-term impact of all this will be on men's self-esteem levels, and associated behaviours, especially men who don't readily adapt to shifts in role dynamics. Unless they are assisted to higher levels of self-awareness and emotional endurance, societal unrest and mental health issues are likely to grow.

On a more immediate basis, psychology articles I have consulted suggest that men – in the face of not feeling that they can satisfy the modern women sufficiently, who have higher expectations of them or are less drawn to traditional relationships – are walking away from dating, and are spending more time with their friendship groups. I have seen this referred to this as the Age of Male Indifference. And this exodus is confusing many women who are noticing the lower number of men attending social functions and approaching women with the intent of initiating dates.

One wonders how women will react in the future to this phase of male indifference, if it continues. With many of the pursuers no longer pursuing, like they once did, will the pursued turn and decide to do their own pursuing? Or will they soften their dating and relating requirements to seek to restore the previous balance? Only time will tell.

Feminism has also arguably increased the opportunity for women to express their masculine energies more fully and even compete with men on many fronts. In this transformation, women are often needed to lead as men once did, take on debt as men once did, and spend time in workplaces that can be both highly unforgiving and masculine in nature. And many such women are excelling in such roles, because their high intelligence is finally being recognised in other walks of life.

Women who choose to walk away from traditional female roles have every right to do so, and I applaud them for their conviction. Some women even choose to play the dual role as mother and father within their families and become single mothers through choice. However, every action has an equal and opposite reaction, so if we don't compensate for this shift through higher awareness, issues can arise in families and in the realms of polarity, and they have in many cases.

If women are accessing their masculine energies more, particularly in business, and less-aware men continue to seek to 'save' a woman who is soft and feminine, can you see the disconnect that is still in transition, and causing disconnection to arise?

We need our societies and communities to be harmonious and balanced, or the consequences will become more dire, with more people giving up on real relationships and turning to heartless 'situationships', which many see as transactional in nature, with both parties focusing on fulfilling their needs, in the absence of love.

And if a partner that you don't truly love fails to meet your needs, they can be easily replaced in today's world of internet connectivity.

Internet connectivity is essentially a double-edged sword for us all in this, being both a threat and a boost to our interpersonal connectivity. Will we thrive if more people seek to be single rather than in supportive unions? And is the growth of single families less about female empowerment and more a sign that trust between the sexes needs repair?

There is a time and a place to be single, but it does not support our inbuilt desire to love and be loved over the longer term, and this could lead to a loneliness epidemic, not to mention further declines in the birthrates that assist economies to grow

Unless a society has a birthrate of at least 2.1 children per family, our society risks stagnation. Some might of course say this is a good thing in a highly populated world.

Still, the bottom line is that we are suffering in love, because we have not fully and consciously adapted to the new order that feminism is creating, and had the appropriate conversations to accommodate it. And, frankly, humans do readily embrace suffering, as bizarre as that may sound!

Perhaps it is time that we did have these more learned conversations, because if men better understood the needs and wants of women and vice versa, our chance of joint happiness would be much higher than they seem to be now.

We need greater consultation, communication and education to make this a reality.

2. Is Social Media Making Us Anti-Social?

Now more than ever are we heavily influenced by the media, and the media world is still evolving. There was a time, not that long ago, when the definition of media meant radio, newspapers, magazines and television; and when our media hits were sporadic, somewhat formal and probably more professionally presented. Whether they were true is another matter!

Back then, if we had a bad experience in a relationship or on a date, we only had close family and friends to share our experiences with, there was no way of sharing it broadly with the world.

Things have really shifted in recent decades. Social media is now 24/7, always available in the palm of our hands, and of course anyone can become a social media speaker and influencer. You just need an account, no employment contract or license.

From a relationship perspective, social media seems to be full of jilted lovers and dismayed experts, firing criticism at the opposite sex, in search of likes, and supporting comments.

The problem is that these posts seem to create 'armies' of people who are being influenced negatively against the opposite sex. Compassion and understanding appear to be in short supply, as followers are whipped into a subconscious frenzy of negative judgements that may be entertaining or informative, but in no way constructive to solving any issues at hand in the dating and relating world.

Many relationship coaches seem to also chime into the conversations, advising men and women on how to behave if they want to manipulate the opposite sex and attract them with cunning tactics that take advantage of their subconscious psychologies.

What seems to be lacking is actual loving advice, advising people on how to become more authentic and aware in their approach to dating and relating, rather than blaming the opposite sex for our own experiences.

All this, I suspect, is denting the confidence and desire of some wonderful people to participate in the dating world. Trust and acceptance are being replaced by fear and low expectations.

This behaviour is unlikely to temper until someone becomes a voice of reason and steps in to solve the drama and chaos with true wisdom and calmness, and provide solutions rather than just pointing out obvious tensions. That's the intent of this book, even if it confronts some readers – it's meant to help not hinder the situation.

Not everyone has social media of course, but most adolescents in the western world do, and this makes them prone to be more influenced than older generations, through the negative gyrations that they are being exposed to and influenced by.

3. The Transactional Nature of Online Dating

The multitude of apps that allow people to find new partners to date online has redefined the way we now 'try' to find love. And I use the word 'try' intentionally, because to some extent it has turned us into 'try-hards' with little patience, and with low or no trust that love will find you when it's meant to find you.

In my book *The Truth About Love*, I explained that when we feel love it is a frequency or vibrational match between two hearts. It can therefore only be a felt experience when two hearts meet.

Two hearts can be in energetic connection regardless of where they are on the planet. There is no such thing as time or distance when it comes to the energy of love, or more precisely the power of our souls. But love will be fully sparked into reality when two hearts meet in person.

Many of us are likely to have an intuitive inkling that a lover is on their way to us; however, this inkling turns into knowing when we come into close contact with a person, and effectively our hearts recognise the frequency of love in each other's presence, and possibly so much more. To find love and fully experience it for the first time with another, our hearts really need to meet in the physical and be present with each other.

And therein lies the key word: presence. In years gone by, people met future partners in person, and in presence. They had limited alternatives. There were no dating sites on which they could go 'shopping' for new partners. People met at work, doing hobbies and sports, at social events like dancing, on holidays and so on. Many of these experiences were recurring ones, like going to the workplace multiple times per week, and as such they allowed for feelings to develop and be deciphered. There seemed to be less chaos in the dating market.

People did not meet through websites, carefully crafted marketing campaigns, or across screens, which can risk fast decision-making, called swiping, based on pictures and colourful descriptions of people's more positive attributes. When they met someone in person for real, they often felt drawn to them, and this was a felt experience. They felt any combination of the following:

- A sexual attraction in their bodies as chemistry
- A level of emotional connection in their hearts
- Curiosity due to aligned interests and/or values, and
- The love in their hearts, triggered through eye contact.

These assessments were substantially felt – not only thought – and were in real time. They were not assessments substantially made through screens and the energy of egoic projection.

People of my generation once screened for lovers in proximity, but not through screens or fee-paying contracts. Meeting someone new was more of a felt experience, than a thought-out and planned one.

Of course this is still possible, but internet dating is now providing such a large proportion of dating opportunities for people on a mass scale that it's become more common to meet romantic partners through it – though lots of first dates do seem to occur and fizzle out once people meet in person. Also, by virtue of its volume of introductions, internet dating is increasing the level of rejections and disappointments with which people need to cope. Ghosting and deleting have become an art form, it seems, as people do it through the impersonal nature of their devices.

Of course, we all know people who have had a successful experience on dating apps and sites. However, I suspect that this represents a relatively low proportion of 'matches' that end up creating real love matches.

And how many truly involve love?

Internet dating has also undoubtedly contributed to the dating market becoming more transactional, and perhaps creating a fantasy world in which instant gratification of our needs has become more likely than the prospect of deep and meaningful connections. It is now very feasible for the participants, particularly the more attractive people, to date multiple people at once.

Frankly, I'm not sure how people justify this approach of dating multiple people at once. If you are focused on multiple prospects at once, you are surely approaching the situation with the expectation of failure.

And what you fear, tends to come true!

If a date doesn't work out, there is no problem, you can just get another one by logging in and swiping away. Potential partners have become disposable commodities that can be easily forgotten and deleted with the push of a button. Push the delete button and they are no more.

Has instant gratification become the order of the dating world, much like internet shopping?

Patience is not a necessary ingredient when you date this way, because there are many sites, with many listed people, offering themselves as potential partners, all over the world.

Love cannot fully thrive in any energy of fear or need. Seeking love is always an indication that someone is in the energy of need, not desire. Dating sites encourage this seeking behaviour on steroids.

In decades past, it was much harder to set up dates, because you had to go out to meet people, and be brave enough to enter a conversation, then swap phone numbers or addresses. Only the very skilled and confident tended to date multiple people at once. This led people to value the connections they made more fully and not enter dates lightly.

Unfortunately, there are many profiles on these dating sites that are also fake or have been set up by scammers. These profiles are designed to manipulate those among us who are more naïve and hopeful.

I recall the first night that I registered on a dating site, I had 104 responses, most from supposedly beautiful women who were all around the age of 31. Funny that! This is not a boast, because I knew that there was no way most of the responses were from valid people. I exited that morning and gave up on the experience.

There are other disadvantages as well, which men and women endure in different ways when going on dating sites.

For women, there are higher rates of digital harassment to contend with, as well as unsolicited content. Younger women, in particular, I am told, are frequently subjected to unwanted explicit images, abusive messages, and stalking.

There are safety concerns of course, since meeting strangers online presents elevated real-world risks, with a significant number of women reporting sexual harassment, scamming, aggression, or physical violence from the men they meet via dating platforms. There are now government guidelines to help women navigate the world of online dating safely in some parts of the world.

Given swiping creates an environment wherein people increasingly make superficial physical assessments of potential partners, women are also once again having to subject themselves to physical objectification, which can be very damaging to their psyches.

As for men, there are increasingly complex issues of competition to deal with, which can of course be highly damaging their motivation and self-esteem, especially following some women's pursuit of what's been termed 'high value men'. A high value man is someone who balances financial stability, physical fitness, and interpersonal integrity, such that they become a highly desirable, successful, and emotionally mature male. It is estimated that less than 5% of the male population are high value men – with some estimates putting this closer to 2% – which mathematically means there are not enough of such men to go around!

Set out below is a diagrammed illustration of how this impacts the modern dating market. ***This is a diagram I designed, based on what I have heard on podcasts, and from other expert commentaries on the internet.***

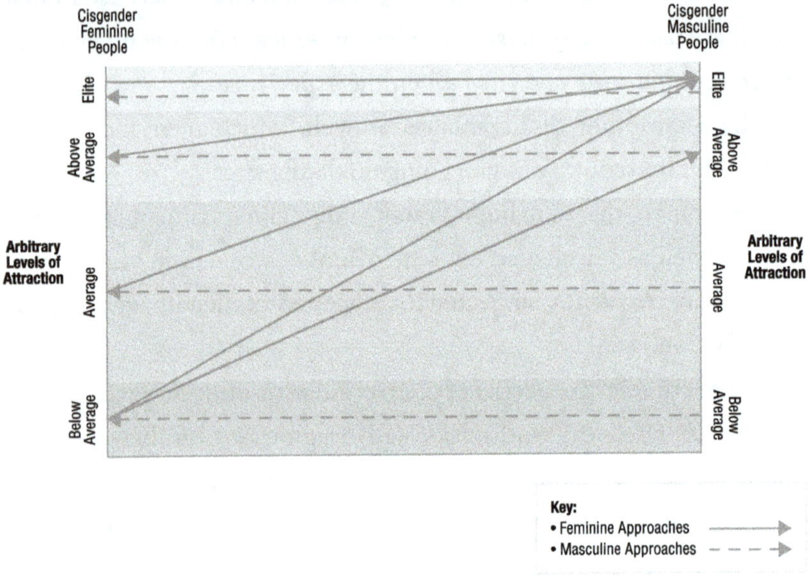

Figure 3: A Visual Depiction of Internet Dating Habits (Estimate Only)

I can vouch for the fact that, men are taught, either directly or indirectly, to date within their perceived 'league', and not significantly above or below it. To do otherwise is to invite the high probability of rejection, which is something our egos hate.

But this new dynamic is putting a small cohort of men in a very powerful position in the dating market, which is arguably not serving most men or women. These men can date multiple women at once if they choose to, and they have little need to commit because their core needs are being met by the constant flow of respondents and admirers.

This position of power was perhaps once held by the most attractive women in society, for they were the hunted species in the dating pool, who men had to approach and court. This appears to have moderated in favour of these 'high value men', although 'hot' women do still have much 'pulling power'.

Traditionally, men were the ones expected to approach women in person to initiate a dating experience, or even a flirtatious moment. But dating websites have changed this dynamic to some degree. Women can now approach men by swiping and messaging them behind a screen, rather than waiting for an approach from interested men. In fact, many dating sites now give women the exclusive right to initiate all approaches. Essentially what was once a conditioned way of initiation in the dating market has been 'turned on its head', at least online. In a way, this is a good thing because it has introduced higher levels of equality for both sexes into the dating world. However, like all in life, it does create ripples of change.

Now we have an even more distorted dating market than we had before. The most attractive women get most of the attention and messages from attractive men, and the high value men get substantially all the attention from the bulk of the women.

Essentially dating sites have become the domain of the elite, which only exaggerates the pain for the more 'average' or less advantaged participants, who are essentially just funding the ecosystem for elite participants, with little to show for it. 'Average' men and women get minimal responses, and average women run the risk of being used by 'above-average' men who may just want to 'pump and dump' them, and really do not value them as realistic long-term partners.

Many people pay good money to be on these sites, with all their widespread promises, only to be constantly disappointed by their experiences and the costs.

The dating sites of course remain alluring, as they promise easy access to love, despite strong love matches being a relatively rare event in our lives.

Anonymity is heightened on these sites, because we are interacting as 'keyboard warriors' with limited accountability and feeling, and potent levels of self-interest.

When you select partners through a screen and a superficial listing of ego-driven qualities, you switch off the intuitive indicators of compatibility within you, which are built to detect whether the energies of passion and love are present. And you switch on your conditioned ego-centric mind, which can be goal oriented and superficial in a highly competitive environment.

It is often said that love is blind. Once you sense it in the presence of another, it is truly a gift. But blind love is less likely to find its way to you by watching a screen.

Unless you are an elite person, the evidence suggests that getting off the couch and going out to meet people is a much better alternative to swiping your way through round after round of disappointment.

4. The Prolific Rise of Online Pornography and Only Fans

Pornography was different in the past, as there was no internet. Access to pornography was thus largely limited to pornographic magazines, sold in retail outlets, and only adults could buy these.

These days, pornography is largely free and easy to access on the internet, even for unsupervised children. And women are setting up multi-million-dollar businesses selling pornographic content to a customer base they have often recruited on social media.

However, contrary to general perceptions, the consumption of pornography is not just a male-driven activity. In 2025, a report by the Barna Group noted that over 44% of women in the USA download pornography regularly. It is now estimated that one third of all pornography is downloaded by women.

In other words, both sexes use it on a regular basis.

The social implications of this reality seem significant.

Perhaps it is a result of the number of sex-less long-term relationships that exist? Perhaps it is a result of the increasing number of people staying single? Whatever the reason, is it certainly distorting and objectifying what we are supposed to look like to be sexually desirable to the opposite sex. And is it giving younger people a false image of what love making can truly be.

While both sexes perhaps use pornography in different ways, I see this as nothing but a sad reflection that men and women are turning to fake, external sexual stimulation, rather than sharing this wonderful experience with each other.

And this probably includes the world's oldest profession, prostitution, which is said to be booming off the back of the digital era, economic pressures across the world, the mass scale of immigration into western nations, and the plethora of sexless relationships we so often hear about, and sometimes end up experiencing ourselves.

5. The Noble Role of Dating Agencies and Speed Dating Events

Few people probably use the services of professional dating agencies, because they tend to be expensive. They are staffed by professionals whose role is to find love for other people, by matching the clients on their books.

No one can find love for you, though others can help you find someone you are attracted to, and through that perhaps love will also arise. Only your heart can establish if a love connection is present when you meet someone.

I accept that these types of organisations can assess compatibility, and their work is a noble cause. However, whether two people fall in love with each other, in any situation, is only possible if their two souls allow it to be so.

One initiative that has surfaced in recent years is Speed Dating. This involves a group of people attending a location and going on a series of mini-dates with the opposite sex. At the end of the event, you can decide whether you want to see a potential partner again.

I attended one of these to try it out. I didn't find love, but I was impressed with the concept, because it allowed people to meet in person, and thus share conversation and their energies face-to face, rather than over a screen.

6. The Rise of the Modern Dating Coach

Social media may be crowded with people offering advice – certainly to men on how to attract women – but there are also professional dating coaches.

After my second divorce, I took the opportunity to engage with some dating coaches and courses, because it had been over 20 years since I had dated. What I found surprised me.

I did two online course, attended an in-person course, then continued to receive dating advice by email from certain renowned coaches.

However, I didn't participate for long because I found it to be lacking in authenticity. The advice I received was more about how to present myself to manipulate the psychology of women – by essentially pretending to be something I probably couldn't be at that time. I was coached in what to say, how to stand, how to text, when to be available, and when not to be.

There was no mention of simply being myself and working on becoming my truth, which is what my work stands for. Instead, it seemed to be directed at helping a man to get sex or a date, rather than truly finding love, and compatibility.

In fact, there was rarely any mention of the word love, and the concept of attraction was used as a proxy for love, whereas they are in fact totally distinct in my view.

What we need is real advice that teaches both men and women how to be their true selves, and how to remove their conditioned thinking so that they can attract and hold a reciprocal relationship with someone who genuinely cares for them.

We need more truth and less manipulation tactics. If someone is not suited to you, that is just life, and although it may hurt, we just need to accept it. Acceptance is a key gateway to peace in the dating and relating world.

Of course, it can help to understand more about the needs and desires of the opposite sex; but learning how to manipulate these attributes is disingenuous in my view.

The best dating coach is the one that lives inside your chest, and trusting it fully is critical.

Chapter 22

Is Marriage on its Knees?

I Do, I Hope

For centuries, marriage has been held up as the ultimate representation of romantic commitment between two people. Traditionally, men have then been the initiators of marriage, being the ones to ask for a woman's hand in wedlock.

But in the same way that divorce rates are rising, marriage rates are starting to fall. And surely these two factors are linked.

According to the *Economist Magazine*, marriage rates are declining in 89% of countries around the world, and it is most pronounced in wealthier and emerging economies. This doesn't necessarily mean that people are not living together, but both men and women are questioning the risks and need to marry, particularly women who are probably opting to live with greater personal freedom if they do not find the ideal partner.

In OECD countries, back in 1970, 70% of the adult population were married. That number is now 50%.

In the United States, the marriage rate has dropped by 60% since the 1970s, with one in four people in their 40s now never marrying.

In Asia, the decline is even more stark in countries such as China, Japan, South Korea and India. In China, for example, the marriage rate has more than halved in the last 12 years, although this may have been impacted by the one-child policy that was in place from 1979 to 2015.

For centuries, sexual relationships were discouraged between partners until marriage was consummated. Marriage also gave many people societal status. However, over the last 50 years these expectations have started to be softened by a society that fully accepts sexual activity at any stage of a relationship, and more fully accepts de facto relationships, including children being born outside wedlock. This is a positive change because it supports our right as humans to be sovereign with the opportunity to make our own life choices.

In the past, marriage was also seen as the best environment in which to raise children. But the breakdown of marriages and modern opportunities to have children outside of a relationship, such as through IVF treatments, has to some extent taken the spotlight off marriage as a necessary option in people's lives, should they wish to become parents.

Men, as the historic initiators of marriage, are also becoming increasingly wary of the value of entering the institution, because of the rising tendency of women to end them, and the material costs that they have witnessed other divorced men endure at the hands of the courts. Women are also exercising their right to enter and end marriages that they believe are not serving their best interests or contributing to their happiness sufficiently.

Divorce can result in high financial costs and legal processes and inflict great financial and emotional pain on both partners when they end, although de-facto relationships can also be very difficult and expensive to exit too.

I have been through two divorces in my life, so I am aware of how difficult it can be on both partners when they end. No one gets married to get divorced, but over the last 50 years divorces have become more common.

I still believe in the sacredness of marriage, despite my two experiences. The wiser I have become the more I have embraced the possibilities that marriage presents. I know that if I marry again, I

will do so with higher awareness and a much higher ability to align with the energy of love. It surprises people that I still embrace the concept of marriage, but it reflects the fact that I have done the inner work to turn my past pain into the gift of higher awareness and self-love, and now I can foresee a different kind of marriage to the ones I ignorantly performed within to be loved.

On a more macro-level the question is, will marriage survive the next 100 years if we don't sort out our relationship issues together?

Embracing the Conscious Marriage Concept

Marriage was originally supported by rules and protocols that made it an essential component of society. In centuries past, marriage provided for a clear delineation between the roles of men and women, almost like a division of labour. We have already outlined these in earlier chapters.

But the world has changed as we embrace a modern romantic model wisely based on equality and higher levels of personal sovereignty.

Frankly, marriage was traditionally adopted because it brought structure to families and even supported human survival. It gave people access to 'permissible' sex and supported the birth of children. But it is now arguably an outdated concept in the more materialistic world we now live in, unless it is supported by a high level of conscious relating skills and commitment to each other.

Marriage was designed to be an arrangement that two people entered for life. It represented a commitment through the good times and the bad times, no matter what circumstances arose. It didn't guarantee happiness, but it was predicated on safety and security, one of the key areas that the human ego craves to ensure its survival.

But in this new era in which relationships have seemingly become more like disposable situationships, and not lifetime partnerships, marriage has quite frankly become a high risk and expensive experience to commit to for many people. It's a 50/50 proposition, according to the statistics. And getting out of them is generally much harder and more expensive than getting into them.

And here is the burning question, why do we continue to commit to something to which we are clearly not committed to, at least in the long-term? Is it just conditioning, or blind hope?

There is a solution!

Let's call it a conscious marriage or partnership. We are entering a new era of consciousness, one in which many people want to be in partnerships that not only support love and passion, but also allow for the deeper growth of both partners. It is a partnership of equals, and it driven by love, not fear.

In my book *The Truth About Love,* I speak about the virtues of conscious relating. We all carry wounds, or frightened aspects of ourselves, which falsely tell us that we are not enough. But we also have loving aspects of our personalities. Conscious relating allows a couple to work on their wounds together, with the power of their love, to allow both people to evolve individually and together, to levels of happiness beyond anything they would have previously thought possible.

No one is perfect, yet modern dating and relating is seemingly all about finding Mr or Mrs Perfect, who can make us happy. And if you are not perfect, or of high enough value or interest on an ongoing basis, your days in that relationship may be numbered. Once you do not meet the needs of the other person's ego sufficiently, you may well be replaced or disposed of, even if your love and commitment to your partner is deep and profound.

Conscious partners help each other to live in love together, in a way that supports responsible life choices and joyous outcomes. They do not scan the environment for the next best person with whom to connect. They build a life together and know that there will be 'speed bumps' to overcome.

It gives both partners the ability to see the truths that are lurking in every dispute and resolve them to allow the partnership to strengthen in love, not atrophy in increasing levels of accumulating resentment, which eventually implodes once it hits a certain threshold.

My advice to anyone is that, if you enter marriage or a long-term relationship, with the aspiration that it will last for the rest of your life, do so in a conscious way with strong doses of commitment and love. This is a skill that can really hold the relationship together, in sickness and in health, and in good times and bad. To do otherwise is to play a high-stakes game out of sheer ignorance, with something very precious, and in fact sacred.

The bottom line is that marriage is divine in its intent. But are we truly consciously aware of what possibilities they offer us and how best to conduct them when we get 'hitched'. The use of that word to describe marriage is a clear sign that normal paradigms of marriage can depict it as more of a burden we must endure, rather than a blessing. For many it has been a burden, but this can all change when we know how to change it.

I wasn't sure how this was possible the first two times I married, but I believe that I know now. Not because anyone has taught me how, but because I have taught myself.

Chapter 23

Active Management of Attraction

The Multiple M's of Matching

Love may be 'missing' in some relationships, but the forces of attraction rarely are, at least at the start. But since attraction can rise and fall as polarity shifts, we need to heed its significance in our relationships.

I wonder how many people are really taught how to maintain attraction and polarity in longer term relationships? Not many, I suspect, unless you make the effort to discover it for yourself. So many of us are 'flying blind' when it comes to maintaining polarity.

To maintain our magnetism with a partner in a relationship, there are six core areas that I believe we are well served to be mindful of. Love is, in my view, the main energy that matters; but these six material aspects, in no particular order, matter in the maintenance of magnetism, and should not be discounted. They vary based on the life stage of a partnership, and the needs of everyone.

1. Mating

We live in a material world, and as this book depicts, physicality in a romantic relationship matters to most of us. It is an important way that we can express our love and/or attraction to another, and meet our own biological needs. Physical attraction, or lust, can be mistaken for love or even overwhelm it; though the one person in the world who we can legitimately assess in terms of their physical attractiveness is our partner.

Beauty is in the eye of the beholder, so we are all attracted to different physical attributes; yet we must also face the reality that some people have a kind of universal set of attributes that, collectively, many of us tend to desire. We are all sexual beings at our core, if we let ourselves be natural in this way, and although it is clearly a choice, our sex lives matter to most of us.

Staying healthy and fit, and applying high-quality self-care, is a positive way to stay physically desirable to your partner, particularly if they also do so at a high level.

2. Meaning

When another person has a deep passion for a cause or passion, we are often drawn to that person. Their purpose tends to create an air of intrigue and admiration that we like to be around. People with passion and purpose – beyond a need for just a relationship with us – can preserve their sense of independence or sovereignty, and this can be very alluring to some.

Interesting and meaningful conversations also tend to make us enjoyable and alluring to be around.

3. Mystery

Our minds are attracted to mystery in another, because it keeps us guessing and intrigued. The human ego craves what it thinks it may not be able to have and thinks that something is precious when it is in rare supply. The longer people are in a relationship together, this element of attraction can diminish, compared to the intrigue that is often present in the beginning, when two would-be lovers first meet.

Keeping some form of mystery in a relationship can help to preserve attraction, even if it just amounts to doing different things together with spontaneity, to introduce novelty into the interactions. Novelty matters to the human mind, even if it is not a prerequisite for the presence of love, because it can keep boredom at bay.

Love, on the other hand, doesn't care who we are, or what we do, it cares what we are.

4. Must Be's

As I suggest in another chapter, knowing what your partner needs and wants is important to maintaining polarity. We can be guilty of assuming what they need or want us to do, or be, particularly if this subject isn't consciously discussed. Changing as our relationships mature is critical to maintain polarity.

5. Merriness

Fun is an important energy in all relationships, but it often gets a lost when life gets busy and obligations start to take over. Too much fun can deflect from the realities of life, but not enough can create boredom in a relationship.

It is a balance that we all need to consider with our partner, and all of us have a different definition of fun.

6. Management

Life comes with a certain level of administration that we must stay on top of, unless we can outsource it. Caring for kids, doing the grocery shopping, cleaning the house, and so on, all need to be considered for a family to function with ease. When we start a relationship, meeting the need for this administration of tasks is often less critical, but if we choose to live with a partner and function in fullness together, our relative contributions to the administrative aspects of life can matter more.

There are probably other areas to be wary of in addition, but these are the six I see as critical to maintaining balance and harmony in a relationship.

In a world where matter often matters more than it truly needs to, we must pay heed to the energies that drive attraction and polarity, and consciously work with them. Love is not a choice, but relationship dynamics are.

In current paradigms, we cannot just rely on love to support a successful relationship. When we get out of balance in life, and prioritise certain aspects of attraction, at the expense of others, we can introduce elements of risk into the longevity or happiness of our relationship.

I don't mind admitting that I did this at different points of my life, overworking and losing my sense of fun at times in the pursuit of financial security. I was not conscious of the full ambit of attraction in my younger days and paid the price for my ignorance. Ironically, the more financial security I created through my commitment to my career, infused greater relationship risk into my life in many ways, as this ultimately cost me wealth in the wake of divorce. It was a cruel plot twist and circle of despair that I didn't see coming!

The difficulty is that attraction can ebb and flow over time, and some of it may be subconscious in the less aware. Love doesn't do this, contrary to mainstream mindsets, unless it is over-ruled by our conditioned minds. This places a greater need for clear communication and conscious conversations with our partners, on what both partners want and need to maintain polarity into perpetuity.

Sometimes it can be easier to excel in areas of our life, like work, because our employers provide clear guidelines to guide us to success. This could include documented team values, key performance indicators, appraisals, operational and strategic plans, and so on. But our private lives are normally devoid of these kinds of guardrails, for obvious reasons.

However, in a more conscious relationship with clearer communication on needs, wants and feelings, and delineation of responsibilities, we give ourselves a higher chance of happiness and success.

Relationships, unlike love, are a choice, and therefore what we consciously choose to do, and be, matters to their longevity and our levels of shared happiness.

PART D

KNOWING OURSELVES IS THE ONLY LOVING WAY FORWARD

Chapter 24

The Loving Power of Self-Awareness

Our Confusion is Clear

The earlier chapters of this book were designed to show readers how complex and confusing romantic relationships have become, and to illustrate how destructive our inherited and conditioned thoughts and beliefs are in dismantling our romantic opportunities.

Most readers may have had their own experiences and perceptions, and may disagree with my observations and conclusions, and that is okay because we are all entitled to our own truths. It is a very complex area of life, which is probably why our current levels of consciousness have not been able to solve the problems en masse.

What is hard to refute, however, from known statistics, is that many romantic relationships are not meeting our original hopes and dreams and are therefore ending in a degree of pain.

We can all argue over who is to blame, and what men and women collectively seem to get wrong, but to some degree this is pointless, and adds little value to the notion that we can turn this situation around. We are in an intense period of change in human romantic relationships, and it will ultimately find a new equilibrium. But this will take some time, and the facing of much pain.

The reality is that our egos are creating a troubled relationship dynamic. But at what cost to our ability to connect to love and happiness. And how is this likely to impact the younger generations following in our footsteps? How will their romantic endeavours unfold, if their mentors continue to show them a world of harm, rather than harmony?

Connectivity is what needs to improve across all aspects of our lives. We need better connections to ourselves, to our lovers, in the office, in our communities, between nations, and so on. And this connection can only become truly enriching when we are in the energy of love, not fear, and can value each other more fully for what we are at our core: beings worthy of love and respect.

The concept of true love that we hold so dear is possible when we know how to find it, but the unconditional love – which we need to exhibit to be able to love others in a true way – can only arise when we first feel it within ourselves.

This ultimate connection awaits those of us who are ready and willing to do the work necessary to find the love and light within ourselves, and more fully embrace all aspects of our masculine and feminine energies. It is in all of us – we just need to understand how to fully embody it, and how to step forward under its spell.

This is not theory, for I have followed this path and can now share it with integrity to those interested in learning about it. This is the key purpose of this book.

The chapters that follow are more focussed on solutions, not problems. Only higher consciousness can solve what might now feel like it's unsolvable. And this higher conscious awareness can be gained on our own, or with the help of others. I suggest we attack it from both angles!

Let's now turn confusion into clarity. Pain can be our stairway to new possibilities in love, if we tap into its wisdom, and rise from within it.

The Choice Between Normal and Natural Relating

As discussed in earlier chapters, we have the choice when it comes to dating and relating. We can either move to a new paradigm of love, in which more pure connections are possible, or we can stay in old paradigms of love and simply get better at playing the normal game.

What will it be for you?

A new more natural game with new rules and new possibilities, or the same old normal game, in which we are more skilled at performing on and exploiting the unconscious playing field that we are already on.

I believe that many of the so-called relationship experts in this world are helping people to take the latter path, by teaching people how they can relate more effectively within the current paradigms of love.

This is no doubt helpful, and I too sought out their advice at different points in my life, before I discovered more advanced ways to relate.

So while accepting that all choices are valid, the choice is essentially this…

Learn to consciously relate to a partner, and to yourself in an advanced way, so that you can relate from a higher frequency of love or awareness, and become a new-age partner, so that the partners you desire find you to be more irreplaceable.

Or…

Continue to date and relate within the known and conditioned paradigms of 'love', which have applied for many years, and just get more skilled at it.

Appendix I gives you my thoughts on the kinds of lessons I have learned that can help you to have a better romantic relationship, without going through the, sometimes, demanding path into deeper self-awareness and conscious relating. If you choose to engage in this normal paradigm of relating, however, you must accept that you are choosing to operate in an ecosystem based significantly on need and value, and less on the purity of love. And in this place, it is important to remain constantly aware of the needs of the people with whom you want to relate, to ensure that you remain appealing to them. Here, polarity must be constantly considered, and even discussed, for it is the primarily glue between your partner and you.

You will also need to be in sync with your needs and express them, so that you can ensure that your partner continues to meet your needs on a consistent basis and prevents you from considering other partnership options as well.

But beware, when need is dominant in our relationships, love can't help but take a patient but vigilant back seat. Love and need are not good bedfellows.

But even if we choose the more conscious way to love, let's be real, we still need to confront the challenges that exist in modern relationships, and actively apply what we know. Each new relationship is like an experiment in love, from which we can learn, even if it does not fully meet our expectations and ends.

One of my key learnings was that in early relationships in my life, I did not learn with my partners in real-time, as they unfolded, and this led to gradual disconnection and separation. I did a kind of reset after my second divorce to learn, in retrospect, from every relationship I had ever experienced, sometimes in isolation, but this could not save what had already become broken.

Self-Discovery is the Road to Recovery and Close Connootion

If a reader has read any of my other books, they will be aware that I stand for the power of self-awareness to create better lives, and a better world for us all, by bringing us to higher states of love and truth, and turning pain into new possibilities.

There is a key truth that I stand for, in that our egos can try in vain to overcome the love that we can experience; but love, in its ultimate wisdom, has the power to overcome our egos, if we allow it to do so, without even trying.

The rest of this chapter is about how to apply a more conscious approach to romantic relationships. Relationship counsellors and dating coaches are probably more adept at teaching people how to manage their love lives within current dating and relating paradigms; though this book does touch on this area of discussion with my own observations, because it cannot hurt to learn about both alternatives, ***and I did both along the way.***

I believe that when someone becomes more closely connected to their own self, this enhances their alignment with love and enables them to radiate more love into any environment into which they step. And in this higher frequency of love, they can more naturally embody a better balance of their inherent masculine and feminine energies and perspectives. This more evolved alignment can then leak into business and community environments, and of course, romantic relationships.

But this must start inside us, through heart-based intelligences, not ego-driven intellects. The more we love and respect ourselves, the more we can love and respect others.

On the flip side, the more hurt we carry from past experiences, the more we are likely to hurt others. Put simply, happy people and countries do not start fights, for they value peace and know that simply being alive in life invigorates them.

So, if hurt people, hurt people, what does that say about unhappy romantic relationships, and those who participate within them?

Two of my books, namely *Where Your Happiness Hides* and *From Pain to Possibility*, in combination, explain the path I took to higher awareness, and the deeper connection to my own love, and why I felt compelled to pursue this calling.

I will briefly summarise it here, but in short, I took a three-phase approach encompassing:

- Acquiring knowledge,

- Experiencing knowing through practical application of my learnings, and then,
- Embodying my knowing energetically.

This process was highly guided by the wisdom of my own heart, and some wise mentors, because the journey to higher self-awareness begins in intellect and transitions into higher intelligence, and its associated energies. It goes from thinking and doing processes in the egocentric mind, to energetically becoming what you know yourself to be, because once you reach a certain level of awareness your soul takes more control of the process, as you become more aware of its wisdom with less ego-based resistance. And it changes your inherent energies, then your outside world.

The journey to higher self-awareness is truly one of discovering what we are not first, as we remove our conditioned thinking, then allowing our hearts to show us who and what we truly are. Accordingly, the same applies to loving unions. The journey we can take together to higher levels of love involves us first determining what unions are not, then defining what we want them to be. This is the opportunity of our lifetimes.

For humanity to progress, we need to go to higher levels of self-awareness as a race. And one key area where we need higher awareness is in love and romance.

On a personal or micro-level, there are essentially two processes, involving higher conscious awareness, that can work in unison to bring forth divine union, within us and with another.

Firstly, we can grow our own self-awareness to lift the frequency of our own love and take us deeper into our natural energetic evolution as sources of love. This is what I briefly outlined above.

Secondly, in our loving relationships we can grow through conscious interactions, with our partners. I have already touched on this opportunity, but will expand on it here, for interested readers.

The beauty of these two processes, when done in tandem, is that they allow us to find our own centre of love and express it with another, who is also on this same journey. And when these two paths to greater self-connection intersect, you have the makings of the journey to true love, because both individuals are growing together, in the absence of need.

On a macro-level as a society, we must continue to challenge more strenuously the masculine energies that tend to dominate our ways of life and encourage all of us to more fully embrace the feminine energies within us. Life will be so much more fulfilling as a society once this process gains traction. Right now, I suspect that we are going the other way in romance, which is throwing polarity and balance into chaos.

Let's consider the micro-level changes we can all make, first on our own, and with our partners, then consider the macro.

A – Micro (or Personal) Level Factors

Our Two Core Operating Systems

Let's recap on our human state of consciousness, and how it can be transformed through the restatement of our belief structures. This is more fully discussed in my book *Where Your Happiness Hides*.

Humanity lives in a state of duality. We are metaphysical beings living a physical life, and we can make decisions from our ego-centric minds, or our loving hearts.

Our egos are basically logical memory banks that can think and reason, and their simplistic role is to project and protect the personality that they have constructed in this life. They respond to fears, and opportunities for validation. You might call your ego your individual identity, or personality. They can witness conscious awareness, but they can never be it. Put simply, our ego-centric minds are very good at creating stories to justify their own perceptions, rather than looking at their own reflections.

On the other hand, your soul – sometimes referred to as your heart, because the two are intertwined through the heart chakra – is pure love and light. It connects you to infinite intelligence and has no fears. It is eternal energy and the source of your consciousness. You might call it your 'what', or the energy of your true self.

Carl Yung, the famous Swiss psychologist and philosopher, once said:

> "The greatest privilege of your lifetime is to
> become who you truly are."

I share this same opinion, which is why my work is focussed on helping people become more self-aware.

In any given moment, we can choose to make decisions from either of these two operating systems. However, most of humanity have lost sight of this reality, for we have collectively been taught that we are separate human beings with physical bodies and minds. Accordingly, we make decisions in our logical minds and have largely lost the art of learning from our feelings and connecting to our true centre of consciousness, which is connected to all things.

Most people suppress the messages or feelings that arise in their hearts and flow through their bodies, and rely upon their logical responses to situations in which they find themselves. This is fraught with danger when it comes to living our lives, because great wisdom arises in our hearts, and the universe has a way of using pain to alter our subconscious patterns and beliefs.

Everything in life has metaphysical and physical aspects to them, and our romantic relationships, like our own selves, are no exceptions. If we only focus on the physical aspects of each other, and our lives together, we lose connection to the greatest power at our disposal, love.

And love is metaphysical. It cannot be controlled, created or destroyed by thinking for it just is, or isn't. Yet how often do we think our way into, and out of, love?

When we allow the love that exists within us to radiate out into a romantic relationship, it can transform our relationships into light and wonderful experiences.

This is the natural way humans were meant to live, in the energy of love, not seeing it as something they must seek and find, or even think about.

Sometimes the only way out of a problem is to go inward to solve it. And so it is with the challenge of creating more wonderful romantic relationships.

The Pain of Protection and Projection

The fact that our egos are conditioned to protect and project us, from the energy of need or fear, places most of us in a kind of self-imposed box or cage of conditioning. We want to succeed and avoid failure, but the two can be diametrically opposed.

The more we seek to succeed, the more risk we are prone to need to take, and this can induce failure, or stimulate the fear of failure within us. The result for many is a life somewhat predicated on fitting in to meet the expectations of others, and avoiding loss, rather than pursuing our own dreams and desires. Our full potentiality is essentially dismissed so that we fit in and stay safe.

The ego is a double-edged sword because it has conscious and subconscious beliefs that dictate the outcomes in our lives. The problem is that we often behave in ways that are determined by our subconscious beliefs, because they unknowingly colour and create our thoughts.

Because these subconscious beliefs are a mystery within us – until we shed light upon them – and allow them to become conscious, we can become ignorant slaves to them, in all parts of our lives, including romantic relationships.

This explains why so many of our behaviours in relationships can be so confusing, selfish, selfless and contradictory. If we are not allowing love to determine our responses and decisions in relationships, we are in our ego state.

The ego is always seeking to increase our perceived sense of self-worth by looking for opportunities to boost our perceived 'value' and image in the eyes of others. It sees itself as a kind of performer.

The more valuable and interesting we perceive or try and show ourselves to be, the more 'lovable' we believe that we are. This is a falsehood because our true value can never be determined by what we do, achieve or fail at. And we are all equal no matter what we strive to become or end up becoming.

From a relationship perspective, the core problem with living from ego is that, when we are interacting with our romantic partners, we are likely to be acting out of fear, and out of the subconscious wounds that we carry and have yet to resolve.

Two people in a relationship are likely to be fine in the good times, because this is easy. It's in the difficult times when our egos can cause most damage. Will they project us for validation, or protect us when things don't meet our expectations?

And will we concede to our need for validation and allow it to override fairness and our sense of commitment when temptation arises?

The minds of men and women tend to be conditioned in different ways, by society, and by the habits and beliefs dictated to us in our family lineage. But they can equally be aligned. We become stereotyped to behave and think in different ways, until we do the inner work to change our own realities, essentially forming our own sovereign belief structures, and clearing off the 'junk' we no longer wish to be defined by, in our lives.

The peace we feel within ourselves determines the level of peace that we can bring into a relationship with another. If our inner world is in chaos and disharmony, because we have unresolved traumas, we will almost certainly establish this dynamic with our romantic partners and then, perhaps, blame them for the experience that we are, essentially, creating for ourselves on purpose. Or we may even look for partners who reinforce our limiting belief that chaos equals love.

This is why someone whose inner world is chaotic or unhealed will struggle over time to be in a relationship with someone who is calm and centred, and vice versa.

It is often said that when we date someone, we are not only dating their hearts, bodies and minds, we are also dating the unhealed wounds that they carry within their egos. This is like a ticking time-bomb, because unless you are highly skilled at assessing another person's conditioned anxieties and pains, you may not confront them until the relationship matures, essentially setting off unexpected problems that we need to address or endure. We sometimes call these red flags.

Of course, when we feel heavily attracted to or in love with another person, we can often gloss over these red flags, essentially repainted them green. However, if both partners love each other, and work together to address these red flags and issues between them in a conscious way, the sky is the limit.

Don't Try to Be What You are Not

If there is one core lesson that my life of dating and relating has taught me, it is that you should always be true to yourself.

But this is not a five-minute fix, it takes work to attain, depending on your starting point.

To love someone fully needs acceptance. Some people enter relationships with someone because they have an idealistic expectation of who someone could become. The word 'could' is a favourite word of the human ego, because it arises when we step outside of what is, and form fantasies of what could be. We project a future state that may never arise.

There is a famous line which is often used with reference to women and marriage. It goes this way: 'Aisle, Altar, Hyme' The quote makes light of the fact that women sometimes marry a man with expectations of what he could be with her guidance, rather than who he is now.

The problem is when we marry or enter a relationship with a person based on what we think they could be, rather than who they are, we are effectively inferring that they are not good enough as they are.

Entering a relationship with someone in the hope someone will change is likely to be a recipe for disaster, because it will most likely result in disappointment for the person with the fictitious expectations.

I had this experience. In one of my more significant relationships, my partner left me, delivering a humiliating letter to me through our counsellor, stating that she was leaving because I had been a 'disappointment', and had never met her expectations of me.

In other words, she was in a relationship with me, hoping for me to become a fictitious person that I never was. And she had never communicated to me what these expectations were, or what we she wanted me to change about myself.

In this moment, I realised that I was being 'loved' in a highly conditioned way, at a purity level way below the love I had given her. In fact, I now doubt that I was ever loved at all by her, and was just a means to an end. Essentially, she had married a person who didn't exist, but one day perhaps could. Shame he didn't know that!

This experience taught me that my one job in relationship, and in fact in life, was to only ever be the true me. If someone could not love the current version of me, without compassionately helping me to grow, then, I now realise, they never properly loved me in the first place; just some illusory depiction of me!

The moment that you stop being the truest version of you that you can be, and start trying to just please another, is the moment you become an inauthentic partner.

You deserve to be loved for who and what you are. None of us are perfect, but when we live under the illusion that we must be perfect, it sets us up to believe that, as we are, we are not enough and not fully lovable. And this is a soul-destroying experience that too many people endure for too long in relationships, out of the fear of being alone.

If someone treats you like you are not enough, and this is a prolonged experience, self-respect requires you to confront it, and if the response is not reassuring enough, you may need to detach from the relationship to honour yourself. You do not need another person's validation to be enough, and the moment that you feel that you do, is the time for you to consider how you can grow further.

Your true self needs nothing, other than your commitment to your own evolution. When you try too hard to be acceptable to another, you have abandoned your own true self, and you will suffer in varying ways, including physically through stress.

You are on this planet to be you, no one else. Everyone else is taken. So, open your heart to your own self-discovery, even if another's heart is closed off to the best version of you that you currently are. Remember, you can never become a better or more valuable person, just a more aware one.

When a person does the work to become highly conscious, they start to see through all the fear and fake behaviours that dominate our dating and relating landscapes, and this awareness encourages them to be more patient as they open to the possibility of a purer version of love gracing their path.

This has been my experience, the closer I have become to being the truer me.

The Pure Benefits of Knowing Yourself

Very few people really know their true selves, because this is not a process we are generally taught. This will confuse readers because your mind will tell you that you do know your true self. This is a falsehood promulgated by the artificial identity in our heads. Your true self is your soul, not your ego-based mind!

Once we connect with our deeper truths and tap into our soul energy, we can enter unity consciousness, and the benefits of this shift are life-changing for all our relationships, including the one we have with ourselves.

These include:

- Increasing your sense of self-worth and self-love

- Discovering what you really love to do and be
- Finding greater peace within yourself
- Becoming committed to giving and receiving love in equal measure
- Becoming less interested in superficial aspects of life, including image creation, unnecessary assets and titles
- Attaining higher levels of self-respect and self-honour
- Becoming more sovereign and independent
- Releasing needs, attachments and validations that no longer serve you and replacing them with clarity about your true desires in life
- Giving you higher composure, because you are no longer beholden to your emotions and feelings, but can make sense of them and integrate the wisdom within them
- Being able to more easily see through illusions and fake representations within yourself and others
- Allowing you to set clearer boundaries in your life so that you are free of external manipulation and exploitation
- Bringing forth greater patience in your life, because you can trust that what is meant to enter your life, including the right partner, will do so when you and that other person are ready to have that experience
- Giving you a higher sense of what you stand for and what you can contribute to the world, and
- Being more able to be alone with yourself, because you value this more than inauthentic relationships.

Knowing yourself allows you the become more authentic, because your inner reality becomes more steeped in truth and transparent ways of living. Here you go from thinking that you know who you are, to feeling into who and what you really are.

Two lovers who know themselves deeply can create an authentic relationship that is steeped in love, and relate without the fear that many people choose to exhibit in their relationships, because they do not need another to complete them. They are both already complete, and well on the way to this place.

The higher your self-awareness becomes, the higher your energetic frequency of love will become. Why? Because your soul energy becomes freer to penetrate all aspects of you with less resistance and radiate out into the world.

And this frequency is felt by the souls of other people who you meet. Your energy is magnetic to the right souls, and when two souls are energetically aligned a majestic love can be the result.

This means that the more you know yourself, the purer will be the love that you can enjoy within yourself, and with another person.

As a person starts to know the truth of themselves more clearly, the people they want to be in relationship with can change, particularly if their existing partner does not want to grow with them. And this can be disconcerting, because change can be painful to go through. But evolution so often involves us facing and growing through pain.

We all want to be in love, but we also want a partner who is sufficiently aligned with us, as we journey through life. We don't need them to be the same or perfect, because this would be impractical and boring. But the more unique we become, the more we want a partner who can be different with us, not too different to us.

Becoming the true you, is a journey that can be very challenging, particularly if you hope to share your life with another person on an intimate level, who does not share your passion for personal growth or deep soul connection.

All Happens for Us, Through Us, Not to Us

If we are to get ourselves out of our romantic mess, there is one truth we need to accept and work with, and that is this:

All in life happens for purpose, and therefore it has been orchestrated by our souls to assist us, to expand our conscious awareness and ability to love more fully.

This principle is a universal truth that can free us from the blame and shame game we so readily endure, with ourselves and with others, once we come to terms with it.

However, as crass at it may sound, romantic relationships are experiments orchestrated by our souls to assist them to grow in self-awareness and evolve, back to the pure love that they wish to experience on Earth. We have not collectively been taught this truth, and it's now a great time to realise it. Your heart already knows it.

So, if every romantic relationship is an experiment, surely that means they can be a success or a failure, like a science experiment in a laboratory. But they only become a failure if they do not support our evolution and we do not learn from them. When we learn to relate, it can change our fate, because the quality of our human relationships is a core input into our happiness.

Later chapters provide more detail on this important subject, as it relates to romantic relationships.

B – Macro (or Societal) Level Factors

Becoming More Aware of our Collective Consciousness

Part of the conditioning we all experience as individuals comes from our individual experiences, though they can also arise through the shared experiences of many, with which we witness and align. Some call it culture, or societal level mindsets; but put simply it's how we relate to each other.

My view is that the patriarchal model of life that we have endured for centuries has left us steeped in more masculine ways of being at a societal level. Feminism and higher consciousness in society, is giving women the rightful opportunity to live their lives as they see fit, but we have past conditioning that we need to 'peel back', before we can achieve the full rebalancing we need in our romantic lives.

The masculine ways of life that we so heavily prescribe to in our lives are clearly alive and well in the dating and relating world, because many people are focussed on value and maximising their images and lifestyles through their interactions with other people, rather than by sharing love and letting it guide them forward.

If romantic relationships start to be seen as another place where we can further our success in life, rather than a place where we can experience the beauty of love, then we can start to see why the relationship landscape is looking at partners through the lens of value, and not through the lens of love.

And if our partners do not offer what another can to help us avoid failure and maximise our perceived levels of success, including maximising our social image, is it any wonder that partners who are not deeply in love will seek to upgrade their partners when they meet someone that they feel can offer them more?

The definition of this more varies by person, but typically in a materialistic society this often comes down to things that the more masculine ego needs to feel whole, like wealth, career opportunities, social recognition, good looks, and the opportunity to compete and win.

Where does love sit in this egoic definition of more? My answer is, way down the lists of many people, for the ego that is making the decisions cannot truly perceive of love, only think it. I repeat, love can only ever be felt, and many of us have grown up never experiencing unconditional love. It is largely extinct on the Earth, like the dinosaurs!

Our societal values and priorities need to be seen for what they are, so that we can make informed decisions and offer the younger generations more support with the narratives forging their futures. Unless we just leave it to individuals and couples to find their own way forward, without any public recognition of the issues that our shared mindsets have created.

We may be like frogs in a heating pot, but perhaps it's time we hopped out of the water to witness what's really going on, before we get too badly burned.

Chapter 25

A More Natural Way to Love

True Love is Always Transparent

Our inner reality must become our outer reality. This means that a person who has found deeper truths within their own heart cannot help but take that into romantic relationships.

The truer you become within yourself, the less you can pretend to be something you are not with others. You will naturally want to experience great love and joy with a partner who is committed to creating a truly authentic relationship with you. You will no longer value drama or be blinded by beauty. You will no longer compete for attention, negotiate for respect, or allow your life purpose to be watered down by the needs of others, even if you love them. You will want to lead your life primarily for you, for you are centred in the knowing of who you are, and who you want to become.

The truer you can become to you, the more you can walk to the beat of your own drum, on your own and with a partner, because you will recognise that your life and romantic relationship are uniquely yours to cherish and design. You also see that romantic relationships can be wonderful, but you can happily survive without one. They matter, but your own life matters more.

When you become truly authentic, you will seek a conscious relationship with a partner who will not 'trade you in' if they meet a more accomplished person or if the going gets tough, for love is the unbreakable bond that keeps you bound together.

There will be no question in either of your minds and hearts that you are together, for each other, with each other and to support each other's life journeys, no matter where that takes you both.

Attraction matters, and it is consciously worked on to strengthen the polarity that is unique to your relationship. But a powerful frequency of love is the foundation of the relationship you share, and passionate intimacy grows as the relationship evolves, rather than atrophy in the passing of time, and the likelihood of increasing familiarity.

Expectation is replaced by truth. You both know that you don't own each other, for you are two sovereign beings sharing a life together, simply because you choose whole-heartedly to do so. You remain united, but also sovereign, through total transparency.

Every day is a new adventure, in which you agree to express your true feelings with each other, so that the relationship can grow in the meaningful exploration of the emotions that arise.

Forgiveness is ever present, and compassion is your default way of interacting with each other. This allows peace to descend onto the relationship, for it is being crafted with love and passion, not the need to win, or have power over the other.

This is the love that we call true love, and the relationship that I just described is what I refer to on the cover of this book as being your ultimate connection. Both partners are in a high state of self-love, and no neediness applies.

The relationship is free of control and rich in equality, even if roles are different. They overflow their love onto each other in equal measure, like a beautiful fountain in full expression.

If you love someone before they even speak to you, or before you even touch their skin, this a special kind of love because it transcends the superficial concepts we often call love. It is a precious love, in a world obsessed by appearances and performances.

True love is built on patience, empathy, understanding and a deep connection between two hearts, which recognise the light within each other and instantly remember the frequency of pure love that they share.

This strong and beautiful connection will not fade, but grow stronger every day, when we learn to nurture it and not let the agendas in our egoic minds limit its potential to give us the ultimate experience in loving relationships.

For those who are willing to do the work to make this possible, you are home in the knowing that two wise hearts have found each other and are not likely to be tempted to give up something that is so precious, for something less real and temporary.

This is not fantasy. This is available to all who wish to experience it.

But we must remember that the best things in life often require high doses of commitment. The universe makes us stronger, before it places the ultimate loving relationship in our arms to hold and to cherish.

Roses are often used as a symbol of love and given freely as a representation of romantic devotion. This has a deeper meaning. Their petals represent the love and light we can offer each other. And their thorns represent the darkness we all share and can overcome together, when we try to do so. We must always remember that we need the darkness to see the light.

Our wounds are never far away from the medicines that we can offer ourselves, and our divine unions. But it helps if we can perceive the wounds that we need to heal.

Unconditional love is possible for us all, but not whilst we cling to the conditioned mindsets we inherited, from thousands of years of the insanity created in the minds of humanity.

All love is unconditional until our minds impose their illusions upon it.

The Contrast is Stark

This advanced form of relationship, which is possible between two highly self-aware individuals, is next level. Contrast the advanced form of loving relationship just described with what we are witnessing in the dating world today. There is a stark difference.

A wise person wants to commit to a mature and conscious relationship, free of drama and the transactional nature that has become so common. This advanced lover has the discernment to trust that the right person will come along when the timing is right, when both parties are ready to share in an extraordinary love experience. They know not when this wonderful match will materialise, but they trust in the magical powers of universal love to manifest it in due course, so that they can then step in to allow it to take its full physical form.

This special kind of relationship is a gift from the universe to those who seek to take responsibility for their own lives, and do the inner work to bring their own hearts and minds into inner harmony and balance, then apply that to a relationship that can match their own high level of evolution.

This is a kind of cleansing process in which those on the path to higher states of purity, purge the wounds and conditioned beliefs of the past so that they can bring forth high vibrational levels of love to a partner who also wants this same experience. They banish their egos, to rediscover their hearts together.

You are constantly receiving loving signals from your soul, and when you take the time to listen to those signals, you can become that unique high-frequency person who could not be rushed into full view, but could only be subtly found and received.

Your soul will not chase you, but it will embrace you when you listen to its wisdom. It waits patiently for you to witness its quest and respond with your willingness to allow it to take its preferred path back to true love.

If there are any wounds still on show when two conscious lovers meet, they know that they can clear the pain that arises together with the power of love.

Each relationship in this world is unique, but the contemporary collective dating world lacks the authenticity, love, truth, trust, and integrity with which an advanced lover seeks to align, because of conditioned mindsets that can affect us all.

I'm not judging the people involved in the current landscape of relationships we witness, for most of them are just being what they have been taught to be and behaving in alignment with the normal – though ignorant – standards that they have witnessed and with which they have subconsciously aligned.

I was in this same 'cage of conditioning' for the first five decades of my life, so I offer this book in full compassion and care, for I too walked this path, unknowingly.

I spent many years learning from my past relationships and life traumas and putting myself through an intense journey of rediscovery to understand and embody the deeper truths of myself. It is called soul-searching for good reason, as I discovered.

When we leave this planet, we will realise that love was all that truly mattered, and that everything else was transitory.

I hope this wisdom helps others who dream that divine and sacred love will grace their path.

Chapter 26

Am I Really in Love?

The Million Dollar Question

Love can only be felt. It cannot be thought. The problem with this reality is that, in a world where have been collectively taught to think, not feel, love is becoming a distant memory, or a thing we confuse with lust and intense admiration for another.

Many of us have forgotten what love really feels like in a romantic setting, because it's not like loving a child, pet, friend or relative. It can be more intense and complex and can get readily confused by the influence of other forces, like lust.

The feeling of real love is different to that which our world has portrayed it as. And when I did the deep inner work, this shift took me by complete surprise.

There is only one way to know if you are in love, and that is to ask your heart in stillness.

It sounds simple, but from my experience it's a skill that needs to be refined. We can all do it, and its free and natural. But how many of us do this, before we conclude that we are in love?

The truth is, if you don't know with certainty if you are in love with someone, the answer is normally 'no', you are not. Your intuition always knows the truth.

The higher your level of self-awareness, the more aware you will become of the love in your heart, and its intensity. This is a given, because the substitutes we often put in the place of love are easier to distinguish from love itself, the more attuned you become to your own frequency of love.

I am often disappointed when I listen to psychologists, and so-called relationship experts on podcasts, talking about loving relationships, because often the word love never comes into the conversation. Most of the time they confuse attraction with love, and lead people deeper into a dating and relating world based on value and interest, not love.

How Do I Feel into and Discover if Love is Present?

Love has become the forgotten jigsaw piece in modern relationships, and we need to start putting love back in its rightful place – as a key force in partner selection.

But how does someone do this if it is not a learned process?

Before you attach to any normal way of seeking someone to complete you, sit quietly with your own self. And I mean really sit in silence, not just with your thoughts – put your phone away, separate yourself from possible distractions or your to do list.

I found nature to be a calming place to do this kind of process, for it is pure love and light.

Next, be present with your presence, and ask the critical question that you want the answer to, like: is this really love, or just attraction that I'm feeling and thinking about? Or, perhaps, is participating in this relationship really in my best interests?

Your soul can't help but process your enquiries through the lens of love, because that is what it is.

Almost certainly, your thoughts will try to interject and tell you that you should be somewhere else, doing something more constructive. However, this is not the voice of your soul, this is the voice of your ego wanting control. It is doing its protection and projection process that it has been taught to do by the energy of fear. It's running interference, because it wrongly thinks it is the master of love and consciousness and does not want to be dethroned from this role – after all, you once gave it the license to own this process.

But ignore this surface-level voice and go deeper to find the more composed voice that speaks from the silence. You will know it when you hear it, because it doesn't negotiate or repeat itself. It is true and clear, and just knows the answer.

You may not get the answer that you were hoping for, but you will get the answer that is in your best interests.

In that answer, you will feel the power of peace, and a sense of relaxation, knowing that you have aligned with an important set of truths.

Learning to hear the voice of your own centre of love is a major step forward, which allows you to live authentically from the energy of love. When you find real love in your heart, and share that in reciprocity with another, you open yourself up to the opportunity to share a path with someone who genuinely chooses you, and is likely to want to grow with you, not just share an experience designed to rescue each other, or allow each partner to receive what a transactional and superficial relationship can give them.

Romantic relationships that are not based on love, do not have the 'juice that is worth the squeeze' in my view, and I think many other people are also starting to work that out. This is why increasing numbers of people are choosing to stay single, even if it hurts to do so. Relationships based predominantly in need and fear are likely to be fragile, particularly if they cease to offer each partner what they were needing.

I know this because I put myself in this place multiple times, and it hurt in the long run.

But in a relationship that has a higher frequency of love at its core, there is the potential for true passion and desire, the kind that is unstoppable. Love is the most powerful force in the universe. Try getting in its way and running interference where it exists, and you will discover what I mean. Perhaps you already have!

When we enter a relationship where love is truly present and we allow love to be the conscious force that takes the relationship forward, we stand a great chance to not only have a fantastic relationship, but to develop one that continues to go from strength to strength.

Love is free, and it can't be bought or sold, but it can set you free. When you listen to your heart, you listen to the voice of love, and the transmission of truth.

Chapter 27

Our Relationship with Self-Worth

You Are of Infinite Value

Most people have a hole in their sense of self-worth. Many of them feel incomplete. Their hearts have been 'broken' by various experiences in their lives, and this has dented their self-esteem, sometimes deeply. This is not their fault.

This was me in my earlier years, because I grew up in a difficult family environment where self-esteem was collectively low. I essentially learned to be the same way and was clueless on how to restore my own sense of self-love, once the damage was done.

This hollowness can be the outcome of our personal responses to difficult relationship breakdowns, but it could have other origins, including different forms of disrespect or disappointments that we have received in other aspects of our lives.

Self-worth is truly infinite in all of us, so any inherent assessment of our own self-worth is an illusion, which we should ideally dismiss. Our life stories are just experiences we have had, which have now ended. They are not our deeper truths.

The truth is that worthiness is what we are. Not what we might think we are. It's actually not even capable of debate in the chambers of our hearts.

Romantic relationships can boost our sense of self-worth, typically when they begin, but they can also diminish our sense of self-worth when they end or atrophy in the passing of time.

When we lack self-esteem, a lover can restore our faith in ourselves, because we feel accepted and loved, often in ways that we seemed incapable of giving to ourselves. However, this sensation is just artificially covering up the cracks in our sense of self.

When we fall for someone, we typically imagine that we have found an unbreakable bond with a soul mate, and a shared future with a partner that we feel 'gets us' and wants us, and this can give us a false sense of identity. The problem is that the reinforcement of self that we experience is not coming from within us but is being predicated on the words and actions of others. And the universe will almost certainly challenge this paradigm within us and may dismantle it.

However, when relationships end, particularly off the back of a partner's decision, it can expose the cracks that were already existing in our sense of self but were vulnerable to rejection or dismissal. As is often said, you see who's been 'swimming naked when the tide goes out'.

After a break-up, some people can go into an ego-based blame mode and start pointing the finger at their former partner. Or they can go into self deprecation, and lose further self-esteem, seeing themselves as a failure.

But what we must always realise is that it is the relationship that fails not us, and often the person who leaves, without truthful conversations, is the one who did not have the courage to face their own demons, so they blame their partner and move on.

It's common for people in this situation to seek the next relationship or version of sexual validation quickly to distract them from the pain that their breakup exposed within themselves. But this crossroad in your life is a wonderful opportunity to learn and grow from the pain that you are experiencing. Losing someone you loved can be incredibly difficult to overcome, and can destroy your trust in love and relationships, but it does not need to be this way, because it can be a great catalyst for personal growth.

These experiences are never accidents of course but are designed to bring you wisdom. If you deal with them consciously you can set yourself up for better experiences in the future and find peace where pain once lived, inside you.

From my experience, if you leave a relationship to enter another, without any period of introspection, you are prone to make the same mistakes you once did, because you have failed to learn from the past, and change your mindsets and behaviours. Some period of learning and integration of your newfound awareness is a critical step as we evolve through relationships.

Not learning from past relationship traumas is the ticket to repeating patterns and further issues. Going inward and finding deeper aspects of your truths is the only safe way to protect yourself from future pain.

Love, in the form of self-love, is your protection from this pain, yet our risk is that we begin to shy away from love, because we see it as the problem that it's not.

Chapter 28

Love is Our Only True Protection

Life Without Love is Fragile

I repeat, when we let our egos manage our romantic relationships, they will often go after value and interest to protect us from our deepest fears, and project us towards what we need to feel valuable to this world. This can, and so often does, lead us away from love and into material safety.

The irony of this distortion is that love is the only energy that can really protect us from our fears and their painful manifestations. ***Without love, life can be very fragile, as I discovered.***

Love offers us emotional protection, for it has our best interests at heart in the long run, whereas fear offers us the high probability of emotional rejection.

Love is the very essence of us, for it is the true basis of all that we are. So, when we think we can separate ourselves from it, we enter a truly unnatural and delusional way of living, that can make our lives fragile.

When we live in fear, we will manifest our fears. This is a 'given'. What we fear comes true in the end, for our souls seek to show us the fears that we possess, so that we can overcome them.

Love and fear cannot co-exist. And love conquers all fear in its own divine timing. As Mark Twain famously said:

"Do the thing you fear most, and the death of fear is certain."

When you face your fears, you are acting out of love for yourself. And in this energy your fears will dissolve.

Our romantic relationships are likely to be challenging and unsatisfying for as long as we enter and co-exist within them out of fear. And this is one key reason why the current world of dating and relating is so messy. In these situations, our thoughts become the ego's way of protecting itself from the truths that we need to see, because the ego is cunning and insidious. It does not necessarily have love in its sights, or your true desires as its focus. It is focused on security above all else, then success, however it defines both.

The soul has your best interests at heart and always uses love as the force to propel you towards what is best aligned with you, even if that is a lesson that can take you one step closer to true love and joy.

Let us consider money as an example to demonstrate these truths.

Our egos want us to be financially safe and successful. But our souls know that the key desire we have in life is to be loved and to love. This is central to our reason for living.

As a result, money can never give us what our hearts truly want. No amount of money will ever fill the hole in our hearts that we will inevitably feel if we lack love. This is why people who go in search of money to fill the void in their hearts will never be able to be rich enough to feel fully satisfied, no matter how big their bank accounts become.

But such a void filled by love itself is the only true cure for the sense of separation we feel from our own souls, and the love that they want us to give and receive.

Love is your only true protector, and projector to a fulfilling life. Any other surrogates for this true protector represent a fake version of what is possible, and what will bring you peace.

The Power of Honouring Love

The human ego creates a separate identity for us, out of ignorance of the truth. But reality is the opposite, for love only knows unity and truth. When we separate from our own hearts, we experience separation in our 3D realities. This is a given. Love, through the intelligence emanating from our souls, uses separation to bring us home to love, within ourselves.

The pain of this separation is the magnet that brings us back to the unity we all truly share. This explains why separation is so common in this world of relationships. A lover may leave us to find a love that they think is purer and needs to be honoured with another. Or we may separate from someone to honour the love that we feel we deserve. A person may leave the family home to live with a new lover. The list goes on. Whatever the circumstances we choose to endure or enjoy for love, we must make these choices from our hearts, or we will suffer the consequences of ego-based decisions, which are out of step with love itself.

Karma has a way of working with love, to make sure that this is the case in the fullness of time. It is not our responsibility to seek retribution in the face of a toxic separation. Our role is to process any associated pain that we feel, learn what we can perceive, and evolve through the experience. Essentially, we turn our darkness into light, when we accept that everything in life happens for us, and not to us.

Honour love always, and it will honour you back. Dishonour it at your own peril.

Chapter 29

We Challenge Each Other to Grow

Greater Presence is the Present We Receive

Romantic relationships, in which love is present, allow both participants to come closer to their true presence, by shining a mirror on the limiting beliefs and negative energies of both partners. The more intense the love, the more intense the pain being brought forth for clearing, is likely to be. In this way, relationships can be highly confronting in terms of allowing two people to grow their awareness together, or separately.

To be blunt, both sexes, by virtue of their offsetting masculine and feminine energies, challenge each other to change. In this way, they bare a gift to each other on a consciousness level. It may not feel like a gift on a purely human level, but it can bring us closer to wholeness, and therefore to deeper meaning in our lives.

When we live from love, and not ego, we naturally adopt more evolved levels of the following energies, which align with love:

- Sovereignty
- Presence
- Composure
- Forgiveness
- Truthfulness

- Compassion
- Acceptance
- Trust, and
- Respect.

And these refined energies, once elevated, change us as people by making us less fearful and needy, and allowing us to see through the conditioning that limits the possibilities in our lives.

For example, if a woman were to reject a man because he did not have a strong enough sense of purpose, or sufficient emotional regulation, they are essentially providing that man with a message from the universe that these areas require his attention to become more balanced.

Similarly, if a man were to reject a woman because she needed too much physical validation, or lacked sufficient emotional regulation, then they are essentially providing that women with a message from the universe that these areas require her attention to become more balanced.

If your partner is overly controlling, you are being given the opportunity to stand in your own sovereign energy and stand your ground for your own purposes. The controlling partner needs to see that their control is not aligned with love.

There are many different examples that could be used to demonstrate the power of this mirroring effect, but you get the picture. It helps to make us more conscious about how we could evolve, by giving us pain from which to learn.

This important process explains why relationships can be such a fertile place from which to grow from, because heartbreak can provide such a massive stimulus for what we might call soul-searching.

Relationships don't have to end to help us grow, however, as we can learn together in a relationship. One way to look at this overall process is that the mirrors that our romantic partners hold up, throw light onto the energetic shadows in our minds, which are keeping us trapped in our small, individuated belief structures.

They show us where we are engaging in life from a place of fear or need, and not the pure desire, which allows us to truly enjoy life and have the adventures that we were born to enjoy.

Healing Doesn't Absolve You from Responsibility

We live in a society where wisdom is not actively sought or applied en masse. We typically seek information and intellectual competence, but not true intelligence or the active application of our intuition.

The more we know ourselves, however, the more we can love ourselves and others. The journey to higher awareness can be challenging and emotionally difficult, of course; so, if a couple are interacting unconsciously within a relationship together, this difficulty needs to be considered, before it tears them apart.

They need to know that every emotion felt and understood, every tear that drops with care, and every conversation that clears the previously toxic air, is a triumph that should be celebrated together, not remembered as some kind of battle without purpose.

Growing together is a great gift we can give each other in a relationship. If we ask our partner to simply be present every day in truth and love, and express that with us in a compassionate way, we are on the path to experiencing genuine intimacy on all levels.

And that is ultimately more valuable than the external representations of value that we so often seek from another.

What greater gift can your partner give you than the opportunity to find deeper aspects of yourself that you previously had not seen? This is the true gift of loving relationships.

In this place, we can drop the swords of despair and allow our scars to fully heal. After all, how many times do we want to keep stabbing ourselves in the back, when love is ready to show us a better, less volatile, way forward.

Chapter 30

Entering Relationships with Higher Awareness

The Challenge of Becoming Truer to You

Once you attain higher self-awareness you become much wiser and discerning in who you relate to or date. Fundamentally, this arises because the person you are becoming is not the person you once recognised as yourself.

And this can mean that you are less drawn to people who may have once held your attention and desire. You enter a quality, not quantity, mindset in your dating and relating hemisphere, in which love becomes non-negotiable. This can feel somewhat lonely, until you acknowledge its intent.

But why is this case?

It occurs because, after doing the inner work, you now refuse to compromise on a single thing you swore you'd never tolerate again, and because you are respecting and honouring yourself more than ever before. In addition, you have finally learned to completely trust your own intuition over anyone's behaviours and promises. You are now able to spot the exact issues that you know will quietly destroy a connection in the future, and can respond to them upfront, not wait until the future when they implode.

The temporary rush of feelings that once hijacked your logic, when you encountered a new person of interest, is now controlled by your heart. Frankly, your heart can now remind your mind what matters, and is finally being heard. And what matters most of all is your peace and happiness, not being involved in a dysfunctional relationship that you already sense might morph into mediocrity after the initial 'honeymoon' experience.

You begin to witness that many people out there in the dating world are substantially unhealed, and are just looking for a partner to take away their inner pain and complete them. They are ignorant to the fact that becoming complete is their job, not something they can outsource to another person. And you finally appreciate that these types of unhealed people are not for you, because they will be unable to love in the way that your heart now demands. You don't judge them harshly, you just accept that they are not the right person with whom you should build a partnership.

The result of advanced awareness is that you open yourself up to a deeper love, and you know that you must be patient in knowing that this love will arise when synchronicity and natural forces bring it into your periphery. And if you are sufficiently open to the right kind of love, you know that it will arise if you truly desire it and want to manifest it.

In the meantime, you can enjoy great peace in knowing that you finally have access to the love you have discovered within yourself. And no other love is needed, even if it is your preference to share deeper aspects of yourself with another soul in union. Love is protecting you in a way your ego never could, by keeping you away from fragile relationships, and this is the greatest protection you could ever ask for or need.

There is one more powerful quirk that will probably arise, in that you can meet someone and feel love, and attraction to them, but the more self-aware you become, the more you know that there is another element to any relationship that you desire, and which you won't compromise on. Put simply, you want someone to grow together with in a conscious partnership.

But this growth must be for you both, and be real, not just some abstract concept you think may be good to try. In any conscious relationship of true substance, you need to both expand, together and individually in the energy of love, not just relate to inflate the egos of one or both people involved, or to fulfill some unhealed needs.

I have been through this experience myself. And it can be lonely, because what you want to experience with a partner evolves to be more natural and advanced, but not normal. The connection you seek now has an extra dimension that most people are not taught to seek in a partner. And that is this extra dimension of expansion and self-development.

These days, to be in relationship I personally require, love, attraction (both physical and mental), and this more conscious element of expansion. I have had a few romantic relationships where this last element was not present, because one or both of us lacked this desire to grow. I know that this arose out of ignorance, not malice.

We were doing our best to make it work, but there was a disconnect we did not overcome. I will never let this happen again, because I know that that dysfunction in a relationship is inevitable if the commitment to expansion – which our souls seek for us – is not present.

And this desire for expansion varies across the population. Many people are happy to stay in normal paradigms of relating, whereas others are not. And all choices are valid.

I have witnessed many couples where one partner has ventured onto the path of higher awareness, often later in life, and the other one has not, and this can create great personal confusion, particularly for the person who is seeking expansion on top of more normal relationship objectives. I hear the awakening partner say things like "I have outgrown my partner" or "I have fallen out of love with them". Without generalising, it is often the case that the love has not gone away between the two partners, but the shift to higher awareness in one partner has moved both partners out of alignment in terms of their level of self-connection, and the frequency of love that they can both hold and share.

Essentially, unless these different desires are reconciled, the relationship can suffer from a different form of reduced polarity, with self-awareness levels becoming a new barrier to alignment. The good news is that this disconnect can be resolved, but it requires a new set of mindsets and practices – which arise from the understanding what is taking place – and a commitment to address it by both lovers.

The more aware partner may also find themselves seeking to share the journey they have embarked upon with their partner, but find that their partner is not interested in matters beyond the normal physical and mental concepts within which most people reside. This disconnection can be a real challenge to maintaining polarity.

This is also why growing together matters so much, once one partner embraces their inner desire to expand beyond normal physical and superficial realities.

True intimacy resides inside of us, before it can take place with another in union. You might say that it begins when a person is into-my-self and seeks to share that wholeness with another without limitations, in the energy of love.

PART E

REBALANCING THE MASCULINE/FEMININE DYNAMIC

Chapter 31

Lighting the Pathway Back to Genuine Love

Some Important Points to Ponder

Starting the journey back to greater harmony and balance between men and women is such a critical endeavour. As earlier chapters showed, the disconnects are stark and seem to be getting more pronounced, because of modern stimuli and shifts in our demographic structures and mindsets.

Before we set out a blueprint for better relationship experiences and explore true love more deeply, there are some key principles that could be infused, reaffirmed and hopefully adopted, as a part of our cultural frameworks to enhance the current dilemmas. Many of these may sound simple and obvious, yet still people struggle to apply them, perhaps because of lack of awareness as to their importance.

If only I had been gifted with the awareness in this book when I was younger, I probably would have had a far more fulfilling and prosperous love life. My schooling included no classes or advice on relationships, other than a one hour talk on sex, which I received at the advanced age of nine!

I have identified twenty-one key principles to consider, and some of them may recap on what is discussed in earlier chapters. When this is the case, I have kept it brief.

1. Putting Truth Ahead of Our Need for Safety

One of the key problems that many of us share in relationships is our propensity to hide our truths, and not fully express them in relationships, because we don't want to hurt our partners or have a confrontation.

Many of us were taught as children that we should be seen and not heard. Our parents may have gotten upset if we too freely expressed what we desired. So, we learned to be compliant and 'keep the peace' at all costs. We did not want to bite the loving hands that fed us. And this pattern can continue into our adult relationships, particularly if love is present, because these are relationships that we wish to keep in harmony, by not offending another.

However, the desire to maintain harmony can lead us into the suppression of our feelings. When we become the perennial givers who strive to keep our partners happy, we do so at our own expense. We may not speak up, and we set a pattern of unhealthy silence in train – because suppressing or distorting truths in romantic relationships is a ticket to unhappiness over time. It may preserve short-term peace, but over a longer period it is one of the worst habits a couple can adopt.

Expression of truth is critical, though it must be expressed with compassion and empathy for the feelings of our partners.

Some people are unable to process negative emotions with ease and can shut down when difficulties arise in a relationship. Others may flare up unnecessarily. This can make dealing with issues extremely difficult for an emotionally available and regulated partner, even if they are comfortable speaking their truth and hearing the truth of others.

Love and truth are inexplicably linked, for both come from the heart, so if truth is absent in interactions with your partner, any love that is present will be tested too.

2. Confidence Attracts, Neediness Chases

Many people enter relationships with a lack of self-esteem, and this makes them fearful of failure and rejection. The reality is that they have a scarcity mindset when it comes to love and sexual relevance. They often fear losing love, because they believe that this opportunity may not come around again. And this keeps them in a needy energy, and thus in a loop of needing constant ego-reinforcement.

This energy may take the form of a need for constant reassurance that they are loved, for attention, touch or compliments, or perhaps they constantly worry about what their partner is thinking about them.

Psychology reports suggest that about half of the population have secure attachment styles, but the other half live in fear and do not trust love. Deep down they fear abandonment and betrayal, and this fear of failure can make them either clingy or dismissive of emotions in relationships.

However, this is normally not their fault and can be rectified – although narcissism can be harder to rectify. They have been conditioned to be this way, because of the experiences they have encountered in life, or the models of relationships that they grew up witnessing.

If you have ever been in a relationship with someone who is needy, you'll know that this energy can become unattractive. The same goes for someone who is too emotionally closed, or controlling.

Self-esteem levels are a continuum, and the reality is that few people truly know themselves well enough to be fully secure. Pretty much all of us have some degree of insecurity or need to be loved and validated. Even beautiful people can look in the mirror and find faults in their appearance.

So, no matter how self-assured you are there is always more you can do to enhance your sense of self. The more you know yourself, the more your confidence grows, because you progressively learn more about your truths. And in this great place the war between your heart and mind can evolve into peace.

It is true to say that people with high self-esteem become magnetic to others, for they are lighter and more confident. These people generally don't need to chase love; it chases them.

Of course, other factors can attract people too, like physical stature and levels of wealth, but the soul-to-soul connection that we all naturally crave is activated by the light within another person's heart. This is the magnetism created by the frequency of love that a person emits.

Generally, of course, we don't like being alone, and social expectations can make us feel inadequate when we are not in a relationship. Neediness can thus form the basis of many relationships, especially where ego-based attraction is present. When we choose partners primarily based on attraction, and not love, the relationship can be put under pressure when needs shift. This is a core reason why people will say that they fell out of love, and this ended their relationship. It is likely, however, that deep love was never present. It was the shifting sands of need that brought down the structure.

Should two needy partners come together in a relationship, co-dependence can then result.

But love itself isn't needy in any way and is always ready to show you the best way forward.

3. Your Light and Heart are Your Real Virtues

The word love is used so often in our society that we have forgotten its truth. Love can only be felt, and cannot be thought, because love is a frequency. When two people with a matching frequency in their hearts meet, romantic love is on offer. From there, each person's frequency can then be disturbed, though it can also be consciously supported and allowed to strengthen.

We always refer to our romantic relationships as our 'love lives', even though a close frequency match may be missing because the relationship is based mainly on high doses of attraction and need, and low or poorly matched frequencies of love.

And yet our hearts still yearn to experience enduring love – not just a version of attraction, which may feel like love within the myriads of emotions that can arise within a new relationship. And this can take composure and patience to properly assess.

Love and attraction can both be potent, but when they arrive together, the dynamic is one of the most incredible experiences that we can encounter.

But we rarely give ourselves enough time to truly allow love to enter our lives as nature intended, despite our souls wanting that for us and therefore always rearranging around us to make this possible. Sometimes we even walk past love, perhaps because we do not like the body it comes wrapped within, or because we have not developed sufficient self-awareness to appreciate who we are ourselves, let alone listen to the voice of love within us.

The ultimate relationship requires love as its cornerstone. Add in other virtues like physical attraction, common interests, and the alignment of values, and you have the structure capable of supporting a wonderful life together, which is not likely to break, just because a more attractive person comes along.

If you are making a cake, you don't bake it without its key ingredients. It won't rise and it won't taste great in the end. That's what a romantic relationship is like in the end without love being present.

What could be more valuable than two hearts that have come together in a loving embrace, and are together in the *petri dish of love*, for the mere sake of discovering the purity of love, and the joy that it can create?

If you want an unbreakable bond and the fairytale romance you always dreamed about, bring it back to love and feel for its presence. Then nurture that love with your partner. It is the great creator and the great healer in all circumstances.

After all, we exist in a universe comprised of love and light at its core.

4. Your Real Value is Internal, Not External

Commensurate with the truth that love can only be found in the heart, is the reality that we look for it in places where it cannot be found.

The eyes are truly the window to the soul, and this is where love is found. When two souls meet through the gaze of our eyes, both souls connect in a way that our minds cannot truly comprehend. They recognise the light in each other. I'm sure many readers are familiar with this unexpected and incredible experience.

It is our normal practice to look at the external qualities of a person when we search for value and interest in a romantic partner. These include factors like:

- Physical looks
- Age
- Apparent lifestyle choices and interests
- Family status
- Religious alignment
- Level of past achievements, and
- Wealth, job status or title

But these qualities are merely external surrogates for love that impress our egos, not our loving hearts. They are valid factors within a framework of attraction.

Isn't it time we asked ourselves what a loving relationship feels like, before we ask ourselves what that relationship is supposed to look like?

Perhaps someone we love doesn't perfectly fit the checklist we mentally designed, and we fear they won't be endorsed by our family and friends? But maybe they have the secret ingredient that we need to bake that truly wonderful cake together!

5. Rediscovering the Power of Peace

Peace is underrated in the world of romantic relationships, yet pure love is always aligned with peace.

Our relationship with chaos and peace can be determined by what we grew up experiencing in our family of origin. If we were exposed to hostile or erratic relationships, we can be drawn to, or turned on by, partners who replicate this dynamic in our present lives. In short, it is what we are used to experiencing.

The less self-aware a person is, the more they are likely to be comfortable in an environment lacking peace and serenity, particularly if they are highly emotional by nature.

If you want a relationship that is deeply embodied in peace, you must take peace to that relationship. And this requires you to be conscious of any wounds that you are still hanging onto from your past, or which you have taken steps to overcome. Remember, you get back what you put out.

It is often said that we are attracted to a person who reminds us of our opposite sex parent, particularly if you deeply loved them. This allows you to essentially reproduce the kind of family dynamic that you understood represented love.

Find the peace in your own heart, and you can then find it in another.

6. True Equality Requires Reciprocity

A really satisfying romantic relationship must be in energetic balance. This means we give and receive love in equal measure. If it is not, then one partner in the relationship is likely to become dissatisfied and may exit, unless a new agreed-upon balance is consciously achieved.

If a person has a secure attachment style in relationships, they are likely to connect and attract to another secure lover. This type of relationship is likely to be more balanced and has a higher chance of lasting.

However, many people can be conditioned by the life they have experienced to be excess givers, or excess takers. And often these two types of lovers tend to attract each other, because they validate and balance out each other's personal imbalances.

In an extreme scenario, a person with narcissistic tendencies may end up in a toxic relationship with a highly empathic person. This type of relationship can be extremely out of balance in terms of the flow of energy between the two partners, and the empath is likely to be the one suffering but believing they are the saviour in love.

It is important to understand your own tendencies in terms of giving and receiving in relationships, to ensure that you don't enter or stay in an imbalanced relationship subconsciously. Remember to always honour and respect yourself in any romantic relationship, or you will invite your partner to give you the opposite energies. Only when we set firm and fair boundaries do we generate sufficient respect to support the presence of love.

A person who has a low sense of self-worth is likely to give more than they receive in a relationship, because they fear losing the partner who they love. A person who has an inflated sense of self-worth is more likely to believe that they are entitled to receive more, and will therefore seek to take more.

When two people are both in harmony within themselves, their romantic relationship can flourish because both parties are more likely to be giving freely to each other for the benefit of the relationship itself. In this energy, there is little or no need existing in the dynamics between them and requiring 'transactional flows' to satisfy the other partner. Love flows freely between them.

Many of the old patterns of behaviour live on in the subconscious minds of modern partners, as this book sets out. They don't go away until higher conscious thinking arrives, and sometimes it takes a make-or-break experience, followed by meaningful reflection to bring on this higher awareness.

Is this the cross-roads we are now at, together?

7. Designing Your Kingdom Together

Too many relationships are shaped by our conditioned thinking, much of which can align with intergenerational habits and the expectations of others.

But why do we want to fit our relationships into some kind of cookie-cutter mould, when as individuals we are all truly unique and, as a result, each romantic relationship commands uniqueness?

I would encourage all partners in romantic relationships to actively participate in the design of their relationship to meet the needs of both partners. Too many relationships try to survive on assumption and personal expectations, rather than on conscious agreements and shared intentions. Yet active and regular discussions about what would make both parties happy is such a critical process that is so often overlooked.

Where attention goes, energy flows, so why not agree with your partner, with intention, what both of you want before committing your energies to a set of behaviours and roles?

If you do this regularly enough you can avoid the trap of creating a relationship that is not maximising your shared love and resources, but might be impressing people who don't really matter.

When you set intentions, you bring forth the tension needed to enforce changes.

8. Avoiding Co-Dependency is Important

You matter, your partner matters, and the shared relationship itself matters. All three require attention and loving care.

Our individual relationship with ourselves determines how we priorities these different components that add up to a romantic relationship.

We are all somewhere on the continuum between selfish and selfless ways of being. However, the healthiest place on this continuum is in the middle of it in the energy of being self-centred. In this energy we value others, but we recognise that we matter as much as anyone, and do not deserve to be dishonoured by anyone, particularly ourselves.

We are all living our lives, not the lives of others, so we need to take full responsibility for our own wellbeing. If we become too selfless in a relationship, we are likely to suffer and can get lost in the belief that the relationship with our partner is the key determiner of our happiness. This can lead us to prioritise our partner and/or family over our own interests, leaving us in a lonely place.

And the irony is that the more you do this, the more needy you are likely to become, and the more unattractive you will become to your partner. By over-committing to your partner, you increase the prospects of your relationship failing. It may seem counterintuitive, but excess availability kills attraction in normal unconscious relationships by creating familiarity and boredom, unless it is openly managed. Scarcity is a key basis of unconscious attraction.

On the other end of the spectrum, if you are too selfish in a relationship, you may also decrease your attractiveness for different reasons, and your perceived lack of commitment to the relationship can bring it undone.

The balance is in the middle with all three components being in sync. If both partners are self-centred, and therefore balanced within themselves, their combined energies are likely to allow both partners to feel whole within themselves, and for the relationship to stay in a harmonic and balanced place.

This can be problematic when a couple are raising a family, because the pressures of this exercise can lead to the romantic relationship, and the respective partners, feeling like they are losing themselves or each other, in these circumstances.

Balancing all the different relationships within a family is important and can only be done in a conscious way. Often, we don't realise this until it is too late.

9. Chemistry Need Not Die, That's a Lie

Attraction matters in our love lives; it's just not love. We live in a physical 3D world, in physical bodies, and one of the most incredible experiences we can have in our lives is to express ourselves sexually with a person with whom we share a love and/or physical chemistry.

Making love to a partner for whom we feel love is a wonderful expression of our love, and therefore it matters. However, in many relationships sexual attraction and activity often atrophy over time.

We often confuse lust for love. While we may understand that 'love making' can be the expression of love, we do not realise it's not love, and that love making can also be devoid of love.

Polarity needs to be nurtured in relationships so that it can be maintained. But to do this we must be aware of each other's needs and wants and be ready to take steps to meet them.

In a world where few men understand the psychology of women, and vice versa, is it any wonder that polarity and sexual desire die, particularly if both partners don't understand themselves either. We are effectively preparing to fail, rather than preparing to be fulfilled. It is hard to stay attractive to your partner if you are just leaving it to chance and not intent. We are what we practice after all.

Maintaining sexual chemistry requires knowing and not just hoping with blind faith that your connection is special and will survive what lies ahead. Many are special, but far from bulletproof.

How many of us are prepared to admit to the world, or even each other, that our sexual relationships are mediocre at best?

Are we so busy protecting our precious artificial identities that we don't want to recognise how much they are destroying our opportunities to experience fulfilling intimacy with the person we love throughout our lives? Perhaps it's time we dropped the cover-ups and expressed with full transparency?

Do our sexual desires mean so little to us that we are prepared to let them perish, just to protect the fake peace we pretend exists with our partner. Should we just put up with the mediocrity until one of the partners in the relationship can't stand the pain anymore and gives in to outside interest, and validation, through an affair?

10. Sharing the Right Current of Currency

Money is an important energy in life, because it allows us to buy the things and experiences that we need or want, but it is not love. A relationship based on the provision of money in return for other services is transactional, and is akin to passive prostitution, although we would never describe it to ourselves this way.

Perhaps real prostitutes are more authentic, because they don't pretend to be what they are not. They offer sex and intimacy for money, full stop. And there is no pretence that love is present in the exchange.

When two people are really in love, the flow of energy between them is freely given and endless. Many relationships start out this way. But if we allow value and other materialistic goals to become more dominate than love in our relationships, these relationships can become superficial and shaky.

When we meet someone new and love flourishes, particularly in our youth, we usually don't care about money and assets. Love seems to be enough. But this can all change if we alter our focus away from love.

Our conditioning is the originator of these superficial patterns in relationships.

Love is our heart's true desire. Not money. It is the real currency we all want in relationships. So, give from your heart as a priority, not your wallet.

We have a generation of men and women who are chasing the approval of the opposite sex, because they do not know their own worth. They need to pursue self-worth and self-mastery, not the recognition of others.

Old-fashioned expectations and conditioned practices, like the ones discussed in this book now need to be wiped clean and reimagined.

11. The Misalignment of Relationship Goals

In the past, men were focused on their career goals, because this was their way of meeting their primary relationship responsibility of being the provider and protector. This was not historically the case with women.

Women were more likely to have relationship goals, because this was consistent with their conditioned role as the homemaker.

As we have moved into an era of greater equality, and the partial breaking down of old patterns of relating, it has become more imperative that couples are consciously aware of their respective relationship intentions and goals.

I repeat, all choices are valid, but making assumptions based on assumed paradigms is a risky way to relate.

12. Partnership v Competition

'Loving' relationships are meant to be partnerships, not competitions. The union between the masculine and feminine is supposed to be a divine union, not a power struggle.

For centuries, patriarchy made this kind of harmony impossible, because of its ridiculous suppression of feminine energies, within women and men alike.

But balance demands equality with agreed roles between both partners, and ongoing compromise. Being in a relationship naturally requires some degree of sacrifice, compared to being single, although there are also huge benefits. We have another person to consider, but also with whom to share our time, potentially parent, and share and mould our life goals.

This can only happen successfully when we come together, care about each other and treat each other as true partners, not customers with different needs to service.

13. What More Do We Really Want?

As human beings we are programmed to expand and want more. This is the nature of the universe of which we are a part. It is constantly expanding. But, unlike many humans, it consciously expands in the name of love.

But, what do we want more of exactly? As our western world has sped up and become more competitive, we have become more programmed to want more of the material benefits of life. This is where we focus our energy and time, chasing money and other material things.

But is this really what our hearts desire deep down? The answer is 'no'. We seem to want more money and an impressive image to show the world that we are worthy of love and admiration, not realising that most people are living their own lives and don't really care about your image at all.

Material things are merely a poor surrogate for love. They matter, but not as much as love.

Increasingly, we are also selecting romantic partners based on who can help bring greater material or perceived value to our lives, and improve our image to the outside world; rather than the partners who can help us home to our own hearts.

14. Controlling the Male Sexual Urge

Many men are highly intimidated by very beautiful women, because they are taught from childhood that their wealth and own personal looks cap the level of beauty which they can date. We call it a 'league'.

Men subconsciously want to own the beauty of a woman, because their egos believe that it will bring them social recognition. The looks of their partner seem to matter more than any other attribute they seek in the opposite sex.

When I was less conscious, I admit that when I met a super attractive woman, I could become mesmerised in her presence, and

a bit overwhelmed. It's common for men to be attracted to women like this, but with higher awareness I have now learned to feel for connection and assess their personalities, before I approach a woman romantically.

Many men will look past female shortcomings, bad behaviours and red flags if they meet a woman who is good looking enough, and who offers them alluring intimacy.

In addition, even if they have decided that they are not looking to have a relationship with a woman, deep inside them lurks a powerful sexual need that they struggle to quell.

Sexual irrelevance is difficult for both sexes, but some men seem to struggle more with this issue, probably because of their body chemistry, and the egoic validation they derive from being desired by a beautiful woman.

So, how can men tame this beast?

Here is my advice:

- Learn to look upon a woman's beauty as a wonderful asset that she owns, not you. It is like a beautiful sunrise or sunset that you can admire but not possess.

- Realise that female beauty is in abundance. There are many beautiful women around and, without positive traits like intelligence and loyalty, it ceases to be as valuable.

Men, when it comes to female beauty, don't try to own something that may end up owning you.

15. Confusing Chaos with Connection

Many people confuse chaos and connection in relationships. Connection, particularly on a mind, body and spirit level, is ultimately what we are all seeking, and love is never chaotic.

A craving for chaos is a sign that someone in the relationship has unhealed egoic wounds that need to be worked on with self-awareness practices.

These chaotic moments can feel familiar if that's what you were accustomed to witnessing and experiencing when you were growing up. Sometimes they are a kind of test that the ego of another is putting you through to test your resolve to commit to yourself.

Either way, this kind of frailty is best avoided if the wounded person is not prepared to recognise that their behaviour is unhealthy and to work on it, alone or with their partner or a therapist.

Chaos can kill connection and needs to be treated with caution.

16. You Will Never Be Enough for the Wrong Person

Our quest to find the right partner in life is both a conditioned one and a desire held in our hearts. This is one strategy where our hearts and minds agree.

However, there is a fundamental difference in the way our two centres of intelligence operate. Our hearts know who the right partner is for us at any point in time. But our egos do not, and they will be busy ticking off their mental checklists to find a match, and often this will steer you away from love.

This owes more weight to the need to let go of our mental constructs and trust our feelings to find the most appropriate partner.

We are always enough. But after repeated relationship problems, we sometimes conclude that we are not. A scarcity mindset can lead us to date the wrong person, even if our intuition is screaming at us to walk away.

Think abundance with confidence. Know your value and feel into this truth. We are all lovable, even if we can find this hard to believe.

If love is present, and a relationship is meant to be, it will be in divine timing. The universe, through our souls, has a plan for all our love lives; our minds don't need their own.

17. Worship is Worthless

When we worship another person and put them onto a pedestal above us, we do ourselves a grave disservice. Few relationships will thrive if they are not properly balanced or based on equality.

We are all equal, no matter what material things we offer another. We all have a heart, and it is the ultimate prize in relationships, even though we rarely think this way.

Remember, what matters in romantic relationships is not matter; it is love, and love only has eyes for true equality and reciprocity. If love is not present, what you are left with is a friend, even if it's a friend with benefits.

18. Romance is Not Love

Romance is not love; it is a process undertaken in the hope that love can be created between two people. It conveys intention and sometimes pretension. But love doesn't care about romance. It just is or isn't present, and our souls cannot be deceived by an expensive dinner, gift, or holiday on a tropical island.

Courting someone in the hope that they will fall in love with you is a crazy concept constructed on the core belief that the things we do can create love. Love comes from being, not doing.

If someone is in love with you, they won't care whether you take them to a flash restaurant, or somewhere cheap and cheerful. And if they do only respond to an expensive experience that you gave them, it's not you they were loving, it was the circumstances they loved.

Bring forth the romance after love and commitment is known to be in place; not before.

19. Sex Has Essentially Become More Affordable

The sexual revolution began in the 1960s.

I was a child at this time, and over my lifetime I have seen it evolve significantly.

Modern dating practices have made sexual interactions more commoditised, in the same way that they have made dates more readily attainable online.

In centuries past, it was more normalised to marry someone to attain a sex life, and this put pressure on both sexes to marry, given the on-going human desire for sexual expression.

Arguably the cost of sex was too high in previous eras, because marriage was seen as a prerequisite for it to be regarded as moral. Those days are well and truly over in western societies.

There is nothing wrong with sex between two consenting adults, if it is offered and received willingly and in good faith, and if it does not harm others inappropriately by being offered secretly in contravention of existing commitments.

Perhaps the new approach in the dating world with respect to sex is more authentic than in centuries past, and has moderated the propensity for people to marry purely for sex? And perhaps this is another reason why marriage rates are falling across the world?

20. What Matches Are We Choosing to Be Loyal To?

Loyalty is a vital ingredient of love, and of great relationships. And like everything in life, loyalty is a choice we can embrace or dismiss.

I witness a world where loyalty can be misdirected away from the areas of life that really matter. And sometimes we do this out of naivety, and our inbuilt programming. ***I have been guilty of this too.***

Consider the sporting teams we support. Many people commit to, say, a football team, and the success, or otherwise, of that team does not seemingly affect our sense of loyalty to it. We will often commit for life to the teams we support and give them our undying devotion, willing them to win.

The same can be said of the employers that pay us. Sometimes we are prone to commit too heavily to our careers and to our jobs, rather than to the families and partners who we openly say we treasure.

I once had a learned boss in my workplace say these prophetic words to me after another late night of work.

"Remember, it's easier to get a new job, than it is to get a new wife."

Wise words, that I probably didn't value fully, until I met my divorce lawyers for the second time.

When our romantic partners, who we say we love, prove to be imperfect or seemingly let us down in some way, we can lose our sense of commitment to them, even accumulating reasons to resent them, then using these reasons to justify replacing them. But sometimes, they are just being what they were taught to be and may think they are doing the right thing by their partner. Compassion needs to be the close cousin of loyalty and truth in romantic relationships.

The question is, which matches are we fully investing in and committing to; and do we offer the right level of loyalty to our lovers, when it is clearly deserved?

21. The Illusion of Trying to Disconnect from Someone You Love

One of the great misconceptions many people share is that, when a relationship ends or breaks temporarily, they think they can disconnect the love that they held with another through thought, and by simply trying hard to do so. But your mind cannot achieve this if your soul does not allow it to be so. Distraction is temporary at best, and in the quiet of the night, deep reminders will arise.

Souls create love-based connections, irrespective of the preferences of our minds. And only they can sever them. Being in a physical disconnect from a person can lead us to think we have control over love, but if there are still unfinished experiences or learnings that two souls are meant to share together, love will remain in place between them and draw them towards each like a magnet, to fulfil what was intended. Time and space are irrelevant to our eternal souls, even if it is not to our 3D minds.

If you have ever had that experience of meeting or being in relationship with someone, and feeling deeply connected to them, but you can't stop thinking about them in the months or years that follow, or in intense cases still feeling their energetic presence, this is what I am referring to here.

Resistance in this situation is futile, and the best thing to do is simply send that other person love, knowing that if there is more to come between you, this will happen in divine timing. Alternatively, you may have not taken a learning that your soul wanted you to take out of the circumstances of the separation, and it is therefore waiting for you to have the realisation that was intended, before it sets you free. Relax in the knowing that love has got this – it is ultimately living you, you are not living it.

You cannot control love, for it is leading you home through the experiences it wants you to have.

Chapter 32

Becoming the Love You Want to Experience

Owning Our Relationship with Love

When our relationships don't work out as we'd hoped, many people have a tendency, ***like I once did***, to try and put the pain behind them, and simply hope for a better outcome next time. Seeing the source of the disappointment as being outside of themselves, they may generalise about the faults of the opposite sex, and then put their faith in a blind hope that a more competent and caring lover will come along in the future to give them what they need or want. They essentially hope for a saviour, and they become a victim or martyr of the past.

If our past experiences hurt enough, we may undergo therapy, or even withdraw for a period, convincing ourselves that we were just unlucky, or just met the wrong people before. Our egos tend to shift the blame to our ex-partners, as we sit in a righteous bubble. After all it couldn't be our fault, could it? But this attitude is the key source of our perpetuated suffering, for it ignores the 'magic mirror' of life, and the reality that all happens for purpose, for us and not to us.

The truth is that we must first become energetically aligned with whatever we want to experience in life. If you want to find true love, or any higher version of love, you simply must be in that energy first. We must start looking at love and relationships in the same way we look at other things in our lives; with a focus on ongoing self-development, not the naïve paradigm of 'it'll be fine next time'. We tend to cross our fingers and try again, or perhaps give up, without substantially enhancing ourselves, and our abilities to relate effectively.

Consider this analogy: if a football team loses, it goes back to its training base, thinks about why it lost, probably listens to its coach and works on improving its skills and abilities, so that it can win next time. Do we apply this approach in our love lives?

Consider these important questions:

- Do we let our past relationships of despair, make us more aware?
- Can we let our past love disasters, turn us into new love-masters?
- Do we want 'no chance romance', or the chance to feel the real deal?

I essentially pondered these questions in the wake of my two painful divorces and other relationship issues, and became determined to learn more about love and myself, so I could hold a more powerful love in the future. I eventually understood that no one was going to save me, only I could do that. If I wanted the love life I had always dreamed about, I had to become the man capable of holding that love first. And this meant transforming myself and taking full accountability for my love life.

So I read books about love, got multiple mentors to learn from, 'audited' my past relationships to own my share of the problems that arose, released my pain and my fears about love, and importantly stopped judging myself as a 'failure' in love, who just couldn't make it work.

And now, after years of this deep introspection, I have emerged with higher wisdom about love and relationships, and excited about what is possible. I made this a priority in my life, and I know that this is not for everyone, but every stepping stone we traverse to higher understandings about love gives us more genuine possibilities, and less blind hope, for a more positive love-life.

Isn't it time to unlearn what we think we know about love, and open to a fresh way of loving that is based in truth?

Here is my blueprint that an individual can follow to find this fresh new paradigm of love, and truly give themselves the real chance to live 'happily ever after'. Consider what hasn't worked in your past romantic relationships and take responsibility for your contribution to these issues. 'Audit' how things went right or wrong, and join the dots, because these dots will expose your patterns of attachment.

1. Release any pain associated with your disappointments from the past, and any associated fears you might hold for the future. At the same time, consider what limiting beliefs you may have had, which potentially sabotaged your past romantic outcomes, and restate them.

2. Elevate love and relationships by learning about them from people and books that are in the know. If you really want a better version of love in the future, step into it. Don't hide from it like it's some kind of voodoo doll out to get you. It is not! It just wants you to grow with it, for you are it.

3. Stop comparing your love life to that of others and judging yourself as anything other than a scholar, and future master of love. Forgive yourself for the past, draw a line in the sand and step over it into a new paradigm of love. Drop any thoughts that you were a victim or a martyr in past relationships. You merely got what you needed to evolve.

4. Imagine what you want your love life to be like and feel like in the future, and work to being in alignment with that dream. Know what you want, and dismiss what you think you need, because life has a way of rewarding wants and punishing needs. If you don't know what you want, and how to emotionally express

it, how is the universe – to which you may be praying for a better love life – going to know how to co-create it with you? Make no mistake, love and great relationships arise from co-creation. It's not up to your version of 'God', or sheer randomness, to give it to you. Commitment is necessary on your behalf.

5. Once you know what's possible, open to love and learn to feel for it when you are out and about. Real connection matters, not the kind you get on the internet, or through an email. So get off the 'couch' or your computer, that you may have retreated to, and venture forth into new experiences where people you are wanting to meet are likely to be. Do what you love as you love and respect yourself, so that you can find that love with another, who also wants it.

I know how hard this is after multiple painful experiences, and I have struggled with it myself.

But the only way to the kind of relationships you want is to face your fears, and not let them hook you, as they will inevitably try and do.

6. Trust that the chance meeting with your next love will happen when you and they are ready for it. Patience matters, because love doesn't care about the timing on your watch. It works off the coalescing of energy. Whatever you are energetically ready for, can't help but appear in divine timing for you. And know that, essentially, what you are looking for is also looking for you.

Become the person who knows that the next time you fall in love, you'll know better what to do. Don't be the person, with his or her fingers crossed, trusting sheer hope, clinging to limited self-awareness and convinced they were simply unlucky in the past. In the kingdom of love, luck is a myth that our unaccountable egos made up to preserve themselves, at the expense of our own possibilities.

If you want the ultimate connection that this book depicts, know that this will require the next level of dedication and commitment, because it defines the path to true love, and dismisses the misconceptions about where it can be found. This is a choice we can all make, or not. However, every step you take towards it will bring you to the potential for higher love, and better relationships. These steps are discussed at a macro level in a later chapter.

Loving Vicariously Through Others

It is not uncommon for many of us to stop believing we are worthy of wonderful experiences, so we sometimes live vicariously through the experiences of others, thinking they have what we want, and that we can substitute their experiences for ours.

Picture a big celebrity, or royal wedding, and stop believing that they have the fairytale you can't have. Love is about how you feel, not carriages, horses, and big budget weddings. They are not you, and you are not them, nor can you ever be. And who is to say that they can experience more from love than you can? Discover your own 'more', and take responsibility for your dreams coming true.

Hiding from love because your trust in it, and the opposite sex, has been broken, is not the gateway to future happiness and sacred union. It is a cage you may never escape, simply because you did not take responsibility for your own full potential. Do you want to get to your deathbed, look back, and regret that you gave up on love when a dose of wisdom may have allowed it into your life?

The bottom line is this: when you become the kind of lover that you want to be loved by, and connect to yourself in the way you want to be connected to, there will be no limits to where you love life can take you. The mirror of love is reflecting the light that you put out. So be radiant, and do not dull the opportunities that life has in store for you.

When you arise in love, love can't help but rise with you, for it is the very essence of you. At some point, the only way to keep it down will be to actively hold it down.

Love is the source of infinite possibilities, once you dismiss the illusion that it's not for you, but it is for others.

Become the lover who learns then returns, not the one who merely sits and yearns.

Chapter 33

Returning to Love Through the Energy of Peace

Turning Peace Back into Passion

Many people are walking away from relationships, and rediscovering that special someone who can love them in a new place of peace, where they no longer need to perform and compete to have their needs met – that special someone being themselves.

Others, however, prefer to dwell in the energy of regret, and stay single merely to enjoy the peace it brings compared to shared love, motivated by the sheer frustration of their perceived inability to make romantic relationships a resounding success. In this, a key question for such people would be: are you living increasingly in a vacuum full of peace fuelled by emptiness, but devoid of the true happiness that sharing our lives with another can bring forth? And are you loving yourself more, but letting others love us less, in a wave of self-protectionism?

Also, are you giving yourselves freedom to feel safe for now – akin to being on a life raft in the ocean on a calm day – but temporarily lost and cut off from the connection with the happiness that you so richly deserve? And finally, will this relief of feeling safe fade, because the highs and lows of being a part of real life and love with another are absent in our experiences? The storms of life won't normally break us, if we are flexible enough to move with the waves of change, and adapt to what confronts us.

Some of us are indeed becoming too sovereign, as kings and queens of empty kingdoms, devoid of the one true richness that this world can bestow upon us. Why, when whether we choose union or singlehood, there will always be benefits and drawbacks to confront?

It can take a lot of energy and mental discipline to keep your heart closed to, and away from, what it really desires. The mind can work overtime to keep us in this loop of denial, and this can be exhausting.

Opening our hearts to love again after repeated relationships have failed to meet our expectations, is a challenge that should not be underestimated. Trusting that someone will love you as you want to be loved, and not 'fumble' your heart again, as you perceive others may have done, is a great test of your faith in love. But this is a test worth taking and passing in my view, once you feel ready to try again.

The good news is that finding greater peace and self-worth within yourself is the gateway to the love you truly seek, for many of us who have had to endure painful detours along the way home to love. They are essential stepping-stones along the path to a higher version of love. A kind of romantic reset, you might say.

When you step away from periods of romantic stress and search inside your own heart, taking responsibility for all that has previously occurred, you open the drawbridge to new relationship possibilities. And when you enter a new relationship with higher self-worth, you send the universe the message that you are ready for a better experience next time and can now better honour yourself in relationship experiences.

Further, if you enter a state of greater peace, your nervous system can reset, and allow you to bring greater peace to your next romantic adventure, and your life in general. Both are important steps forward. And the length of time that this evolution takes is truly an individual experience. There are no set rules here to be obeyed, for love knows no rules, nor cares about time.

One positive of people stepping away from dating and relating for a period is that they can get to know themselves better and find new areas of personal self-expression. And perhaps in this void, in which men and women are seeing the other side finally valuing themselves more, and not just chasing the validation of relationships, they can start to value each other more as partners in life. After all, doesn't absence make the heart grow fonder?

If we use the period of being single wisely, this peaceful break can give us the opportunity for that wonderful reset many of us so desperately need to have. Fresh starts must begin somewhere. Why not embrace the opportunity to be in a new energy of peace and quiet, which affords us the chance to relax back into being ourselves, and not see ourselves as the other half of a struggle we may have once felt compelled to take part in?

Humility is always the first step to mastery, and for me taking time out to reset my relationship with love, was one of the most valuable gifts I could have ever given myself, even if it confused other people who knew the old, busy me. I had not previously shared all my struggles with people I knew, so only I had any comprehension of how much pain I needed to process.

I eventually reached a point where I knew I was ready to open to love again, but this time with my new understandings, and a new resolve to enter and enjoy the dating world as someone open to learning. This time I sought someone who wanted to grow with me in the energy of love. I suppose you could say it was time to return, play and learn, as a brand-new me who was humbler and more discerning.

When we take the opportunity to step back and redefine our own lives, we take away the need for duty to call and define it for us.

I no longer plan to let the world write a script for me to perform in love. I am now the lead actor in my own 'romantic movie'.

Chapter 34

The Fundamental Steps to the Ultimate Connection

The Ultimate Reward Awaits Your Attention

This book is predicated on the belief that true, or unconditional, love is both possible and natural for human beings to experience; firstly, within themselves and then secondly, with another, who is also on route to this vaulted place of love and bliss. When two lovers devoid of need come together in union, the ultimate connection, and the promise of the ultimate romantic relationship, becomes possible.

Readers need to understand that true love is quite rare, although many couples will be convinced that they have already found it. This is normal, particularly at the start of many relationships, because our egos tell us, and want to broadcast to the world, that we have met our Mr or Mrs Right, and that they are 'my one and only soul mate'.

But the real pathway to true love has been lost in the annals of time and substantially deleted from our way of loving. This chapter explores this ultimate step up to the highest form of romantic relationship available on this planet. It is time we remembered what our hearts have always known is possible, but our minds forgot.

True love is, essentially, a reward for becoming more self-aware, and allowing the energy of love to guide us forward, because we have removed the blocks that held us back from it. You might say that true love is a birthright, but not a given right, which we can make the focus of our attention and intentions in life, if we want it. But it is a felt experience, not a thought one, and therefore must be embodied within us.

We already have it inside us at our core, so why not let it out of the 'dungeon' that our distorted egos have locked it in. Out of sight and out of mind, you might say, but never far away.

One of the greatest fantasies on this planet, which many of us have been sold and told to believe in, is that true love is the result of good luck and could happen at any minute if we meet the right person. On the contrary, it is almost certain that we will first meet the right, wrong person instead, who can help us clear any needs, wounds and fears, which will be holding us back from the experience that we seek. This encounter with our right, wrong energetic match, can be challenging if we approach it with the wrong and naïve intentions. But, if we know we must grow through our relationships and personal experiences, then we can set ourselves up to share a sacred form of love, and an unbreakable bond with another. Who doesn't want that?

The missing link for most of us is understanding that, to attain the ultimate connection with another, we first need to attain it within ourselves. And this can be achieved alone, or by consciously creating it through loving relationships with others, or a combination of both.

Unless we are in the energy of unconditional love, and therefore complete within ourselves, we cannot establish this ideal match with another soul. I hate to be the bearer of bad news, but fulfilling a fantasy is impossible, no matter what your mind, or the hope that it generates, is telling you.

In earlier chapters, I explained how the process of attaining higher awareness about ourselves, and states of love, can unfold. I specifically explained the core steps that I applied to my journey to find higher states of love within myself. These were taught to me by great masters of love, but some people may not need all the steps. It depends on where they are at, and where they want to get to. And in later chapters I put forward 'blueprints' of what a person who makes this journey with commitment can become within themselves, and how they are likely to naturally behave in romantic relationships as a result.

But what are the key high-level phases that can collectively get us to this experience we all aspire to have, but which are so rarely understood? The picture below summarises the core steps needed to make this journey possible at a high-level for most of us, though the journey will of course vary somewhat depending on the person.

I say most, because there is a small cohort of fortunate few who are already energetically aligned with unconditional love, and can step into this paradigm with little to no soul searching. As I have said, though, this is rare, and only a miniscule number of people will have this experience without doing the deep inner work to get there.

Our egos, of course, will try to tell us otherwise. Our ego-centric minds are not in the right energy, and ironically because of their wounds and limiting beliefs, represent the main barrier to the experiences we all want to have in love. They set the goal, then destroy it, out of fear and ignorance. You might call it an 'own goal', to use a sporting analogy. This is why so many relationships end in separation, or atrophy into mediocrity. If we simply expect others to be able to give us true love, even when we are not ready for it within ourselves, we will be sadly disappointed.

Love arises in presence, not performance. If we are performing rituals to be loved, we are fundamentally sacrificing love, on the altar of fear, and we have lost the plot. Our love lives should not be like performances, where we are putting on a show to be recognised and valued.

But our souls know what true love feels like, for they are always in that energy.

Consider the following picture, for it depicts the core steps through which most of us must arise, to be capable of the ultimate love connection with ourselves, and then another.

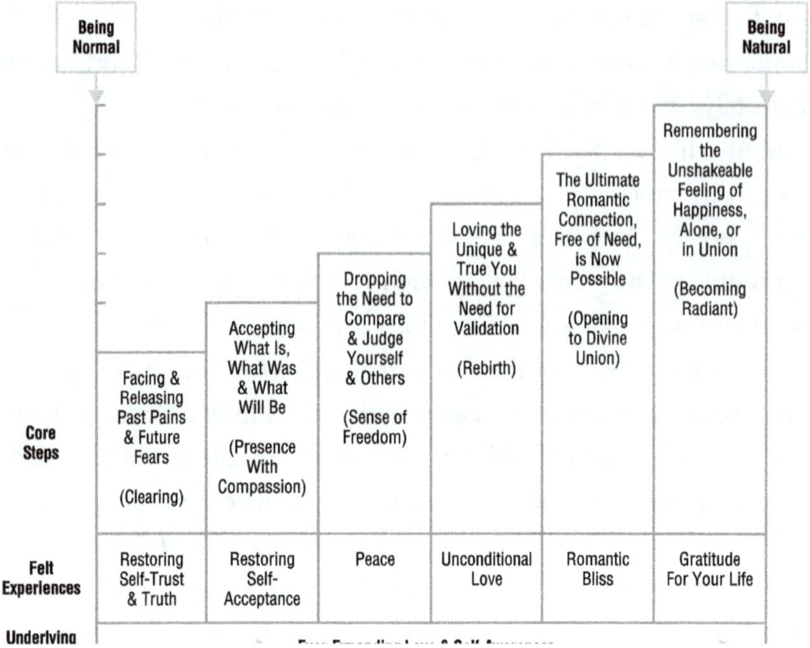

Figure 4: Core Steps to Connection & Romantic Bliss

The key points that this diagram brings forth, which I seek to reinforce, are:

- The extent to which an individual, or couple, need to face and clear their pain and fears, is a matter of circumstance and will be determined by the levels of conscious awareness that they hold, and the relationships or frequencies of love with which they are in-tune.
- Unconditional love is born out of the energy of peace. Only when a person is at peace within themselves, and can bring peace to a relationship, is true love possible.
- True peace is only possible when we are substantially clear of the pain of the past and our fears of the future. When we are accepting of what was, is and will be, we can approach life without the physical and emotional pain that was once buried within us, and the psychological distortions we experience when we face the future with apprehension.

- This brings us into presence, and out of the loop of living in the future and/or the past. Only in presence is the feeling and expression of pure love within us, truly possible. But it is easier said than done to arrive at this point, as this book and my other books demonstrate.
- Only when we lose our propensity to compare and judge all that we encounter, can we truly love without conditions.
- Once we can love ourselves, and everything else in our lives without conditions and without needing them to be different, we can start to fully accept the uniqueness of ourselves and any potential partners who we meet. This is a core step to personal and relationship bliss. Unconditional love within us can bring us into our natural radiance and can spark an unshakeable happiness that is not dependent upon any external circumstances or relationships in our lives, because it is a felt experience arising from within us. It becomes our in-built frequency of love, and happiness, that is beyond the influences of our minds.
- This experience of being in a state of unconditional love is like being home in a state of ongoing peace, which allows us to experience the radiance within all of us and share it with others. It is a state of bliss and stillness that needs no movement backwards or forwards to be sustained. It can hold its pleasantness and joy in any given moment, regardless of what circumstances rise or fall.
- This state is not a temporary high that lights up the sky, within our often-dark minds. It is a wisdom offering you the power of choices, and the core opportunity within these choices is to create a life that you love, from the power of love, in every moment.
- The wisdom within this ultimate love can bring you to new and wonderful possibilities, or the alternative, depending on what you ultimately choose to apply it to.

True love with another can never be perfect on this planet, for our human side makes that virtually impossible. But the right choices, made through intuition and the power of pure love with another – who sees the world from the same paradigm that you do – are gifts you will never want to lose, or stop unwrapping.

The 'Magic Trick' to Being Able to Love Unconditionally

It is so easy to think that we are loving unconditionally, but frankly this is rarified air for most of humanity. Not impossible, just rare. To really love ourselves unconditionally, or others, we must embrace the energies of compassion and acceptance. We are all where we are, doing what we are doing, for purpose. But again, this is easier to understand conceptually, than it is to apply in practice. In other words, it is easier said than done.

Earlier in this book I referred to the mirror effect of life. Essentially, we get reflected to us what we need to return to our natural state of being. Natural synchronicities facilitate these learning opportunities, which we can either embrace or ignore. What this means is that we are exposed to the negative traits of another, to show us that we have the same potential for darkness within ourselves, as they have. The same goes for the positives of others.

When we compare ourselves to anyone else, and judge them as better or worse than ourselves, this rating and ranking process is the source of separation between them and us – physically, emotionally, energetically, or in all these ways.

The 'magic trick' that will allow you to love unconditionally is to witness the traits of others, and if they trigger judgement within you, reflect on why this is the case. What you will always find is that you have the same capacity for goodness, or darkness, as they do, buried deep within yourself. This opens you to self-development.

Going through this conscious process as a matter of course, is a trait many successful people possess. I have heard it described as one of the traits of the greats, because successful people learn from the many interactions and connections they have with others, without judgement.

You may not want to admit this, or find it incredulous, but we do all need to remember we are all the one source and live in a 'soup' of energies and conditioned ways of being that we all share. As is often said, no one is a criminal, until they commit their first crime; but faced with extreme circumstances, we all have the potential to break the law.

It is totally liberating to take this perspective – that we are all of the same potentiality, and source of consciousness – into any relationship, for it allows us to be compassionate to the plight of everyone and understand that we have the same potential to fulfil, or let ourselves down, as any other soul on the planet. We all get what we need, before we get what we want, to help us grow. And we all make mistakes.

When we enter a romantic relationship with another person, an important attribute we can adopt if we want to love them unconditionally, is to see that their weaknesses and issues are no more than the product of their experiences, and in essence are just illusions that are ingrained in their minds, which are not their truths. And of course we have the same potential forms of shortcomings within ourselves, although we may have already spotted them and done the 'work' to let them go.

The important thing is that if two people love each other, and consciously work to grow together, there is no obstacle they cannot overcome to develop their love life together, and passion for each other, if they want it to be full of joy. Commitment to each other, and a dose of patience and compassion, are needed.

Loving someone unconditionally from a distance, however, may be necessary, if they are not prepared to meet you in a conscious way, or work on the potential attributes of the relationship.

Love awaits our attention patiently, but if our minds don't want to align with its infinite wisdom, it may be forced to 'take a backseat' in our romantic relationships.

Dropping Our Victim Mentalities

One of the reasons that we struggle to recover from romantic pain, and step forward into new opportunities, including unconditional love, is because we allow our egos to make us the victims of our disappointing experiences. To protect us from further pain, they create stories of hardship and loss, and place us in these stories as the innocent victims, or 'fallen angels', who have been 'hard done by'. True love is not possible in a victim mentality.

When we are live from our hearts, the love that we are will not buy into any illusions of us being a victim. Instead, it will allow us to grow through what has taken place, embrace the new experiences that present themselves in our lives, and to step forward with curiosity.

Abandoning Judgement, Adopting Discernment

A key tenet required to enter the energy of unconditional love lies in our ability to shift from judgement to discernment, as we embrace life, and interact with others.

There are differences between the processes of comparing and judging, and the process of witnessing then discerning, which can assist us to become unconditional lovers. When we compare two different things, or people, from our judgemental minds, we are likely to create separation in some way, because this process leads us to rate things as better or worse than another. But when we witness things with an open heart and use discernment, merely to see what really matters in a situation, we open ourselves up to the possibility of greater compassion and love descending into the circumstances.

Unfortunately, our normal propensity to relate through the lens of comparison and judgement has taught many of us to function within dysfunction, and in fact perpetuate this dysfunction, whilst we convince ourselves that this is as good as it gets. It is, at best, a conditional form of low frequency love.

The Journey from Delighting to Becoming Delightful

We spend much of our lives trying to be loved by de-lighting others. 'De' is a Latin prefix that means to 'away', so to 'delight' means to give your light away. This analogy matters in the context of this part of the book.

So often the process of trying to be delightful is done through an external offering, which we make by dimming our light to make others happy. And in this process we can drain our own potential to be happy, or light, within ourselves. We may give another our love, or some other form of offering, to attract their attention towards us, and in the process we can diminish our own sense of self. This is our well-trodden path to pursuing completion by loving others.

But when we stop trying to perform in this way, and instead activate the light within us, and for us, first and foremost, we can't help but become magnetic to others. The light within us needs nothing to be complete and radiant, and when we stop dimming it to impress others, we activate greater frequencies of happiness that we already hold within us.

The radiant you becomes magnetic to the person who can witness your inner glow, and remember the light that you are. Your radiance is your truth. So instead of trying to give your light to others to find happiness, why not find your own radiant light first, then shine that light onto another who is also radiant and can't wait to share theirs with you. This is the gateway to the ultimate connection.

None of us have the responsibility, or even the ability, to make another person happy or activate their light, but we do have a responsibility to be radiant within ourselves.

The ultimate relationship awaits those who embrace what love, and a dose of higher awareness, makes possible should they choose it. This is a paradigm shift in a world that sold us the concept of need-based relating and competitive dating.

The light of love is calling us home. Now, isn't that worth exploring, and not ignoring?

The Irony of Finding Peace

There is a quirky anomaly buried in the process of moving towards peace, from my experience. Confronting pain and your fears can be tough, because we may be finally facing things we once suppressed or denied. And this can feel as real and raw as the original process would have been, had we faced the associated pain on a timelier basis, in more trying and active circumstances.

The human subconscious mind can store painful memories indefinitely until our psyches surrender their hold over the emotional stories of our lives.

So, from my experience, once you find peace after facing fear and pain, you may also need to find peace in the process you had to go through to find this peace. This sounds like a riddle, but it can feel very real in the thick of the battle with your own 'demons'.

When we take on our accumulated pain, we must eventually forgive that pain for being present in our lives. As my book *From Pain to Possibility* explains, emotional pain and some forms of physical pain, are just messages from the soul that something needs to be faced and turned from darkness into light, from the negative into the positive. Pain awaits the alchemy that only the balm of love can apply to it, to take it away.

This is the opportunity that we all face together, and within ourselves, in tandem with love. When we remember the power of love, and the truth that it holds for us, we can face our pain together and turn our shared pain into a deeper love. But first we must accept that we are where we are, draw a line in the sand and step over it into a new paradigm of peace.

Forgiveness is the key, even if the coming together gets tough at times. Our pain may well be our eventual source of great gain.

Chapter 35

My Blueprint for Individual Happiness in Romantic Relationships

My Loving Advice

The contents of this book are designed to bring awareness to the problems we encounter in modern-day dating and relating. But there is only a limited point if it does not also offer readers sustainable solutions and hope to apply to their own lives.

Many experts will tell people how to create a relationship by 'playing the current game' cleverly. In other words, they advise people how they can be successful by manipulating the rules of the game as they currently stand, and having a stronger or healthier ego.

I'll leave that approach, primarily, to the dating experts and relationship advisors, who I recognise are trying to help the masses adapt and succeed in their dating and relating endeavours by simply working with what exists, and not by stepping away from the malaise, and forging a completely new paradigm of love.

However, I do truly believe that the only way forward is to fundamentally change the game of love, and the skills of the players taking part. And this is where my advice is different from others – because I believe that the human ego is the enemy of harmonious relationships, and not its ally. In fact, unconditional or true love requires the human ego to be substantially melted in the fire of love.

My recommendations and observations are thus more about sustainable and structured transformations, rather than incremental adaptations. What I offer is not therapy, but a complete and natural redesign of the way we love.

This is because our human souls can see straight through inauthenticity and will punish it in the end. ***My views might therefore be harder to implement, but more permanent and sophisticated in the long term, than what I experienced in relationship therapies.***

If we just keep teaching people how to be temporarily successful in a fake world, that world is not going to change for the better, and more tears will be shed as hearts continue to break. It will just continue to be the same old game, which more people become better at manipulating to their own advantage. But what is the point in improving your ability to play chess if you really don't like the game, and would prefer to be playing scrabble?

What we really want in our love lives is a natural experience that fulfils us because it is based around truth and love. And these two properties can never be faked.

This is what the world of lovers is really craving. Everything else is just window-dressing and aesthetics. Our love lives should be fun and enjoyable, but it can't be a game that is based on fear and control.

Some people might argue that all of life is one big game, because it is just an illusion of light. But that doesn't mean we can't change that game, so that it better aligns with our true purpose in being here in the first place. And that simple purpose is to discover the light and love within us, and to create the life that we love. What we do and what we achieve is just the outpouring of this love that we all are.

The bottom line is, if we want a more wholesome game of love, we need players with greater awareness to take the field, who are prepared to become even more whole themselves.

This chapter provides my views of what new-age aware lovers can become when they learn more about themselves, and how love naturally operates.

It is supplemented by details encapsulated in the appendices, provided for readers to consider:

> Appendix I: A checklist of my key learnings in romantic love for both men and women to consider.
>
> Appendix II: A set of questions for couples already in romantic relationships to consider together, for the benefit of their relationship.

Specifically, the rest of this chapter offers a blueprint in the form of key areas of advancement that could assist to create new-age men and women capable of bridging the romantic gaps between them and creating far less turbulent relationships, in which they can both grow in love.

In the next chapter, I will also offer a blueprint for community leaders to consider, to improve the broken paradigm of romantic relationships in modern family dynamics and bring peace to the families that are the bedrock of our communities.

Any steps we can take to move up the continuum to a higher embodiment of these qualities are likely to help us all.

The Common Attributes of Advanced Lovers

The key to becoming a person who the opposite sex wants, and is more likely to commit to in the long run, is to essentially become less needy and fearful, and truer to your authentic self. This involves becoming deeply connected to your own heart, such that you can readily connect to the hearts and minds of others.

You can become this through:

- Not needing another to complete you.
- Believing in real equality in your relationships regardless of gender.

- Believing in the power of love and prioritising it in your life.
- Feeling for love, not thinking it.
- Not fearing being single, if that arises, because you love your own company.
- Being able to wait patiently for the right lover, rather than compromising too much on what you really want, and using partners as temporary fillers.
- Being capable of giving and receiving in equal measure in a relationship.
- Knowing that lovemaking is an expression of love and valuing its role in relationships.
- Always honouring yourself first and foremost in relationships, whilst also honouring your partner, because you accept that we are all here to live our own lives, not sacrifice it for others.
- Respecting the spiritual or religious beliefs that you and your partner adopt and practice, even if they are different.
- Being capable of enforcing and maintaining appropriate boundaries, so that you both feel safe and respected in life. Setting and enforcing fair boundaries with other people is how we establish meaningful respect, as a powerful compliment to love.
- Being conscious of the kind of collective conditioning spoken about in this book and through taking steps to allow it to be assessed and dissolved in your relationship, as you see fit.
- Taking steps to address your own limiting beliefs and wounds either alone or with your partner in a conscious way. This allows you to be less enslaved to your feelings.
- Being emotionally open and capable of going inward to process emotions before you project them onto others.
- Being fully present with those you love and desire, not constantly worrying about the future or the past.
- Being committed to love as well as aspects of attraction, because you want the full package.

- Being able to express love to yourself and another with truth, trust, compassion, and acceptance.
- Being prepared to openly design the relationship that you share with your partner, so that both feel sovereign and in union at the same time.
- Being committed to growing together and as individuals as your relationships unfold.
- Not expecting perfection from yourself, or those you love, because you know that this is impossible.
- Knowing what you want and need in a relationship and not staying too long if these are not being honoured properly, after you have made your partner aware of them.
- Not having a predetermined view of what your partner should be or become, because you know that will unfold as life evolves.
- Honouring and respecting the achievements of your partner as well as your own, because you know that your relationship is a partnership that helps each of you become more, it is not a competition to be won.
- Trusting your intuition in your relationships and expressing what you feel with compassion and care.
- Being able to honour reciprocity and sovereignty within your relationship, rather than exercising control, as you know that there is no love in control.
- Understanding that romantic relationships do not necessarily last forever, because people can come into your life for a specific experience, and therefore a lifetime commitment cannot always be expected.
- Reaffirming your love to your partner every day, in words or actions, though you don't need a written contract to stay.
- Understanding that love is the primary currency between two lovers, not superficial currents of connection, like money or status.

Conscious lovers see through the normal game of love and want the truer, more natural game of love instead.

Defining the Qualities of the New-Age Man

The additional qualities that the advanced, new-age man possesses, and which will make him magnetic to women, on top of the generic ones listed above, are:

- Understand that your masculine energies, and to a lesser extent your feminine energies, are important factors that attract women into your life, so you respect these aspects of yourself, to preserve the polarity with your lover.
- Not seek to have physical or financial power over a woman, because you understand that together you are a team with complimentary skills and energies. Never inflict physical harm on any woman – EVER.
- Not seek to pay for more than your fair share in your relationship or on dates, because you have come into alignment with modern concepts of equality (unless this has been agreed upon by you and your partner). Such an approach can however, make logical sense because of different levels of wealth.
- Remain in touch with your emotions, and are prepared to express them with truth, while also not being unstable emotionally or in need of emotional rescue by your partner.
- Not be beholden to the physical beauty of a woman. You know you can admire this wonderful quality in a woman but will never allow it to own you. You know that her beauty is hers to own, not yours to keep. So, stay composed and fully present in her presence, no matter how beautiful she is. She is a person with a soul, before she is a body to make love to.
- Control your desire for a beautiful woman when you meet her and respect your commitment to your current partner.

- Be fun but composed in a woman's presence because you are a mature man.
- Understand that it is not your job to be the saviour of damaged women, like some knight in shining armour.
- Not carry the fearful energies of the excessively 'nice guy', because you have recognised the damage it can do to your magnetism and sense of self in life. The 'happy wife, happy life' mantra is not one you align with, because you know that you matter too, and to subscribe to such a view prevents equality and conscious communication in your relationship, which risks its longevity and happiness.
- Not embody the high ego of a Bad Boy, nor use this dismissive style of energy to manipulate the opposite sex.
- Remain composed under pressure, not out of image creation, but because this is your natural state of being. You cannot be manipulated by the will of others, including that of your partner.
- Develop a deep purpose in your life, and cannot be swayed from this path, regardless of who goes with you, because while pursuing the wrong woman will cost you dearly, pursuing success will not cost you your chance to be with the right woman.
- Contain your ego in the company of women. They are often intuitive, and know when you are 'big noting' yourself just to carry their favour.
- Honour and respect yourself in life, including in relationships, never allowing a woman to dishonour or disrespect you at your own expense. You respectfully communicate your authentic values and rights, no matter what circumstances arise.
- Are prepared to listen to the ideas and guidance of women, though always trust your own intuition in relationships too.
- Have and maintain your own friends and interests, to prevent you from losing yourself within your relationship and becoming too available and co-dependent.

- Respect your body and stay fit and healthy, not for the validation of women, but out of your own self-respect.
- Have no unhealthy addictions that get in the way of a fulfilling life with your partner.
- Lead in life in the areas where this is natural and in the common good, not out of conditioned habit. Encourage your partner to lead where this is sensible for her (or him).
- Never harm others just to prove that you are strong. You know that your true strength and protection come from love and compassion, not your ego, or fists. Be empowered but not needing power over others.
- Have the discipline to tend to the core administrations of life, including a fair share of housework and caring for children.
- Know that money is an important energy of life, but you will not obsess about it, nor use it to try to buy the love of women, because you know that money is not love.
- Are never beholden to, or controlled by, your emotions, because you always take the time to go inward and understand your emotions before you express them with your partner.
- Understand your role as a father and be committed to protecting and guiding your children, and followers, to a positive life. This does not change, even if the children are the offspring of your partner, and not your own biologically. They are souls that have come into your life to be loved, so honour that.
- Never take steps to disrupt another relationship, even if you are attracted to a woman who is already committed to another man, out of respect to both participants, even if she wants you. You instead honour her commitment to the other man, even if she is reluctant to do so, unless she becomes free. This is integrity, in action. Remember that what you put out, you get back.
- Allow your partner, or date, to be in her feminine energies on suitable occasions, because you know that this is natural for her, and this assists your polarity together.

- Recognise the intelligence and intellect of your partner, and the goodness in her heart, not just her looks.
- Are loyal to the core, but not at your own expense.
- Recognise that if a woman rejects you that is a valid choice by her, and it does not invalidate your worthiness to be loved.

Every man has the capability to attain these qualities if they are committed to nurturing their own sense of self-worth.

I recognise that this is a long list to consider, and few men will embody all these advanced attributes fully until they have embodied powerful levels of self-love.

Of course, attempting to move into these energies in a progressive way and being conscious of them is a wonderful journey to undertake, which would enhance your love life immeasurably.

To be embodied, most self-improvement ideas need to be understood and valued first, then applied before they become a new habit. I'm not saying you should fake it till you make it, but understanding what makes you more desirable to the opposite sex, and doing your best to consciously behave in alignment with them, will eventually allow you to be aligned with them fully. We become what we practice, after all.

I firmly believe that women are rising on this planet, and their feminine energies are challenging more men to grow as well. We men can either hide from this or respond with the courage to evolve. The false identity of the age-old gentleman we so proudly thought was honouring women by being chivalrous, was subconsciously suppressing them too in many ways, all the while convincing itself that it was virtuous and saving them.

Isn't it time we redefined the concept of the new-age gentleman, so we can have truly modern families that deliver happiness and love, rather than just the thought of it.

May more evolved men step forward with higher awareness of self and a higher dose of the wisdom that women truly desire.

Defining the Qualities of the New-Age Woman

The additional qualities that the advanced, new-age woman possesses, and which will make her magnetic to men, on top of the generic ones listed above, are:

- Understand that your feminine energies, and to a lesser extent your masculine energies, are important factors that attract men into your life, so you respect these aspects of yourself, to preserve the polarity with your lover.
- Remain in touch with your emotions, and are prepared to express them with truth, while also not being unstable emotionally or in need of emotional rescue by your partner.
- Know that your beauty strongly influences men, though you do not need to seek their validation or use them to manipulate men, as you know your true beauty lies within you.
- Know that you are right to expect your partner to do his fair share of the child raising and housework duties, so you are never placed in the stressful juggling situation in which many women find themselves on this front.
- Honour and respect yourself in life, including in relationships, never allowing a man to dishonour or disrespect you at your own expense. You respectfully communicate your authentic values and rights, no matter what circumstances arise.
- Are prepared to listen to the ideas and guidance of men, though always trust your own intuition in relationships
- Never tolerate your partner being physically, sexually or mentally abusive, because you honour yourself – far more than the average woman who allows herself to be abused seven times before she takes substantive actions.
- Understand that it is not your job to be the saviour of damaged men, like a mother nurturing a child – your partner is not a child, so you need never seek or hope to change or develop him into

someone other than the man who he already is, as that is a job for him alone.

- Remain composed under pressure, not out of image creation, but because this is your natural state. You cannot be manipulated by the will of others, including that of your partner.
- Develop a deep purpose in your life, and cannot be swayed from this path, regardless of who goes with you, because while pursuing the wrong man will cost you dearly, pursuing success will not cost your chance to be with the right man.
- Are never beholden to, or controlled by, your emotions, because you always take the time to go inward and understand your emotions before you express them with your partner.
- Have and maintain your own friends and interests, to prevent you from losing yourself within your relationship and becoming too available and co-dependent.
- Respect your body and stay fit and healthy, not for the validation of men, but out of your own self-respect.
- Have no unhealthy addictions that get in the way of a fulfilling life with your partner.
- Know you have every right to initiate dates, and even marriages, because in this world of equality you can choose, as well as be chosen
- Always either fully or equally fund dates or experiences for you and your partner to enjoy, because you have come into alignment with modern concepts of equality (unless this has been agreed upon by you and your partner), and this is the only logical approach in a world of true equality.
- Select a partner primarily based on love, not on their ability to provide, because you have the ability, opportunity and responsibility to do that for yourself.
- Never take steps to disrupt another relationship, even if you are attracted to a man who is already committed to another woman, out of respect to both participants, even if he wants you. You

instead honour his commitment to the other woman, even if he is reluctant to do so, unless he becomes free. This is integrity, in action.

- Allow your partner or date, to open up to you, as this is a sign that he trusts you, and you therefore encourage him to be vulnerable when he needs to be. You are worthy of being in deep emotional connection with your partner, so do not settle for less, unless this is your preference.
- Be loyal to the core, but not at your own expense.
- Respect that a man's emotional calmness is often a sign of strong emotional regulation, or a learned behaviour from societal expectations, not a weakness.
- Are honest with your partner about any reasons for not being intimate with them for an extended period, and even discuss this with your partner; because – although your body is yours alone to own and offer – you know it is not fair to keep any significant relationship issue from your partner, or to deny yourself the opportunity to have their help in resolving it.

What I have defined above are the traits of advanced men and women who are rich in wisdom and self-determination, because they are able to escape the complex web of insecurities that currently make modern dating and relating difficult to navigate. ***In saying that, my observations are general in nature, and of course, could be added to in consultation.***

Such men and women do not want to give up on love, so they will be committed to embracing love's wisdom, even if they must work hard to make this a reality.

The best pathway to becoming the lovers I depict is totally achievable when you commit to knowing your true self, not by just faking it till you are making it.

Chapter 36

My Blueprint for Societal Level Happiness in Romantic Relationships

The Natural Arc of Human Transformation

Our society is paying a high price, because we are struggling to make romantic relationships as fulfilling as they could be. Obviously, individuals and couples need to take their own steps to grow into the kind of lovers who can radiate love from within them and magnetise each other. But, as I outlined in earlier chapters, there is also a collective or societal 'system' of preconditioned mindsets around romance that we become inculcated within.

In my book *From Pain to Possibility*, I outlined the Natural Arc of Human Transformation (the Arc) and put forward the proposition that it follows a core three-step process involving:

- Understanding, to
- Knowing, to
- Becoming.

Understanding is a mental analysis of what we have, and are, currently experiencing to bring forth clarity to a situation.

Knowing combines this understanding, of what is and has been, with the power and clarity of our feelings, so that we can start to experience what is possible. It takes us from knowledge to a state of knowing through experiences.

Becoming arises when we leave the old states of being behind, and step into the energy of the new possibilities that we have decided we want to be. It's a kind of rebirth.

If I was a community leader who wanted to make a difference in this important area, these are the steps I would prioritise under the Arc:

Understanding:

- Understanding WHY we have a problem in the first place. I hope this book helps in this regard, but I know many other people out there will be able to add to it, and even challenge it, and I welcome that.
- Understanding WHAT the costs of the pain we have experienced have been for individuals, families and communities, for they are clearly significant.

Knowing

- Having mature conversations about our feelings and behaviours, so that we can formulate the way forward, and start the healing and forgiving process. Once we KNOW what is required to improve this mess, and what is acceptable to adopt within our polarised factions, we can start the transformation process with clear intent.

Embodying

- And finally, we can start to become what we seek to be: a happier and more mature society that values our differences and constantly strives to BE more than we have ever been before, individually and together.

The path to achieving true and sustainable transformation is through the core steps from UNDERSTANDING what went wrong, to

KNOWING what we can improve, and, lastly, into BEING what we seek to become.

We can only grow substantially through higher awareness, and this is encapsulated in the first three steps. Stepping into what we discover is Step 4, and this is where the magic can start to take place, because we are able to manifest what we have imagined together.

This process is natural, but far from normal, because it cannot be done if we are protecting our artificial identities, and protecting our long-held illusions about what should be.

We must face truths, which we have probably never challenged before, to become free of the shackles and prisons we have put ourselves in, unknowingly. What could be is only constrained by our limiting beliefs.

We must know ourselves to grow ourselves, and discover new, endless possibilities for happiness.

This is the plan I offer a world in the pain I once suffered through, until I stopped to face it and erase it.

Concept 1: Understanding Why We Need to Change

First, we need to agree on the reasons why disharmony is resulting in the problems that exist today. This book encapsulates my views, but for the sake of completeness here is a summary:

- Most individuals have not done the self-awareness work needed to confront their own wounds and shadows, which dwell within their egos, and make them prone to be needy and seek personal validation from relationships.

I personally witness a growing awareness across the population of the importance of this kind of self-development work.

The kinds of wounds we collectively suffer from often detonate in relationships, particularly if a strong feeling of love is present, and therefore, need to be exorcised not just within any relationship, but within the relating people themselves.

It is quite common for people to embrace this kind of self-development after a major crisis, or series of crises in their lives, because the pain they were enduring became so overwhelming that it could not be masked or covered up any longer.

This was certainly my experience.

Feelings are the doorway to better self-understandings if we embark on this kind of journey to higher self-awareness, and negative thoughts and expectations are the enemy, for they normally spring from our egos and our limiting beliefs.

This kind of deep soul-searching is discussed in more depth in this book.

- Identifying and agreeing on the collective social conditioning that is limiting the ability of men and women to attain equality and balance across their respective energies and perspectives. Many of these linger, although they no longer match social paradigms that arose from feminism and higher social justice.

I have attempted to identify these in this book, but I'm sure there are many more.

Many of these are old-world habits and outdated belief structures that can now be discarded, given the ending of many old-fashioned and patriarchal principles and rules. It is time for equality to truly descend into our lives, together.

- Men and women are largely ignorant of the psychology and needs of the other, and this is distorting the polarity between them. They are taught how to be what, and who, by their families of origin; but truly are not educated on how they can better relate to the opposite sex. Our education system can assist with this opportunity.

Our differing bodies and energy mixes do make us different and suited to different roles to some extent. We confuse the term equal with being the same. We are not the same in many ways. Men are generally stronger physically and are more suited to physical roles. Women are generally more suited to caring and nurturing roles. Intellectually of course we are the same.

Do men really understand what the average woman will be attracted to at different stages of their lives, so that they can accommodate their needs and wants, and vice versa?

Personally, I don't think so. There are often criticisms of the other, but not many informed conclusions.

We tend to engage out of blind hope 'on a wing and a pray' that we will jointly get relationships right. Do we want to keep rolling the dice in this way, or act with greater conscious awareness?

It is often said that love is blind, but perhaps we can consciously help it find its way home without stumbling at the doorstep.

- Conflict management skills are critical in a relationship, yet are they adequate to assist people to settle disputes and avoid ongoing resentments that can tear relationships apart?

We are all good at having fun together, but being able to get through periods of dispute is, in some ways, more critical to preserve relationships.

We can't tell parents how to parent, but we can build this into education systems and courses to teach our children how to resolve differences in relationships.

- We have forgotten how to feel for love, because we now do a lot of partner selections through screens, and not in person. We also look for value and interest in another with our minds, before we feel for love. This has lessened the level of presence we share when meeting new people and normally love requires a degree of presence to be properly detected.

The process to detect love has become a lost art in modern society, because we generally ignore our feelings and let our ego-centric minds control our lives and our relationships. Love is best discovered when the human mind is silenced for a short period of time, yet we are more accustomed in modern life to be comfortable in noise and structure.

- Technologies designed to make the dating process easier and dates more accessible, are exaggerating underlying issues in the dating world. These systems now act as a lifeline for people who want love in their lives but can't find it.

However, they are also introducing higher risks into the market, like scammers and sexual predators, with whom many people are not well equipped to handle.

Can the owners of these systems somehow design them to provide a better platform to promote more valuable information, which could explore compatibility at a deeper level, rather than focusing on what people do and look like?

This current suite of information plays to attraction, but not emotional connection; although I know some platforms do seek to align people in a more sophisticated way, such as through values and life preferences.

But are we considering relationship values, and perhaps different styles of conflict resolution?

- Both sexes believe that they need to convince or induce someone to love them, when this is a false narrative. My book *The Truth About Love* explains how love really works and what it is. Love cannot be created, destroyed or controlled by the human mind, because our egos are not consciousness. This requires us to relax into love, not wrestle it to the ground, or put it in chains.

Education on these realities would assist to take away the naivety we hold onto when it comes to love and help people to relax and be more patient in the dating world.

Unfortunately, ignorance is not bliss when it comes to romantic relationships. It is akin to Russian Roulette, with three bullets in the chamber.

- As the traditional primary initiators of relationships in society, many men struggle to deal with the pain of rejection. This is a big issue for many men. Women also have the tough task of saying yes or no, sometimes in a hurry. Both accepted roles can be incredibly difficult. We need to be compassionate to the emotional difficulties both roles create for those having to do them.

If men had a greater understanding on how to turn their pain into wisdom and new possibilities, we could lower domestic violence rates across the western world, where this is all too common.

More education for our younger people could also equip them to better handle these processes and not be damaged by the choices that are made.

- The art of conscious relating has been lost in modern western society, and probably has been for centuries. We are prone not to express our feelings with truth, because we fear hurting the person whom we love or admire. Ultimately, this causes more problems than it solves.

Advanced relationships are based on conscious relating practices, which recognise that relationships are a great avenue for people to grow together in truth.

Teaching these concepts to aware adults and young people would set society up for greater happiness and authenticity in relationships going forward.

Concept 2: Understanding the Pain and Costs of Relationship Problems

The personal pain and costs associated with relationship breakdowns and separations are huge and varied in their impacts. As divorce rates rise and marriage rates continue to fall, we are facing a stark message about the associated trends.

These include:

- Loss of mental health. Repeated failures in relationships can be debilitating for many and lead them into depression. There are whole industries of professionals dedicated to assisting with this issue, but they come at a huge cost to society.

- Often when a family breaks up and partners separate, a family that used to live under one roof will now need to live under two or more. This has an added cost in terms of rent and mortgage costs on that family. There is currently a mass shortage of housing in many western nations. Many experts blame this on mass immigration practices and issues of housing supply, but family breakdowns are having their own impacts on the housing market that are not small and have been aggregating for decades.

- Relationship breakdowns are notorious for damaging the mental health of children and can cause them to repeat the patterns of their parents when they reach the age when romantic relationships apply to them.

In addition, children are often denied access to one or both of their parents, and their respective families, because of access orders or family disputes. This can impair their development because they may not be receiving the benefits of both maternal and paternal guidance in their lives to help them mature in a balanced way.

- Relationship violence, and even murders, can result from the blame games and emotions that generate intense pain in relationship disputes. Even if couples stay together, this violence can become an unwanted feature that families and even neighbours must endure, and which children grow up unfairly witnessing, to their detriment, and even repeating. Women are the main victims of physical abuse.

- The financial costs of divorces and other de facto separations can also be extraordinarily debilitating. Divorce lawyers are not cheap, as are filing fees, not to mention the child support and maintenance/alimony costs that can burden parents for years after the separation takes place.

The net wealth of many people can be eroded greatly after a separation, particularly if it becomes a permanent life situation.

- The social implications of a relationship market that is breaking down could also be significant. Are we heading for a loneliness epidemic amongst cohorts of men and women, who are essentially unable to form strong long-term relations, and seem to be giving up in increasing numbers? And how do young men behave socially if their social standing is permanently disrupted by relationship disappointments? Will they become violent or anti-social in some way, or turn to drugs and alcohol to self-medicate?

And what impact will all this have on the birth rate over time? An economy requires each woman to bear 2.1 children on average to help that economy or society grow. At present it has dropped to 1.6 in America, the world's biggest economy, and as low as 0.6 in South Korea.

This means immigration is the only other viable alternative to grow a population, in the absence of organic growth. Immigration, though, can cause cultural issues if it is not sensibly managed.

The costs of all this disruption to people's lives are clearly significant.

Concept 3: Knowing What is Possible to Fix

Conversations must be had on these topics, rather than letting chance and ignorance find its own way to a sensible solution. It would be fanciful to expect this to be resolved without a suitable commitment to solving the key issues.

No one can force people to change in these areas, but as new levels of awareness take shape, it can be like a pebble hitting a pond and causing a ripple out across society. Change may be slow, but the main thing is that it reverses the tide of disharmony that is currently destroying our lives in so many ways.

If there is a war or major disruption in a society of some kind, community leaders often come together to discuss the problems at hand, agree on responses and with the help of the media and community groups, implement the changes that are needed through higher community awareness.

A key issue causing the

problems seems to be the age-old conditioning that is corrupting the mindsets of men and women and playing out in dating practices and technologies despite the move to a more egalitarian society.

These issues are causing animosity between the sexes and the long-term implications on human happiness could be terrible. Better societal awareness of how these can be dismantled needs to be contemplated.

The bottom line is that few people know themselves enough to really be well-equipped to handle romantic relationships effectively, and this is a failing of our societal structures and the ways we interact with each other.

There are debates raging on social media, but most of the commentators doing the damage are fringe personalities with sporadic followers. Together they seem to be spreading a vitriol that is having much damage on the world of relationships, because young people are 'glued' to scrolling through this form of media 24/7 and they tend to believe what they hear, even if it is imbalanced or biased.

Many of these posts are provocative rather than compassionate, and seek to point the finger rather than seek peace.

A shift to educating our youth on the power of developing self-awareness practices, would set our communities up for a time when we are populated with a higher proportion of people who know themselves, and can live more authentic lives, without the need to hide behind artificial identities.

Concept 4: Embodying What We Want to Change

To make meaningful change in this world, we must be in alignment energetically with the change we seek. So, to create more conscious and loving relationships, rich in self-awareness and truth, we need to be that increasingly as a community. And we need role models and 'heroes' who others can look to and try to emulate.

To create better romantic relationships, we must align individually and together with the harmonies we seek to establish. Many couples have been able to do this, but even more have not.

We don't need more rules and regulations; we need more compassionate understandings of the situation at hand.

A more conscious way of relating will naturally require higher conscious awareness on all levels, starting with teaching people how to address their own wounds and conditioned mindsets, and then showing couples how to create a conscious relationship.

However, I am not naïve to the reality that many people will not seek to choose this approach and will prefer to stay stuck in their limited identities, with their traditional mindsets. But this is okay, for all is a choice.

At a societal level, communication and education are the only effective ways forward. We must therefore consider:

- Introducing information into education systems, particularly for our youth, which helps people to adopt a fresh approach to their own personal development. We teach children about core intellectual subjects in schools, like sciences and mathematics, but we spend little time and effort teaching them how to understand themselves and other people, including those they love.

We may teach some sex education classes, but do we teach the advanced skills children will need in life to create great romantic relationships and family dynamics? We could leave this to the parents, but they probably don't have the time to teach it themselves, or the wisdom to even know it.

And are we helping our young adults to witness and dismiss the ridiculously outdated conditioning that they have absorbed all their lives, and which will almost certainly have an impact on their dating and relating experiences once they commence?

Our young adults need a better blueprint for what it means to be a fulfilled human being, and lover, in this modern world we inhabit. Otherwise, many of them will suffer, simply because we and previous generations have effectively let them down. This nexus needs to be broken.

Frankly, I do not want to see younger people suffer from the shocking consequences of being the joint creator of broken families, as I experienced. And that includes my own adult children.

This is not a small task, but perhaps just as important as teaching kids how to do chemistry or biology? After all, they have their own biology and chemistry to master first!

We could also teach adults, including mental health experts, more about human consciousness, rather than just about mastering the mind and making their egos stronger. We need optional egos, not stronger ones. Consciousness goes way beyond the mind, and in fact a strong mind will often house a strong ego, and high doses of projection and protection behaviours, rather than truth.

- In terms of communication, we need the various media outlets to become more aware of the subliminal messages they are putting out into the community daily.

That's not a criticism of them, for they are also immersed in the 'normal' paradigms that most of humanity is drowning within.

There is limited ability to control social media, but mainstream media could be a different story, once public commentators put forward the virtues of change in our society, in the way we view love and self-mastery.

For example, in movies does the tall, secretive, emotionally unavailable, rich guy always need to be the one who gets the gorgeous woman? There are reasons why we crave this kind of plot – because it meets our conditioned mindsets and soothes our nervous systems out of familiarity – but it doesn't have to remain this way.

- And can we create more in personal ways for people to meet and initiate romantic relationships? More organisations do now host 'speed dating' events, for people of varying ages, which I applaud; but perhaps advanced creative minds can come up with other new ways to circumvent our reliance on dating sites.

The stage is set for a wiser approach to remedying the shocking relationship outcomes we are collectively creating in western society.

Perhaps we need to take a leaf out of the books of other less advanced countries, which are less focused on money and materialism, in the way they approach their lives, and the greater harmony they appear to offer each other as a society?

We may not be as advanced as we think in the modern world at loving each other, but a golden opportunity awaits us all, when we can embrace the energy of love, and trust, and allow it to take our romantic relationships to a whole new level. This, after all, is our natural state of being and our true birthright.

It's time we loved from a higher place of purity and passion, and conducted our romantic relationships together, as the love that we are, for the love that we deserve, and with the love that we can openly share.

We are all good enough, as we are now, to experience this new possibility. But anything less than this, is not good enough.

PART F

CONCLUDING THE JOURNEY HOME

Chapter 37

Rising Above the Normal into the Natural

You Can Never Go Back

One thing that my deep journey into understanding, knowing and feeling into deeper states of love has shown me, is that once you experience this miraculous journey, you will never, ever want to go back to the old version of love that you once accepted as normal. You will now crave the more natural version of love you have remembered within you, and you will seek to share this with someone in a matching frequency of love. This advanced normality is our natural state.

When you extract yourself from the normal paradigms of romantic relationships, and witness their deeply flawed beliefs and fearful behaviours, you will no longer be able to tolerate the thought of being a part of it ever again. You are home in your heart, after years of being lost, and you want the sacred union that this book, and the wisdom of others, has helped you witness.

The big question is: will you invite yourself to experience the full gift of love that awaits you? All you need do is open your heart and embrace an experience of yourself that you were, essentially, taught to forget. It is just a journey home to the memory of the real you.

I'm sure that some readers will want this incredible experience of a truer love, whereas others will be content with where they are at – either choice is valid. But new and endless possibilities are sitting in the shadows and are waiting to be revealed to those who are ready to shine their light upon them.

I hope this book has shown readers, where to point their torches!

Like the planet we live upon, we are the product of pure consciousness having a physical experience. The physical matters, but it is not our full truth, and we must look beyond what we can see and touch to discover the possibilities that await us. And this also applies to our romantic unions.

Consider this analogy: we have been listening to love songs for many years, and often the words are hypnotic and alluring, as they bring forth concepts of love that we find familiar. But the hidden frequency of love lies, not in the thoughts we receive in our minds by listening, but in the frequency of the music that we receive in our bodies. These vibrations are what can truly activate our hearts and propel us into deeper states of love, if we allow them to do so.

Remembering the feeling of love and living from this wonderful energy that you already are, is the secret to creating sacred romantic relationships, and a life that you will love, together. The core illusion that we fall victim to is thinking that we can master love in our heads. It must be felt to be expressed in its fullness.

When we let our hearts create our relationships through the infinite power of love, we will discover a purity within them, steeped in passion and pure intimacy. But first you will need a partner who is also committed to having this ultimate experience. And this may require patience and trust, unless you already have this gift.

An unbreakable bond awaits the lovers who choose to embrace a higher path in their love lives. When the love is equal and reciprocal with another, there is opportunity to come together for the primary purpose of love, as love and in love, and to express that in our physical realities.

Imagine a world in which people, once again, value love above all else, not just their own unique idea of it. This is possible when we learn from our painful pasts, let go of our fears of our future, stop judging each other as not enough, and refuse to give up on what is possible when love takes over.

The journey into true love awaits those who are the seekers of their own truths. Are you one of them?

Chapter 38

My Ode to Romantic Harmony

My Verse for this Universe

I am not a recognised poet, but I feel called to feel into and express my greatest sense of appreciation for romantic harmony, and the wisdom I have gained over the years.

"I entered the dating world with advantages galore,
Tall, athletic, and committed to forever-more.
I grew up watching fairy tales and rom-coms in black and white,
But nothing prepared me for what then came to light.

I was programmed to be her saving grace,
The shining knight, to put a smile on her beautiful face,
The provider, the protector, the warrior, wrapped in one.
So, what could possibly stop this rising son?

Beauty was, of course, my primary goal,
And the target of my endless toil.
But what took place was all too sad,
Beauty in exchange for money – this advice proved very bad!

How could this willing hero find himself in so much pain?
Why follow a master plan when there was so little gain?
In hindsight, the currency he now sees that really matters
Is the one thing that never shatters.

His self-respect, forged from the burning ashes,
Is now reshaped in the fire of love.
His phoenix now rises to brand new heights,
Ready to sample life's greater delights.

He now knows that greater awareness, of love and life,
Could have kept him well out of strife.
But harmony is worth its weight in gold,
And the true story of love should now be told.

Love, I see now, was always the prize,
And only found in someone's eyes.
This reality gave me many surprises,
And has helped me see love's other disguises.

I have come to witness a major truth,
That love has no real substitute.
We can try to block it all we like,
But love always prevails through the dark of night.

We can find interest in another, and ascribe them a value,
But your soul dismisses your ego's chatters.
Fully aware and never in doubt,
What it desires is all that eventually matters.

You matter more than you'll ever know,
And you are enough, no matter where you go.
So, don't be deceived by what you were taught,
Relationships without truth and love must be bought."

I dedicate this poem to a world that unknowingly craves what it already has in infinite abundance: love.

Chapter 39

Concluding Remarks: Choosing Our Love of Life Over Old Habits

Is it Time for a Quantum Leap Forward?

Modern romantic relationships are struggling on many fronts, and quite frankly are due for a quantum leap. For far too long, masculine and feminine energies have been at odds with each other, and not in the harmony that nature intended.

At a deep level, humanity has moved away from its natural state, and we now find ourselves at the mercy of our individual and collective conditioning that essentially programs us to think, then behave, in old habitual ways that no longer serve us. To be honest, this is not our fault. It is the fault of the 'system' of life that we have subconsciously inherited and learned to comply with, without enough introspection.

But make no mistake, for many of us ignorance is rewarding us with counterfeit love lives that are very expensive to maintain. Why not liberate ourselves from these, and receive a more genuine currency of love?

We can blame whatever our egos decide, but we have chosen this 'screwed up' experience, together with our eyes closed. The blame game is futile, and it's time we drew a new line in the sands of time and stepped forward in love together.

Our dating and relating habits are not bringing us the peace and happiness we all deserve. They have caused centuries of shame, dysfunction, and humiliation for millions of people, including the children who witness them from within our broken families. But that can end too, when we choose it.

We date and relate often to achieve success, rather than feel fulfilled, unaware that fulfilment is the only sustainable way to real and ever-lasting success, because success without happiness is always likely to feel hollow to the human soul.

If you disagree with this then, congratulations, you are probably one of the fortunate few who seems to have got their romantic relationships right! This is a super-power. But these people may still seek to learn new ways to keep their relationships strong, and even to take them to new levels. None of us are perfect, or bulletproof.

Ignorance has become a shield between what we have subjected ourselves to, and what we really want. But do we want to be in love with our lives, for the rest of our lives, or to live in mediocrity with each other? And do we want to continue to live with hardened hearts, or open them softly, with discernment to the experiences they desire?

This choice is stark but real. Of course, it would be easy to do nothing and let people suffer in silence! ***Personally, I won't stand for that.*** We need to know that we are capable of so much more and, once and for all, choose it.

True Peace Lies in Our Joint Forgiveness

When we recognise how significant our conditioning has been in influencing the way we relate, and how much it overrides and damages the natural connections that we are meant to enjoy, we can truly forgive each other for what has unfolded, and start again with compassion and a new sense of curiosity as to what is possible.

It's time we took heed of these famous words from Rumi and embraced what is possible in love, to create a better future for us all:

"If everything around you seems dark, look again.
You may be the light.
Don't lose yourself inside your pain,
One day it will become the cure that heals you."

I invite all my readers to come on this journey from pain to possibility in their love lives. The higher we climb in love the better the view will get, for us all.

The Wise Ones Must Show the Way

We can put spaceships on the moon and connect with billions of people every day through the internet. But we seemingly can't use the more natural connection between our hearts to create happy relationships and societies on this planet. And this seems to be getting worse!

The suffering we put ourselves through in the name of love is like a Shakespearian tragedy playing out on a mass scale every day. If we are to live in peace, we need to overcome our amnesia and rewrite the script, which we can do through a bigger dose of awareness, and a few lessons in how to invite more love into our lives. We can break some of the old-fashioned and outdated habits, by teaching people greater truths about love, and helping them to understand the true intent about relationships, and how to maintain polarity and peace.

Like an usher in a movie cinema, there are many wise ones who have been through the darkness of separation and abandonment, who I'm sure are now ready to shine their lights in the hope of revealing a better way forward. And it would be so powerful for them to do so with a united voice.

Many of these wise ones have been to hell and back in their romantic relationships, but will never go back there willingly, because they now know the different addresses of heaven and hell, ***as do I***.

Knowing the truth of yourself redefines you and what you want in life. Once you know yourself as love, you can never imagine a relationship that does not respect it as a sacred gift. The superficial no longer matters. Fantasies are no longer of interest and intimacy is no longer negotiable to those deeply in the know. Chaos is no longer valued, nor chosen, over calm composure, and genuine care.

You start to see your individual programming, and the collective conditioning or 'system' for what they are, and you no longer want to play the old stale game of love, which you know is so prone to end in tears. You are home in your heart, and you want to share this with someone else who has also found this divine space. This is the ultimate experience in love that we all deserve.

Ironically, our love lives have become somewhat separated from love as we pursue its modern proxy: value! And one of the big problems with value as a driver of romantic relationships is that loyalty can stop when the perceived benefits of being in relationship with another end. When will we start valuing love over superficial measurements of self-worth, and stop valuing ourselves against measures created by a system we didn't even invent?

Recognising Ourselves as Love

In the Introduction, I posed the concept that he or she who needs nothing gets everything, because love is nothing and everything all at once. But what did this mean, beyond sounding like some kind of riddle? If you have read this far, there is more to this wisdom for me to share. And it goes like this...

We are essentially nobodies (because we are just energy) in bodies, trying to attain what we already are: pure love. And it is only when we drop the struggle to be anything other than what we already are, can we become our true selves and experience higher forms of love.

The lesson for our romantic relationships, which this wisdom can offer, is that we are so busy trying to be loved, because we fear that we are not, that we forget we already are completely lovable by the right person, once we simply surrender to this possibility, and open our trusting hearts and minds to love in a more intelligent way.

And if we love from a place of need, then we are not fully present in love, and our partners merely become a means to an end. In this place we are essentially expecting them to prove to us, and the world, what our hearts already know is true: that we are worthy of being loved.

Can you see how crazy this is?

When we finally realise that we are already pure love and start living from our all-knowing hearts, we can date and relate in the energy of love, with another who is also wanting to share the passion and purity of love, together – as love, with love, and for love. Here there is no need and no fear.

In this wonderful place we are home, in heaven on Earth. And we didn't even need to die to rest in this beautiful place of peace.

This kind of bliss is your birthright if you want it enough, and know that you are enough to experience it. I believe it's time that we stopped settling for the kind of mediocre love we have been ignorantly trained to endure.

Reimagining Our Love Lives

Some people may be confronted by the contents of this book, some may even call it dynamite. Some egos are sure to be hurt, as they seek to stay in their victim mentality, which seemingly resolves them of responsibility for their own demises. ***I accept this, if they do, because I once lived in that place too.***

Dynamite is used to remove obstacles, so that new foundations can be laid and something new can be built. This is something our society needs with respect to romantic relationships, for we need a long-overdue restructure in the way we approach and conduct them.

Deeper connection to our own true selves, and then to others, is the sacred code we need to activate to discover greater happiness and fulfilment. This divine coding is within us all, even if it remains dormant for now. We are all here to love the lives we lead. It's waiting for our combined attention, and sincere intentions, even if it will take an extended period to rebuild. But we must start now to rebuild the trust that has seemingly been broken inside so many hearts.

There is no limit to how far we can take this forward, for love possesses the infinite powers of creation. We are at a crossroad, where we can go all the way to true love and enjoy the ultimate connection with another; or we can take new but incremental steps forward, and enjoy our more normal love lives in a wiser way. These different choices are available to us all, and this book tries to accommodate the spectrum of choices that we can make.

When growing up, we were all taught that true love awaited us in adulthood. Many of us have stopped believing in this possibility, after going through romantic pain. But I am here to confirm to you that it is still available if you want it. The question is how badly do you want it?

We should not look for our sacred love where we think we lost it. We need to look above what is visible, to discover where it has been waiting to be found, in the realms of higher intelligence.

It is time that we followed our hearts, without fear, rather than letting fear lead us away from our hearts. We can choose to move away from survival to a more creative way of loving in a brand-new reality. We can thrive, not just seemingly survive, within what we call love..

Many people have struggled in romantic relationships, ***like I once did***, but we must embrace the upside that is possible in the presence of a fuller level of awareness. Each time we fall in life, we build our intimacy with the ground, but if we look up and not down, this can only ever show us the way to rise to higher heights.

I trust that, armed with the wisdom in this book, readers can now embark on a wondrous journey to higher forms of romantic relationships, with curiosity and great optimism, which will inevitably create their own sources of momentum.

Once a mountaineer has climbed a great mountain, hills no longer ignite his or her sense of adventure. And so it is with the kind of love we are all capable of feeling and expressing. We must start taking steps up to the summit of love, which this book may have helped you glimpse in the distance.

Let's rise in love, not fall into it, because the 'more' that we can enjoy, is already waiting for our whole-hearted embraces.

And that 'more' is bliss!

Appendices

Appendix I

A Checklist of Key Learnings for Those Seeking Romantic Love

Key Learnings to Assist You

Set out below is a list of the key learnings that I have had because of my 'educational' romantic life.

These learnings have been recognised from the depths of joy and pain, and I offer them to assist any readers who may benefit from considering them. May my pain, not be in vain!

Whether you choose to do the work to find true love, or simply want a better relationship to help you find deeper happiness, this listing may help you on your journey forward.

- Forget what others have told you about how a great relationship should look, and consider your own wants and needs. Write it down for clarity if it helps. Clarity overcomes confusion.
- Always seek to be the real or true you in your relationships. If you pretend to be something you are not, you are only setting yourself up for disappointment, once your pretence ends.
- Love can only be expressed in presence, so do your best to be fully present with your partner, especially when it matters most.

- Do not put limits on love, for it knows who you are meant to be with, and who you end up with may surprise you, simply because you offered yourself trust and patience.
- Sit down with your partner (if you have one) and agree what your specific relationship should look like. What are your key expectations of each other? What roles should you play? What would make you both happy?
- Don't just rely on internet dating to meet partners. You are likely to find that closer connections can be felt better in person than on a screen. Do what you love, such as hobbies you are passionate about, because this is a great place to open to love.
- Never ignore sexual denial for too long, because it is normally a symptom, not the disease, in a relationship, which generally indicates that attraction is fading, or the frequency match of love has shifted. Living without intimacy for too long can harm your self-esteem.
- Your inner reality must align with your outer reality. You will not find harmony with a partner unless you are at harmony within yourself, so learn to go inward and understand what your feelings want you to come to terms with or let go.
- If you are single, work on your self-awareness. If you are in a relationship, work on your self-awareness. Never stop, for this is the best way to take your life to a whole new level.
- Do not fear being single, for it has many advantages, including high levels of sovereignty. There is a time in your life when being single, rather than in a relationship, will help you grow in the ways you need.
- Feel for love and attraction in that order, before you think them.
- Don't get sucked into the traditional conditioned expectations around relationships that are spelt out in this book. Remember:
  –Men: you are more than your money and what you can give to others. You are not someone else's future; you are your present.

–Women: you are more than your looks, and you have every right to determine your own fate, with or without a man in your life.

–Men and women: perhaps a partner is a wonderful bonus in your life, not a necessity you need to be happy.

- Determine if you are in love with the person who you are with, or whether the intensity of love you feel has shifted. If you are in doubt, consider the methods discussed in this book to answer this question.
- If someone pushes you away with disrespect, walk away out of self-respect.
- Use any pain of separation as the fuel of higher self-discovery and awareness.
- Avoid setting too many expectations in your relationship, so that it can unfold at its own pace. Unfold with the natural expansion of a relationship with patience. Remember, expectations are always the enemy of fun and joy.
- Understand that all relationships are experiments, and that they may not last forever, like they do in fairytales. Enjoy what the relationship brings to your life, and if it ends earlier than you had hoped, let the other person go, even if this leaves you with pain to process. You deserve to be loved and desired.
- Never let yourself become an option to a partner, because one day you may find you are no longer the preferred one, simply by being imperfect.
- You need to bring peace to a relationship for it to bring peace to you. If you are not at peace, do the work needed to get there, then engage with a partner who is also at peace in life. If you are already in a relationship, find peace together.
- The higher your frequency of love, the purer and more fulfilling will be the relationship that you are able to attract into your life. So, work on your own sense of self-love as a priority.

- Trust your intuition in a relationship, and judge someone on how they behave, not on what they say. Confront inconsistent or unfair behaviour, or you will validate it to your own detriment.
- Recognise that not everyone will be attracted to you or fall in love with you. Nature has its own plan. You are not invalidated if another does not choose you.
- Remember to have fun with your partner. We sometimes think that being serious makes us more meaningful, but fun is an essential part of life.
- Your friends and family cannot feel what you feel about another person, so do not listen if another person tells you who you should or should not love or be with.
- Being physically attracted to someone in a romantic relationship is important, but love trumps looks always, for it is eternal, and is what the eternal aspect of you desires.
- Put up boundaries to people who repeatedly disrespect or dishonour you in your life, for they are energetically expensive to be around and could lessen your sense of self.-love.
- The best relationships have loving connection as their cornerstone, in addition to powerful attraction. Feel for both.
- Select someone who is aligned with you on a mind, body and spirit level if you wish to create a wonderful relationship.
- People say age doesn't matter in a romantic relationship, but stage does. It will be difficult to feel fulfilled if you both want different things out of life, even if you love and care for each other.
- Ending a relationship with another is the final act of love, which you can offer another soul and yourself if necessary. If you do not choose them, set them free to be chosen by another.
- You can end a relationship in one or two brief sentences. Further discussions are likely to arise, but make your decision abundantly clear, so that there is no room for doubt or confusion. Fast pain is good pain.

- If you suspect that your partner is having an affair there is a good chance that they are. Do not ignore the red flags and your screaming intuition. Act with an appropriate level of surety.
- If you don't know if you love someone, even after feeling into it, you probably don't.
- Love is a vibrational match between two souls. It is possible to lose and restore this match if you follow conscious relating practices.
- A sense of betrayal is just an emotional response to someone choosing not to honour you. Accept that all happens for a reason and do the inner work to let go.
- If someone leaves you in a way that lacks truth and integrity, don't seek to 'get even'. The universe will always balance the scales through karma. Take your learnings, process your pain, and move on. Remember that whatever took place happened, for you and through you, was at the direction of your soul – so there was a part of you that enabled it to occur.
- If someone dishonours you, remember that you have allowed this behaviour in some way. Feel into the pain and never dishonour yourself in that way again.
- Before love gives you what you want, it will give you what you need to help you grow. Consider what you really want so that the universe can help you manifest it.
- When your feel negative about your partner, always go inward first before you go outward and go into blame energy. Your feelings are yours to own, before they are expressed.
- Love can solve anything, if you let it do so and listen to the wisdom in your heart. Agree with your partner how you will sort out disagreements, because this is incredibly important to help your relationship evolve and not evaporate.
- When you realise that you were in the wrong, own it and do the work to change. Do not protect an unfair position.

- Always be truthful with yourself and a partner. Hiding truths is always a zero-sum game.
- Even if you love a person deeply, accept that they may not be right for your future, or your now, and let go.
- Letting go of love is one of the hardest things in life, but your self-love must always come first, even if this means letting go.
- Never allow yourself to become an option, particularly a second or disposable option. If a person loves you, they will never make you an option, particularly a disposable one.
- Understand your relating style, because it can explain your conditioned responses to a partner's words or actions, and can influence the kind of person to whom you are attracted. These are fully explained in many articles on the internet and books by renowned psychologists.
- Make sure you understand your emotional wounds and from where they originated. The clues are often found in the attributes of your family of origin, and of course your feelings.
- When a relationship ends, search inside the pain and take the lessons it offers. Do this before you enter your next relationship, or you are highly likely to make the same mistakes again.
- Understand that true love is not possible unless you have grown sufficiently to love yourself completely too. But the relationship that your heart draws you to, is the next one you are ready to grow through, so embrace it with all your heart even if it's not perfect.
- Do not mistake chaos for attraction when interacting with partners. Unconsciously wounded people tend to be less in control of their own emotions.
- There is no love in control, because love does not operate in the energy of control. If your partner is excessively controlling, this is a possible red flag or a wound that could be addressed.
- Accept that the beauty of another person is not yours to own. It can be admired, but do not let intense beauty intimidate or

distract you. Highly attractive people are not perfect. They may not be drawn to you, but there is no 'league' that puts them above you. You can play in any league that accepts you.

- Never put a partner on a pedestal. We are all equal and great relationships require equality, not worship.
- Your masculine and feminine energies can be altered by awareness work, and as this balance changes it can alter the polarity of the person to whom you are attracted.
- Only stay friends with an ex who respected you. However, you may also need to let them go to respect a new partner.
- Never give up on love, because it will never give up on you.
- Forgiving another is always for you and not them. A lack of forgiveness is energetically and emotionally expensive to you.
- Do not cling to a relationship that is bad or mediocre. After trying to fix it with your partner or a counsellor, move on, because life is too short to be unhappy for too long, particularly if your partner is not as committed as you to the enhancement.
- If you are trying very hard in a relationship, there is a good chance that the relationship needs to change or be dissolved. Love does not need to try hard, but it does demand commitment.
- Remain self-centred in any relationship, so that you don't get lost or over-give to your own detriment. Needing someone else to complete you is not a winning strategy.
- Never commit to a relationship to which you are truly not committed.
- You have many soul mates, so do not buy into the mistaken belief that there is only one person with whom you can find love.
- The old saying 'if it is meant to be, it will be' is true if you are dealing with relationships that are pre-ordained by two souls. Otherwise, this is not true.
- Always trust your heart for it never lies, unlike your conditioned mind.

- If someone lets you down and cheats on you, insist that they do the inner work to remove the wounds that led to the indiscretion. If they do not do the work, they are likely to repeat this painful experience to your detriment and your exit may be the best option.
- Remember, money is not love and it never can be.
- When you let go of a relationship that is not right for you, you allow the space for a better one to enter your life.
- When issues arise between you and your partner, remember that negative energetic resonance does not go away just because you hope it will. Energy remains in place until it is altered by the force of love.

Appendix II

A Set of Questions Couples Can Use to Develop Their Relationship

For Those Already in Relationships

Set out below is a set of questions for couples to consider with respect to creating a more advanced relationship. They are not designed to be a post-separation fix. I will leave that to the relationship counsellors. This is designed to be a proactive tool to prevent issues before they arise.

I do not expect this list to be complete, and professional therapists would likely have their own valuable contributions to make.

- How conscious are you of the core beliefs that you both hold in life, and from where they arose? If you are not sure how to surface these, please refer to my book *Where Your Happiness Hides* for possible guidance.
- What do you define as being fully present with your partner? How do your definitions differ?
- Issues will arise as you date and relate to each other. Do you have an agreed approach to handling disputes and disagreements?
- Do you really understand what your partner needs and wants from you, and how changes in these can be discussed and resolved between you? You may even consider researching the

psychology of the opposite sex to enhance your relationship skills and understandings.

- Do you understand what each of you finds of value and of interest in the opposite sex, and in each other specifically? How can you stay attuned to any changes in this paradigm, so that your partner can adapt as needed?
- How important are physical looks, career success, or money to each of you, and how can any differences be resolved?
- How do you plan to grow together so that you do not grow apart?
- What are your core values in life, and to what extent are these aligned or in contravention?
- What is your attitude to the expression of emotions and feelings, and to what extent do you expect your partner to help you solve your issues? Does one of you get angry, whilst one shuts down in a dispute?
- How do you plan to resolve all issues that arise, or will you leave some unresolved?
- How do you plan to recognise and celebrate experiences in your relationship that take it to a new level of fulfilment or awareness? It's not all about problems!
- What are your core love languages and how would you like these to be met by your partner?
- Do you understand your individual relating styles and how these may compliment or clash with your partner's style?
- What are you views on the conditioned mindsets that have been discussed in this book, and how you will handle them together going forward? For example:

  – Who generally pays for what and when?

  – How will sexual and intimacy needs be discussed and met?

  – What are each of your views on your right to have same-sex friendships?

  – Are you exclusive to each other, or both available to date other people?

– If you hear advice from friends, family or on social media that worries you, how should this be dealt with between you?

- How truthful or open do you expect each other to be about your pasts, and what approach should you take about what gets disclosed, particularly with respect to ex-partners?
- What do you both believe is the appropriate mix between fun and doing tasks to fulfill life's administrative responsibilities?
- What is a healthy mix of time and energy that you should both devote to your own interests, rather than the relationship itself?
- What fears, insecurities or validations do you feel that you both have, which may assist or threaten the relationship over time, and how can your partner assist you to handle those and help you overcome them?
- How do you personally like to process pain and difficult experiences in your life, and how can your partner assist with this?
- How will you both handle family expectations and interferences if they arise?
- What are both of you planning in terms of the size of your family in the future? How many children do you both want?
- What personal development and spiritual practices do you both intend to undertake, together and on your own? How will you both share what you are learning about yourself or the world?
- How defensive are you both about criticism from the other, and what is the best way and time to raise these kinds of issues?
- If problems arise in your relationship, how will you raise these with each other and discuss the problems?
- What is your level of commitment to the other, and how should personal truths that arise be discussed with compassion?

Acknowledgements

I would like to thank you, the reader, for spending your valuable time reading this book. I consider it a great privilege to share my learnings and discoveries with people on a similar journey into higher awareness.

I acknowledge the beautiful souls who have interacted with me in this life and held their magic mirrors up for me to see myself more clearly within. They have helped to make this book possible.

I am particularly grateful to the women who have shared romantic relationships with me during my life. They were all incredible women, and they helped me to see what is possible when love and higher awareness is present. All of them helped me grow as a person, which is an amazing gift.

I want to again thank my dear friend and long-time mentor Charles Kovess. In the wake of my second divorce, he gave me the support and advice I really needed to get through one of the most challenging periods of my life, and he did it out of the purity of his own heart, expecting nothing in return.

In terms of the production of this book, I wish to thank Zena Shapter for again bringing greater light and clarity to my words. This is the fifth book she has helped me to create with her wonderful editing skills and sharp mind.

Her husband, Bill Shapter, provided his graphic artistry to the diagrams and pictures in this book to help it come to life for readers.

Julia Kuris designed the covers for the book, and her creative genius has again brought this important book to life. She is so blessed in her creative abilities.

Again, I thank my wonderful children for always encouraging me on my journey to my own truths. They all had to endure some of the relationship dysfunctions that I contributed to and endured. I thank them for their love and support in helping me find my light through the darkness. I love them dearly, and they continue to teach me much about life in their own beautiful ways.

About the Author

Mark discovered the concepts embodied in this book after his love life was punctuated with repeated doses of separation and romantic disappointments. He tried extremely hard to make relationships work for much of his life, with limited success.

This led him to undertake deep enquiries into the important topic of love. He consulted far and wide, including holding discussions with some very learned human and metaphysical mentors to get a better understanding of this powerful energy.

He witnessed the disappointments of fragile relationships in his own family and witnessed how hearts were torn apart in the cauldron of conditioning and ignorance of what could be, including his own. He also grew up in a world dominated by men and witnessed the pain and anguish that this had caused the female role models in his life, and the world at large.

Facing the disappointments of his love life with pure integrity and a passion for learning, has allowed him to unearth deep wisdom about relationships, which he now shares in this book with readers, to help others avoid what he endured, or recover from pain.

Mark believes that the modern family is a core component of our social fabric that is under intense pressure as romantic relationships continue to struggle. And this problem does not get the attention that it deserves.

Many men and women are dating and relating in the energy of fear because of their heavily conditioned mindsets, rather than being in the energy of love. To solve this dilemma, Mark believes that we need the truth of love, and a greater dose of self-awareness. We need to understand each other and come together under an umbrella of patience and compassion to reimagine a new and shared vision of what our romantic relationships could be like.

Mark is an expert in love and connection and has written five ground-breaking books on how a person can attain higher levels of self-love, then apply it to important areas of their life, including relationships, living a happier life, becoming a more conscious leader, resolving pain and completing spiritual journeys back to universal love and intelligence.

He is not a psychologist by training, but has been to the university of life, and after years of deep self-reflection into relationships, including his own, he wanted to offer a world in pain, the insights that have helped him to move from pain to new possibilities.

He welcomes the feedback of readers, because he knows that his views represent just one perspective, developed from his life as a 'straight' man, and that deep wisdom can only come forth from opening, not only to your own thoughts and feelings, but also to the feelings and perspectives of others.

We need the new-age man and woman to step forward now, so that we can break the ongoing cycle of distrust and disconnection that men and women so often endure together.

Mark lives in Sydney, Australia, and has five wonderful children.

Should you wish to discuss any part of this book in greater depth,

Mark can be reached through his website at mark-worthington.com, or by email at mark@mark-worthington.com

www.ingramcontent.com/pod-product-compliance
Lightning Source LLC
LaVergne TN
LVHW050758061126
851857LV00012B/607